ROCKING THE BOAT

Welsh Women who Championed Equality 1840-1990

ROCKING THE BOAT

Welsh Women who Championed Equality 1840-1990

ANGELA V. JOHN

Parthian, Cardigan SA43 1ED
www.parthianbooks.com
First published in 2018

ISBN 978-1-912109-50-0
Edited by Francesca Rhydderch
Series Editor Dai Smith
The Modern Wales series receives support from the Rhys Davies Trust
Cover Christine Kinsey, Taith – A Journey/olew ar gynfas – oil on canvas/183x122cm
Typeset by Elaine Sharples
Printed by Opolgraf, Poland
Published with the financial support of the Welsh Books Council
British Library Cataloguing in Publication Data
A cataloguing record for this book is available from the British Library.

For my sisters Celia and Cindy
with love

Contents

Acknowledgements

Exploring the lives of different women across time and place was exhilarating. It was also demanding, since at times I felt as though I were researching and writing seven full biographies. So it follows that I am indebted to many people and although they cannot all be named here, I want to record my gratitude to everyone who helped with queries.

I am especially indebted to Paula Bartley and Sian Rhiannon Williams who read the typescript in its entirety. Thanks are due to Sue Morgan and to Sandra Holton for reading essays and the latter also provided source material. I am grateful to Katherine Bradley for her comments, for her generosity in sharing research and for accompanying me to Ewenny and Laleston. Mark Pitter valiantly deciphered code in Myvanwy Rhŷs' diaries. Neil McIntyre's help was invaluable: the person who has done the most to publicise Frances Hoggan's remarkable life, he generously shared his research. Daniel Williams permitted me to read an article about Hoggan pre-publication and I am indebted also to Beth Jenkins. Sue Crampton kindly shared her work on Edith Picton-Turbervill. Alun Burge has kept a keen eye on sources for me, for which I am grateful.

It was wonderful to talk to Jean Thompson about her memories of Olwen Rhŷs and I have benefitted greatly from communication with descendants of my subjects, notably Anne Eliza Cottington and other Haig descendants of Lady Rhondda, and Menna Gallie's cousin the late Annest Wiliam and her granddaughter Rhiannon Davies. Thanks also to David Herman. I am grateful to Jeremy Picton-Turbervill and to Roger Ford. Thanks to Justine Hopkins and the Michael Ayrton Estate (Margaret Wynne Nevinson). The Clark material is included courtesy of the Alfred Gillett Trust and I am grateful to Julie Mather and staff at the Arthur Clark Archive, Street, Somerset.

Many thanks to the librarians, archivists and staff at the following: Amgueddfa Cymru/ National Museum Wales; BBC Written Archives Centre, Caversham Park, Reading (Matthew Chipping); The Keeper of Special Collections at the Bodleian Libraries, University of Oxford (and Colin Harris, once more); the Bonds and staff at The Great House, Laleston; Boston University (Howard Gottlieb Archival Research Center); British Library (especially John Boneham), British Library of Political and Economic Science (Archives Division) and its Women's Library Collection; Cardiff University Special Collections and Archive; Columbia University in the City of New York (Rare Book and Manuscript Library); Fales Library at the Elmer Holmes Bobst Library, New York University; Glamorgan Archives; Greater London Record Office; Jesus College, Oxford (the Principal, Owen McKnight, Helen Gee and Lodge staff); Llyfrgell Genedlaethol Cymru/National Library of Wales (especially Siân Bowyer, Nia Daniels, Iwan ap Dafydd and Jayne Day); The Learned Society of Wales (Sarah Morse); University of Michigan

Library; Modern Records Centre, University of Warwick; Museum of London; MLA; The National Archives, Kew; Newnham College, Cambridge; North London Collegiate School Library; Oxford High School Library; People's History Museum, Manchester; Pembrokeshire Libraries; Poyston Hall, Pembrokeshire (David Ellis); Royal Society of Medicine; Sherborne Girls; Society of Antiquaries of London; Library of the Society of Friends; St. Anne's College, Oxford; Swansea University Library and South Wales Miners' Library; the Wellcome Library; the YMCA of India.

Thanks also to: Cathy Clay, T. Robin Chapman, Claire Connolly, Ann Dingsdale, Neil Evans, Brian Harrison, Marged Haycock; Ann Humfrey, Geraint H. Jenkins, John Jenkins, Elin Jones, Sue Jones, Hilda Kean, Ceridwen Lloyd-Morgan, Karen Morgan, Kate Murphy, Sheila Rowbotham, David Smith and Mari Takayanagi.

I thank the Honourable Society of Cymmrodorion where an early version of the essay on Lady Rhondda was given, also the organisers (especially Maredudd ap Huw) of the Sir John Rhŷs Centennial conference at the National Library of Wales, December 2015 ('From the Celtic Hinterland'). My lecture there provided the basis for the fourth essay in this volume. Thank you to the University of Wales Press and to the editors of the journal *Llafur* who published earlier, shorter versions of the essays on Margaret Wynne Nevinson and Menna Gallie respectively.

I am grateful to Non Evans for her expertise. I remain indebted to Francesca Rhydderch for her skilful editing. Many thanks also to the artist Christine Kinsey, and to the series editor Dai Smith. The Parthian team has been immensely helpful: Gillian Griffiths, Nikki Griffiths, Marc Jennings, Elaine Sharples, Barbara Whitfield and Maria Zygogianni. Finally, a huge thank you once more to Parthian's Richard Davies.

Illustrations

Their Lives at a Glance

1843	Birth of Frances Morgan, later Hoggan (FH)
1858	Birth of Margaret Wynne Jones, later Nevinson (MWN)
1867	FH becomes a medical student at Zürich University
1870	FH awarded MD (second woman in Europe)
1872	Birth of Edith Picton-Turbervill (EP-T)
1874	Birth of Myvanwy Rhŷs (MRH)
1876	Birth of Olwen Rhŷs (ORH)
1880	FH first female member of British College of Physicians and gives evidence to the Aberdare Committee on education
1883	Birth of Margaret Haig Thomas, later Mackworth then 2nd Viscountess Rhondda (RH)
	MWN gets a degree at St Andrews University
1898	MRH gets a First at Cambridge University
1899	EP-T goes to India with the YWCA
1901	ORH gets a First (Home Student) at Oxford
1905	MRH awarded a degree at Trinity College, Dublin
1911	Staging of MWN's drama *In the Workhouse*
1913	RH arrested and imprisoned for suffrage militancy. During these years MRH and ORH are officers in Oxford Women's Suffrage

	Society. MWN's suffrage activities include the Cymric Suffrage Union
1914-18	MRH, ORH, MWN, EP-T and RH do war work
1919	Birth of Menna Humphreys, later Gallie (MG)
	EP-T first woman to preach at statutory Church of England Sunday service
1920	RH starts *Time and Tide* with all-female Board
1920	MWN made a JP & first woman to adjudicate at London's Criminal Petty Sessions
1922	RH starts claim to sit in House of Lords
1924	ORH gets her MA at Oxford University
1926	MWN publishes autobiography
	RH becomes first female president of the Institute of Directors and *Time and Tide* editor
1927	FH dies
1929	EP-T becomes Labour MP for The Wrekin
	ORH becomes lecturer for forerunner of St Anne's College, Oxford
1932	MWN dies
1933	RH publishes autobiography
1936	EP-T goes to Hong Kong and Malaya on Royal Commission
	MRH's book on medieval history is published
1939	EP-T publishes autobiography
1945	MRH dies
1950	RH becomes first woman president of a Welsh college
1953	ORH dies

1958	RH dies
1959	MG's first novel *Strike for a Kingdom* published
1960	EP-T dies
1970	MG's *You're Welcome to Ulster* published
1986	Publication (in the US) of MG's final novel
1990	MG dies

Introduction

Ask most people within, as well as beyond, Wales to identify the first Welsh woman to become a Labour MP, and chances are they won't know the correct answer. Question them about which woman held the most directorships in the UK in the 1920s and was also, in that same decade, the first female president of the Institute of Directors, and they are likely to be hard-pressed to respond. Get people to identify the first female British doctor to gain her MD in Europe and they will probably mention Elizabeth Garrett Anderson. The correct names – Edith Picton-Turbervill, Viscountess Rhondda and Frances Hoggan – feature in this book, along with those of four other Welsh women. None of them has received the recognition they deserve, in part because they made their names beyond Wales.

These essays are not, however, simply stories of forgotten Welsh women achievers beyond the borders, even though they focus on remarkable, versatile and resilient pioneers. Rather, they seek to challenge the way in which individuals tend to be labelled and perceived as 'belonging' more or less exclusively to either Welsh or English history with the result that their full significance is neither scrutinised nor appreciated. This volume is especially concerned with *how* life stories are told. Each essay demonstrates a different way for the biographical historian to tackle this and so raises questions about the very nature of how biography is constructed.[1]

The first focuses on the medical pioneer Frances Hoggan, born Morgan (1843-1927). Rather than following her from cradle to grave, it primarily concentrates on one period in her life, putting the spotlight on the fifteen years from 1870 to 1885. Based in London at that time, she was remarkably busy, both professionally and in pursuing causes and campaigns. Many of these would today be called 'alternative'. At the same time she played an active part in advocating educational reform for girls in Wales.

Another essay narrows the 'slice of life' approach even further by concentrating on 1922, one eventful year in the life of Lady Rhondda (1883-1958). It shows her juggling her varied interests, from her bold and often forgotten claim for peeresses in their own right to take their seat in the House of Lords, to negotiating business deals, developing *Time and Tide*, the influential weekly she owned and later edited, and founding the Six Point Group with its progressive claims for gender equality, all while facing the breakdown of her marriage. This is the shortest essay in the collection, since I have written a lengthy biography of Lady Rhondda, and the centenary of the winning of the (partial) vote for women in 2018 has drawn attention to her through, for example, Welsh National Opera's cabaret-style opera: 'Rhondda Rips It Up!'[2]

Myvanwy Rhŷs (1874-1945) and Olwen Rhŷs (1876-1953), daughters of a Welsh academic family in Oxford, are the subjects of an essay that adopts a familial focus. The sisters' activities ranged from women's suffrage and First World War famine relief work to hard-fought struggles for academic achievements. The sisters' lives are examined in the light of the expectations placed upon them as part of a renowned Welsh family. The essay considers how they coped with these demands, both collectively and individually.

The essay on London-based Margaret Wynne Nevinson (1858-1932) – writer, assiduous Poor Law Guardian and much else – takes a themed approach and focuses in particular on issues of gender and national identity in an individual's life.[3] The final essay, about the 'exile' novelist Menna Gallie (1919-1990), concentrates on fiction and the importance of place and politics to this writer, examining how she used History but also how History has treated her.[4]

'The Good Life of Edith Picton-Turbervill' (1872- 1960) from Glamorgan, is the longest essay in this volume. It most closely represents the traditional biographical life and times approach. As Sue Crampton argues, she deserves better than merely being commemorated by the names of two cul-de-sacs in Telford.[5] She was described in the 1930s as 'One of the great crusaders of our time in righteous causes'.[6] She won her parliamentary seat, The Wrekin in Shropshire, in 1929 at the so-called flapper election when women over twenty-one were finally able to vote. Fourteen women were returned – a record – though these plucky women sat with more than 600 men. Edith Picton-Turbervill was part of a Labour government headed by Ramsay MacDonald but still new to power: it was only their second time in office. She became the first female Labour MP to introduce what became a successful private members' bill. In the 1930s she authored an influential Minority Report on the persistence of child slavery in Hong Kong and Malaya. An early advocate of women priests and a powerful figure in the YWCA, she was also the first woman to preach at a statutory Church of England service.

The essays deliberately utilise a range of both biographical approaches and sources. Edith Picton-Turbervill's publications are examined, with parliamentary papers providing a vital tool for discerning the priorities for this public figure. Although Frances Hoggan's progressive handwritten observations about the links between physical health, education and exercise have been used here, printed sources, especially newspapers and pamphlets, dominate in her case.

In contrast, the essay on the Rhŷs sisters draws primarily on family letters, diaries and their father's personal papers. Family papers also inform the essay on Lady Rhondda. Fiction has been central to the analysis of Margaret Nevinson and Menna Gallie's lives, though having known the latter personally provides an extra dimension to this study.

All these women were well travelled. At a period when most Welsh women's lives were circumscribed in terms of the freedom, money and opportunity to move far within Wales, they were especially privileged. Frances Hoggan studied in Switzerland, visited and wrote about several continents. The Rhŷs sisters added to their educational achievements and flair for languages by taking courses in Europe. Both Frances Hoggan and Edith Picton-Turbervill were involved in changing the lives of women in India and the latter travelled extensively as an MP. Menna

Gallie lived in England and Northern Ireland and visited America. London-based Margaret Wynne Nevinson lived in Germany both as a young single woman and later at the start of her marriage. Lady Rhondda was an inveterate traveller and was also well known internationally as a businesswoman.

The subjects are united by the fact that each one, in her own distinctive way, sought to challenge convention, to upset presumptions and disturb the equilibrium, particularly in relation to women's rights. How much they rocked the boat depended on class, personality and opportunity, crucially allied to the prevailing culture and attitudes of their time. [7] Frances Hoggan's life encapsulates well the tensions between her position as a Victorian woman keen for change yet limited in how far she could champion this without sacrificing her hard-won professional standing, let alone her personal respectability. Her choices reflect her awareness of the need to negotiate carefully, to undermine and subvert. She spoke out but remained aware that sounding reasonable could sometimes pay dividends.

The essays span a period of a hundred and fifty years, from the 1840s when Frances Hoggan was born, to 1990 when Menna Gallie died. The latter was able to be considerably more forthright in expression than her predecessors – though her reception remained essentially gendered – and she wove the personal into the political. Her predecessors would have viewed the concept and potential of equal rights rather differently from her. Menna Gallie had been born in 1919, the year after older women first got the right to vote in national elections and just before the Sex Disqualification (Removal) Act enabled women to enter a number of professions previously barred to them. So the time span of the book reveals a gradual – albeit bumpy – journey towards the modern woman of the late twentieth century.

The half dozen women who precede Menna Gallie in this volume were all supporters of women's suffrage in one form or another. Frances Hoggan, active in suffragist causes from the mid-1880s, reminds us of the long, yet often neglected, lead-up to the more dramatic years of early twentieth century suffrage activity. The variety of progressive causes she espoused also demonstrates that the demand for the vote was the natural concomitant of wider concerns about women's education, employment and much else.

The three women born in the 1870s – Edith Picton-Turbervill, Myvanwy and Olwen Rhŷs – were also moderate suffragists, active in Mrs Fawcett's National Union of Women's Suffrage Societies. But whereas the Rhŷs sisters were following their pro-suffrage parents in becoming leading lights in Oxford suffrage circles and organisation, Edith Picton-Turbervill risked the ridicule of her large and conservative family in her espousal of the Cause.

Margaret Nevinson took a different route. She began as a moderate suffragist, then joined Mrs Pankhurst's Women's Social and Political Union. But in 1907 she became a founder member and prominent figure in the breakaway group, the Women's Freedom League. It specialised in passive resistance. Her suffrage activity reveals a few of the many suffrage special interest groups. She was, for example, national treasurer of the Women Writers' Suffrage League and a leading figure in the Cymric Suffrage Union. Here her demands for citizenship were intertwined with an expatriate's somewhat romanticised notion of Wales.

Margaret Mackworth (née Haig Thomas), who became Lady Rhondda in 1918, was a suffragette. Like the other Margaret who had to face rats being let loose and the force of a water hose at the Women's Freedom League meeting she chaired at Sutton in Surrey, the future Lady Rhondda had mice thrown on the platform when she spoke in Aberdare, along with herrings, ripe tomatoes and cabbages.[8] Sulphurated gas, snuff and cayenne pepper pervaded the hall.

It made her even more determined. She became the secretary of Newport's Women's Social and Political Union and in 1913 set a letterbox alight for which she went (briefly) to prison. Although halting her militancy during the First World War, she effectively reminds us that the suffrage story did not end in 1918 when women over thirty got the vote. Lady Rhondda remained committed to extending voting rights to younger women, and it was thanks to the pressure of people like her that the full enfranchisement of women was achieved in 1928 and female peers took their seats in the House of Lords thirty years later.

Yet whilst suffrage invariably attracts attention to an individual, it formed only part, albeit a memorable part, of these women's long and busy lives. Both Margarets were arrested pre-war for suffrage activism yet both became Justices of the *Peace* in the 1920s. Moreover, all of these women's lives were crucially intersected by war. War work dominated between 1914-18, from Lady Rhondda's influential positions in organising women's recruitment, to the Rhŷs sisters' Quaker relief work in Serbia and France. Menna Gallie's war work (for the Inland Revenue) was in the Second World War.

The majority of the women were from Liberal backgrounds. Lady Rhondda's father – whom she adored – was a Liberal MP and the Minister who first introduced food rationing during the First World War. The Liberal Prime Minister Asquith's opposition to women's suffrage made Lady Rhondda wary of party politics but Margaret Nevinson admitted that 'in spite of Mr Asquith, I incline to Liberalism'.[9] In contrast, Edith Picton-Turbervill and Menna Gallie were socialists, the former in contradiction to her family and even her twin sister, the latter reinforcing her Labour heritage. It was *social* equality that was paramount for Menna Gallie.

Religion seems to have been central to the lives of only two of the seven women. This challenge to the stereotype of the faithful female Welsh worshipper is accentuated by the fact these two, Edith Picton-Turbervill and Margaret Nevinson (the daughter of a Church of England clergyman), were committed Anglicans rather than Nonconformists.

Menna Gallie had been brought up to attend chapel regularly but lost her faith. In an unpublished piece called 'The Fear of God'[10] she recounted returning as a middle-aged woman to the annual Cymanfa Ganu (singing festival) in Ystradgynlais. 'I sat', she wrote, 'rigid with denial. I would be critical, sophisticated, Cambridgewise, but the tides of music had me engulfed, had me swallowed'. She admitted that she 'felt the fear of God' in that chapel. Yet her comments are as much about her unease with life in Cambridge and the way that memory and romantic nostalgia encroach, delude and unmask us, as they are about any brief revival of religious belief.

All seven women were writers and public speakers. Frances Hoggan published medical research and spoke on many subjects at home and abroad. She wrote articles and pamphlets that ranged widely, from advocating women's public conveniences to medical reform for women in India, and race relations in America and Africa. She was also recognised as an authority on education. So too was Olwen Rhŷs, though her struggle to have her degree recognised, despite becoming a lecturer in French at Oxford, sums up well the difficulties that she, her sister Myvanwy and countless other clever, educated women faced. Both sisters published academic work. Edith Picton-Turbervill was a leading figure in the struggle for women's visibility within the Church of England and wrote books on the subject. She also made a number of radio broadcasts.

Menna Gallie was a popular broadcaster but is better known for five novels set in Wales, England and Northern Ireland. The first appeared when she was forty. She was most popular in the United States. Margaret Nevinson wrote fiction alongside newspaper and journal articles and a play that helped to change the law for the dispossessed. Her autobiography, as its title *Life's Fitful Fever* suggests, was as bitter as Edith Picton-Turbervill's *Life is Good* is celebratory. Lady Rhondda's inter-war autobiography *This Was My World* was enigmatic, focusing mainly on her childhood and youth and betraying little about her remarkable achievements as a businesswoman and editor of *Time and Tide*.

All seven challenged authority in public and, to some extent, in their personal lives. They make us question our assumptions about Victorian domesticity and 'traditional' values and point up the value of 'Biography as Corrective'.[11] Frances Hoggan apparently became a teenage mother. And, quite apart from all the obstacles that this posed, she faced barriers in Britain from a medical profession implacably opposed to women doctors. She became a student in Zürich. The setbacks she experienced on account of her gender helped to shape the nature of her rebellion. Later she spent many years as an extremely active widow and international figure.

Whereas Frances Hoggan appears to have enjoyed a companionate marriage to a supportive, unconventional husband in the same profession, for Margaret Nevinson the fact that her husband, Henry W. Nevinson was, like her, a writer and pro-suffrage, was no recipe for marital harmony. This was revealed in her husband's diaries, in comments by their artist son C.R.W. Nevinson and in her printed remarks disparaging marriage and motherhood. In her circumstances, rocking the boat seemed preferable to rocking the cradle. The Nevinson marriage was deeply troubled and, seven months after Margaret died, Henry Nevinson married the woman with whom he had spent most of his free time.[12]

Three of the seven women never married. The Rhŷs sisters remained single and relied heavily on each other.

Edith Picton-Turbervill lived intermittently with other independent women. Lady Rhondda divorced her husband and lived with women for the rest of her life. Menna Gallie, the most modern of the seven, not only achieved greater social mobility than the others. She also led, in some respects, a more conventional life than these Victorian predecessors: she married a philosopher,[13] accompanied Bryce Gallie to his academic posts at Keele, Belfast and Cambridge, and had two children. She had, though, been a university student (at Swansea) who married, on graduation, a lecturer at the same university and their early married life was, like those of their contemporaries, fractured by wartime separation. And as those who knew Menna Gallie could attest, she was never one to hold back when it came to speaking out against perceived injustices to whoever cared to listen, whether that involved dining at High Table, hosting one of her famed dinner parties or risking confrontations in print or person in Northern Ireland. All seven women also defied time, living into their seventies or eighties, and four endured two world wars.

Collective biographical essays about individual lives have a long history, dating back to Plutarch. The inclusion of women is comparatively recent, but Florence Nightingale was one of the four figures comprising Lytton Strachey's *Eminent Victorians* published in 1918. Before that there were hagiographical Victorian volumes about female figures – usually monarchs, mothers of heroes, saints or 'literary lights' – as exemplified in T.J. Llewelyn Prichard's 1854 collection *The Heroines of Welsh History*, and W. H. D. Adams' *Child-Life and Girlhood of Remarkable*

Women.[14] In 1934 the essayist Janet E. Courtney produced *The Women Of My Time.*[15] It made a somewhat breathless dash through female educators, politicians and professionals. Lady Rhondda was one of four women discussed under 'Personal Service' and meriting one of a small number of photographs.

Since the resurgence of the women's movement in the 1970s, group biographies have multiplied. Barbara Caine's study of the Strachey sisters is one of a number focused on women within a family.[16] Caine also put feminism under the spotlight in her essays on Victorian feminists, whilst inter-war feminists provided the framework for Brian Harrison's *Prudent Revolutionaries.*[17] Sheila Rowbotham's beautifully crafted *Rebel Crossings*[18] identifies a group of feminist freethinkers and their evolving ideas as they travelled from the old world and the old (late nineteenth) century to the new world of the twentieth century and America.

But *Rocking the Boat* is less tightly bound by time and acquaintance. Not all of the women in these essays did – or could have – known each other. They are distinguished by having become privileged professionals, by championing equality with the pen and in person and by the fact that they were all Welsh. All seven women declared a residual loyalty to Wales, though *gwladgarwch* (love of one's country) could cover a wide range of emotions and practices, whilst there were also competing notions of what it meant to be British. The extent to which these women identified with Wales and Welshness depended, as the essays show, on their upbringing, company, timing, location and even expediency. They expressed (both over time within individual lives as well as in comparison to each other) a number of different perspectives and ambiguous relationships to Wales as well as divergent models of nationhood.[19]

Three of them spoke Welsh. Menna Gallie's first language was Welsh – she claimed that she learned no English before the age of eight – but although she did some translation work, the language of choice for her own novels was English. She came from a small coal mining community in south-west Wales, more than just physically remote from the worlds she came to inhabit in later life. Unlike the other six, she was from the working class, and proud of it.

The Rhŷs sisters were also Welsh speakers and had been born in North Wales. However, they lived most of their lives in Oxford where their father was an eminent Celtic scholar and professor. Their cultured mother was a former teacher. Part of the intelligentsia, with progressive parents, they were well travelled and enjoyed a superior education: Oxford High School and Bangor followed by Cambridge for Myvanwy and what became St Anne's College, Oxford for Olwen.

Margaret Nevinson had a sympathetic father: a Welsh-speaking clergyman in Leicester, he believed in fostering his daughter's education. However, her mother was wary of ambitious girls and saw marriage and motherhood as her daughter's destiny. Margaret thought differently. She became a teacher of Classics at a prestigious London school whilst also studying for and attaining a degree at the University of St. Andrews, via an early form of distance learning.

Frances Hoggan, born in Brecon and raised in

Glamorgan, also had a clergyman father but he died when she was a child. Her mother's family were well off and eventually she received the higher education that permitted her to inch her way towards acceptance in the medical world.

The future Lady Rhondda was from the wealthiest family. Her father's family fortune was based on the South Wales coal trade, hence the title he chose and bequeathed to his daughter. She grew up in the Monmouthshire village of Llanwern, received an excellent education in London and Scottish schools but although she entered Somerville College, Oxford, she left of her own volition after two terms.

Edith Picton-Turbervill was unable to get that far. From a distinguished South Walian family based at Ewenny Priory near Bridgend in South Wales, she was, in some respects, the most rebellious of the seven young women. She trained as a missionary but was the only subject of these essays not to have attended university. Her work in India was as much prompted by a need to prove that she was of use as it was by her religiosity. Her story reveals not only a wide range of interests but also how attitudes could shift over time.

Although all these women spent most of their lives outside Wales, to ignore their (often complex) relationship to their particular conceptions of what Wales signified for them, fails to do them justice. Historians of England and of medicine might be aware of Frances Hoggan as a doctor in London and an international figure but might not appreciate why and what she did for the education of girls within Wales. By the same token, the essays in this volume reveal a side to her, as a mid-Victorian London-based activist, that is missing from Welsh historiography.

Putting the pieces together involves, for example, matching up the suffragette Margaret Haig Thomas/Mackworth with Lady Rhondda, consummate Bloomsbury editor, and seeing Edith Picton-Turbervill of Ewenny alongside the YWCA worker in India, the politician in Shropshire, Hong Kong and Westminster as well as the Anglican preacher. It means reconciling Menna Gallie's lived experience of an increasingly turbulent Northern Ireland with her wariness of Welsh nationalism. This does not result in flawless or neat, rounded subjects – far from it – what has been called 'the biographer's cohering touch'[20] can set in stone a life that was invariably more complicated, contradictory and messy than a biography suggests. But it does at least allow for alternative and nuanced perspectives.

Occasionally we can glimpse the subjects of this book coming together. In August 1882 Frances Hoggan and Myvanwy and Olwen Rhŷs's mother Elspeth spoke at the same event at the National Eisteddfod at Denbigh. And in Sir John Rhŷs's papers is a letter from Frances Hoggan to Elspeth Rhŷs. She asks after the children, explains that she and her husband are going to North Wales for a fortnight's summer holiday and wonders whether they can recommend a place to stay with good mountain air and fishing. She hopes that once she is back in London, the Rhŷses will spend a week staying with the Hoggans.[21]

Frances Hoggan's great-aunt, the niece of Sir Thomas Picton, was a Warlow. Edith Picton-Turbervill's surname was Warlow before her family changed its name and she was immensely proud of being descended from the hero of the Napoleonic Wars. There is no evidence, though, that the two women met despite being distantly related. But it seems very likely that Margaret Nevinson knew Edith Picton-Turbervill through the Church League for Women's Suffrage and their commitment to peace after the First World War. Not long after Edith gave her seminal sermon from a Lincolnshire pulpit in 1919, Margaret also found a compliant bishop, Dr David, Bishop of Edmundsbury who enabled her to address a mixed congregation in a Suffolk village church.[22] And, during the Depression, Lady Rhondda and Edith Picton-Turbervill signed the same letter to *The Times* objecting to women being paid less Unemployment Assistance than men.[23] As the honorary treasurer of the Oxford Women's Colleges Fund, Lady Rhondda probably knew Olwen Rhŷs.

These essays can be read as discrete studies of the individuals concerned. Put together, they also provide a glimpse into the shifting obstacles and opportunities facing educated Welsh women of the nineteenth and twentieth centuries who ventured beyond Wales. They reveal the protean nature of biography and its role as a possible corrective to other forms of historical writing. Above all, they help to show why and how these feisty women challenged the status quo over a century and a half. Wherever they were, they ensured, in various ingenious ways, that they effectively rocked their boats.

Notes

[1] The Danish historian and biographer Birgitte Possing has recently identified eight categories of biography. She describes them as Mirror (or Didactic), Hagiography, Personality Portrait, Interpretive, Prism, Life-and-Times, Polyphonic and Prosopography (or Collective). In practice, however, historians tend to deploy several categories within one work. Birgitte Possing, *Understanding Biographies: On Biographies in History and Stories in Biography,* pp. 68-84, University Press of Southern Denmark, 2017.

[2] Angela V. John, *Turning the Tide: The Life of Lady Rhondda*, Parthian, 2013. The opera tours Wales and England in the summer and autumn of 2018. Lady Rhondda is also one of the fifty suffrage activists included on the new sculpture of Millicent Fawcett in Parliament Square.

[3] This is an updated and expanded version of an essay that first appeared in R. R. Davies and Geraint H. Jenkins, *From Medieval to Modern Wales: Historical Essays in Honour of Kenneth O. Morgan and Ralph A. Griffiths*, University of Wales Press, 2004, pp. 230-245. Thanks to the University of Wales Press.

[4] This is an expanded and updated version of my article in *Llafur*, 9/3, 2006, pp.46-57. Thanks to Llafur/The Welsh People's History Society, to Archif Menywod Cymru/ Women's Archive of Wales, and the Josef Herman Foundation where earlier versions were given.

[5] Sue Crampton has written a fictionalised diary of parts of Edith Picton-Turbervill's life, based on her autobiography. See Idem, *A Head Above Others*, Perigord Press, 2013, pp.3-81. Picton Close and Turbervill Close are in Telford, Shropshire.

[6] George A. Greenwood in *Great Thoughts,* October 1936.

[7] See the discussion of the indicators of the 'potentiality' for

Victorian female leadership in Pam Hirsch and Mark McBeth, *Teacher Training at Cambridge: the Initiatives of Oscar Browning and Elizabeth Hughes,* Woburn Press, 2004, p. 118.

[8] Margaret Wynne Nevinson, *Life's Fitful Fever: A Volume of Memories*, A&C. Black, 1926, p. 212; John, *Turning the Tide*, pp. 63-6.

[9] Nevinson, *Life's Fitful Fever*, p. 284.

[10] Menna Gallie Archive, National Library of Wales, Aberystwyth, ML1/1. Interestingly, there are four different versions.

[11] A term used by Nigel Hamilton in Hans Renders, Binne De Haan and Jonne Harmsma, *The Biographical Turn: Lives in History,* Routledge, 2017, Chapter 2.

[12] See Angela V. John, *War, Journalism and the Shaping of the Twentieth Century: The Life and Times of Henry W. Nevinson,* I.B. Tauris, 2006; Idem, *Evelyn Sharp: Rebel Woman 1869-1955*, Manchester University Press, 2009.

[13] Her maternal uncle was the Welsh scholar Stephen J. Williams.

[14] Published respectively by W. & F. G. Cash and W. Swan Sonnenschein.

[15] Published by Lovat Dickson. Note Courtney's opening words: 'It was a wonderful piece of good fortune, *if one must be born a woman*, [my emphasis] to come into the women's world in the later nineteenth century', p. 5.

[16] Barbara Caine, *Bombay to Bloomsbury: A Biography of the Stracheys,* Oxford University Press, 2005. See too Idem, *Biography and History*, Palgrave Macmillan, 2010, Chapter 3.

[17] Idem, *Victorian Feminists*, Oxford University Press, 1992; Brian Harrison, *Prudent Revolutionaries: Portraits of British Feminists between the Wars*, Oxford University Press, 1987.

[18] Sheila Rowbotham, *Rebel Crossings: New Women, Free Lovers, and Radicals in Britain and the United States,* Verso, 2016.

[19] For a critique of popular stereotypes of Wales and an exploration of competing, co-existing images of Welsh society during part of this period (1890-1914) see M. Wynn Thomas, *The Nations of Wales 1890-1914*, University of Wales Press, 2016.

[20] See Robert Douglas-Fairhurst, *Becoming Dickens: The Invention of a Novelist*, The Belknap Press of Harvard University Press, 2011, p. 6.

[21] John Rhŷs Papers, B1/1/2, 20 July nd. but c.1882, National Library of Wales, Aberystwyth.

[22] Nevinson, *Life's Fitful Fever,* p. 284.

[23] *The Times* 12 February 1935.

1

Speaking Out

The Many Causes of Dr Frances Hoggan

In July 1911 a sixty-seven year old Welshwoman called Frances Hoggan addressed the grandly named First Universal Races Congress. Held in London, it sought to bring together, 'in the light of science and the modern conscience',[1] intellectuals, activists, government officials and others in an unprecedented effort to promote inter-racial harmony.

More than fifty countries were represented and at least 2,000 attended. It was described at the time as 'a world parliament'[2] and although its achievements – and what was achievable – have since been debated its very existence at a time of unrest and growing international tension made it a landmark event. It has recently been hailed as 'A rich and compelling episode in modern world history' and 'a laboratory for thought and action'.[3] Speakers included Dusé Mohamed Ali who, in the wake of the Congress, edited the *African Times and Oriental Review*, and the Indian statesman G. K. Gokhale as well as the renowned African American sociologist, writer and activist, W. E. B. Du Bois. As the literary and cultural studies scholar Daniel Williams has argued, he not only played an important part in the proceedings, but his perspectives also influenced the paper by his friend, Dr Frances Hoggan.[4]

Her subject was 'The Negro Problem in Relation to White Women'. She began by commenting how, in Africa and America, there was an emphasis on the danger black men posed to white women. She then questioned why 'so little feeling comparatively is shown when the white man is the aggressor and the victim has a coloured skin'.[5]

Unfortunately, given this progressive approach to her subject, Frances Hoggan could not be heard. Acoustics were woefully inadequate in the vast Kensington hall and, lacking modern microphones, she had a particularly difficult time with what the *Manchester Guardian* described as 'her very tiny voice'.[6] Mrs Archibald Little came to the rescue, acting as 'a human megaphone' and, as the speaker uttered her words, so Mrs Little repeated them, shouting them out to the audience in her booming voice. Luckily Frances had a sense of humour and was 'laughing hard' as she spoke. The audience joined in by laughing too.

Papers had anyway been circulated in advance and the formal sessions were merely summaries, with many of the most valuable exchanges taking place informally over the four-day event.

This transnational gathering boasted eminent figures from across the world. British delegates included the economist J.A. Hobson, and activists Annie Besant and Tom Mann.[7] Women speakers were very much in the minority. So who was Dr Frances Hoggan?

She was a Welsh medical and educational pioneer who championed women's rights throughout her long and distinguished career. Yet until recently her achievements have been neglected. Although female 'Firsts' of the Victorian era have tended to receive publicity, even here she was short-changed. Elizabeth Garrett Anderson has long been lauded as the first British woman in Europe to get a degree in medicine (awarded in Paris). Yet Frances Morgan, as she was at the time, gained her MD at Zürich University three months earlier in March 1870 when she was twenty-six.[8]

Frances Elizabeth Morgan – Fannie to her family – had been born in the centre of Brecon in mid-Wales on 20 December 1843, close to the birthplace of the eighteenth-century actress Sarah Siddons. Brecon would later claim Wales' first female town councillor and mayor: Gwenllian Morgan. And it was from here that recognition of Frances' achievements came, via the Brecknock Society. In 1970 on the centenary of her graduation, Onfel Thomas published a booklet about her.[9] A service was held at Brecon Cathedral, where an inscribed brass font ewer dedicated to her memory was presented to the cathedral.

Yet fourteen years later the surgeon Emyr Wyn Jones lamented the fact that Frances was *still* scarcely remembered in Wales or England, despite being 'one of the most distinguished women born in Wales'.[10] Articles by the medical doctor Neil McIntyre followed, stressing that Frances was, inter alia, the first female member of a British College of Physicians, one half of 'Britain's first medical marriage' and the first British woman to do 'high-quality medical research'.[11]

In the early 1990s the educational historian W. Gareth Evans described Frances as 'undoubtedly one of the leading feminist pioneers of Victorian Wales'.[12] More recently Daniel Williams has assessed her relationship with national identity, race and empire.[13] The Learned Society of Wales has recognised her significance by presenting since 2016 an annual commemorative Frances Hoggan Medal.[14] This celebrates outstanding research by women in any area of science, technology, engineering, mathematics and medicine (STEMM research). It is open to women resident in Wales, of Welsh parentage or with demonstrable connections with Wales.[15] And in that year the Welsh language television series *Mamwlad* (which explores the lives of Welsh female figures from the past), featured a programme about Frances.[16]

So the achievements of Dr Frances Hoggan have been belatedly recognised and, even though she is not a household name, she is now better known, at least in Wales, than she was just a decade ago. This essay will focus on her little known humanitarian and health education causes in England during the 1870s and first half of the 1880s, most of which were woman-centred in personnel and/or purpose. It will then assess the significance of her educational work for Wales during this same period. For Frances, the treatment of women by a nation, organisation or profession became the litmus test for gauging its worth. But what first impelled her in this direction?

Frances was the eldest of her parents' five children. Her father, a Pembrokeshire man, was the curate of St John's Priory in Brecon (now its cathedral) at the time of her birth. Georgiana, her mother, was the daughter of a naval captain from the long-established Philipps [sic] family of Cwmgwili, Carmarthenshire. In 1845 Frances' father was appointed vicar of St Mary's Church, Aberavon (Port Talbot), where Dic Penderyn, wronged martyr of the Merthyr Rising, had been buried fourteen years earlier. This Church of England Living on the South Wales coast was combined with that of Baglan. Yet whereas Aberavon itself was perceived by visitors as 'dirty and disagreeable'[17] and too close to both the new docks and large copper works, the hillside village of Baglan with its Norman St. Baglan's Church, was considered rather more salubrious. This was where Frances and her family lived for the next six years.

Frances' mother's first husband had died within a few weeks of their marrying and in March 1851 she lost her second husband (Frances' father) to typhoid fever and pneumonia. That summer the family moved a little further east to the small market town of Cowbridge. The youngest child was only five months and the eldest (Frances' half-brother from her mother's first marriage) nine. Frances was seven.

Although Cowbridge boasted one of the best schools in

Wales, this Grammar School was for boys only. All that existed for girls like Frances was 'the merest elementary private school'.[18] Not until 1896 was Cowbridge High School for Girls established. This was in the wake of the Aberdare Committee on intermediate and higher education in Wales and consequent legislation and improvements in the provision of girls' education. The lack of decent education locally meant that ten-year-old Frances was sent to a school in Windsor run by a family friend.[19]

In her evidence to the Aberdare Committee in 1880, Frances described uninspected, old-fashioned schools 'where girls were required to work an inordinate number of hours, and where it was a perfect jumble of lessons with no connecting thread running through them'. She added: 'My own personal experience of school life was exactly similar'. It was all the more remarkable that she persevered and took her education further. Frances had, though, received a lesson in gender inequality that she would not forget.

Unlike many middle class daughters whose fathers died prematurely, Frances was not impoverished. Her mother was from a wealthy family and Frances was well connected. Her cousin Thomas Greenish, a chemist in London, was president of the Pharmaceutical Society.[20] By 1858 she was in Paris with her mother where she passed an examination in general education. One account suggests that she was studying with private tutors in Düsseldorf by 1861 as a precursor to making medicine her career.[21]

According to McIntyre, Frances became pregnant and, aged sixteen, gave birth to a baby daughter Elise/Elsie in

Brussels that October.[22] Her mother provided a home for the child. She was presumed to be Frances' younger sister or a niece. When Elise entered North London Collegiate School, Frances' mother signed as parent/guardian. A reference from Frances stated that she had known Elise for eleven years. Later Elise briefly studied medicine then married a Cardiganshire clergyman in 1857.

There is no absolute proof that she was Frances' child. The lack of conclusive evidence or even any hint from Frances herself in later years leaves a slight question mark, not least because she was a progressive woman and feminist who did not shy away from difficult issues. But McIntyre makes a compelling case and Elise's descendants corroborate his findings. Were she Elise's mother, Frances certainly covered her tracks well, though this would have been necessary. Her father had given evidence (when he was Aberavon's vicar) to the 1847 Report on the State of Education in Wales. Here he had stated that the loss of chastity before marriage was 'unhappily the scandal of the Principality'.[23] Meanwhile across Britain daughters from respectable moneyed families went abroad to have their babies out of wedlock – the essay on Margaret Wynne Nevinson provides one example – though Frances appears to have already been on the continent.

She faced huge obstacles gaining acceptance as a doctor and, if she were the mother of an illegitimate child, could hardly have risked acknowledging the situation if she wished to be taken seriously as a professional in Victorian Britain. As late as 1885 there were only forty-five registered women doctors. For these pioneers there was not only the personal need to succeed but also the responsibility of setting an example for others, in addition to the scrutiny they faced from society.

Frances became a governess in Paris, saving money in order to study medicine. Then she, Sarah Goff, an Irish heiress, and Ellen Phillips, who was from a wealthy Quaker family, worked under the tutelage of Elizabeth Garrett (later Garrett Anderson) in London as the first pupils in her new Dispensary for Women and Children. Garrett had become a pioneer female licentiate of the Society of Apothecaries in 1865, qualifying her to join the Medical Register (practitioners who were not included on this Register forfeited any legal protection).

At the beginning of 1867 the three young women passed – Frances with honours – the Society's preliminary examinations in Arts.[24] *The Times* acknowledged that they had succeeded in Latin, Geometry and History but made clear that this was a far cry from doing dissections.[25] The Society of Apothecaries provided the sole route in Britain for the medical qualification Frances needed. But in the first of a series of reversals that must have had an impact on her views on equal rights, it promptly revised its regulations, deciding only to accept as Licentiates those who had attended public lectures at recognised public medical schools, none of which accepted women students.

The consequences proved (though only in retrospect) beneficial for Frances and her career. In order to circumvent the British restrictions on aspirant women medics and what she called the 'disgraceful epithets' used against them in English medical journals,[26] Frances enrolled at the University of Zürich,[27] along with Louisa Atkins, niece of the 3rd Earl of Derby. Atkins graduated five years later, as was customary with medical students, but Frances completed her medical studies in less than three years and took a course in Sanskrit. In the same year as she started at Zürich (1867), Nadezhda Suslova from St Petersburg, also born in 1843, graduated there with the first medical degree awarded to a woman in Europe. Frances followed in 1870.

The Swiss scientist Auguste Forel (later professor of psychiatry at Zürich's medical school) was a student two years senior to her. In his autobiography he recalled that when the anatomy professor Hermann Meyer protested that his laboratory would not provide a 'decorous' environment for a lady, Frances replied 'with sovereign confidence' that it was 'much more shocking and improper to make exceptions here. We wish to study the subject without restrictions of any kind'. Meyer capitulated. Forel later noted that the 'seriousness, the aristocratic calm, and the queenly superiority of this remarkable girl' commanded 'such respect from us all that none of us would have dared to make a tactless or sarcastic remark'.[28] Nevertheless, Forel and fellow students were not quite sure what to make of her. His ambiguous remark that she was becoming increasingly like a male student ('elle deviant de plus en plus synonyme d'un étudiant du sexe masculin')[29] reflects his slight unease.

He was, however, impressed by Frances' composure and performance at the public defence of her thesis (written in German) on progressive muscular atrophy. So many attended in the spring of 1870 – more than 400, including 50 women – that the viva was moved to the university's largest hall. Frances' supervisor Anton Biermer criticised her findings at length. Yet Frances understood correctly that muscular dystrophy was an organic disease of the nervous system, whereas his belief (already in print) was that it was a muscular disease. Undaunted, in her half-hour response Frances stressed that her interpretation was derived from the use of sources in English. Biermer conceded that she had provided an impressive defence and that her 'scholarly earnestness and zeal' had made her 'a worthy model for the women studying here'.[30] After such a public encounter in her twenties, it is hardly surprising that Frances went on to champion women's rights.

She remained in Europe briefly, studying and practising midwifery in Vienna before moving on to Prague and, according to Onfel Thomas, Paris.[31] She would, however, have returned to London before the Siege of Paris (part of the Franco-Prussian War) in September 1870. She established herself in private practice in London's West End (at Granville Place, Portman Square) at the end of that year, qualified but unregistered. That same year a Dr Bennett wrote in the *Lancet* that women as a body were 'sexually, constitutionally and mentally unfitted for the hard and incessant toil' demanded of doctors. Women had not advanced the understanding of science, so what right, he asked, could they have to mental equality with men?[32] Since male doctors had to fight for their own social position in British society – in 1881 *The Modern Review* stressed that most doctors did not come from the 'top drawer' of society and that this was a '*parvenu* profession' – they were especially sensitive about the 'invasion' of women.[33]

In March 1871 Elizabeth Garrett appointed Frances as

her first assistant physician at St Mary's Dispensary for Women and Children, and (from 1872) its successor, the New Hospital for Women in Marylebone. Frances worked at this pioneering hospital staffed by and for women until 1877, when she resigned. Although it has been claimed that this was due to concern about Garrett Anderson's frequent recourse to risky abdominal surgery and in particular her opposition to an ovariotomy (seen by many as both dangerous and unwise), it seems, that this procedure was not carried out at the New Hospital until a year after Frances had left.[34] The Managing Committee noted that Frances' 'kind and skilful labours' had 'done much to raise the Hospital to its present position'.[35]

In 1871 Frances helped to found the National Health Society, along with Dr Elizabeth Blackwell. Blackwell had qualified in 1849 in the United States, and a decade later become the first English woman on the Medical Register. Another founding luminary was Barbara Leigh Smith Bodichon, educationalist and artist, one of the Langham Place Group that had discussed women's rights in the 1850s. Frances became the National Health Society's Honorary Secretary (its rules ensured that women were in the majority on its executive).[36] It advocated the 'steady and wide diffusion of sanitary knowledge' to all and stressed the value of sanitary and hygienic education in schools, coining the saying that 'Prevention is Better than Cure'.

The Society for Promoting the Employment of Women had also been founded in London's Langham Place (by Barbara Bodichon, Jessie Boucherett and Adelaide Anne Proctor in 1859). It encouraged the training – with interest-free loans – and employment of women in a number of occupations, some of which, like bookkeeping, had previously been the preserve of men. Frances became a member and represented the society at a congress of delegates of German societies promoting female education and employment in 1880. A fluent German speaker, she explained what had been achieved over the past decade in England.

Frances married George Hoggan in 1874 but, unlike many women of her time, did not have to sacrifice her public and professional fortunes. If anything, she became busier than ever. This daughter of a Church of England clergyman was married in a Registry Office followed by a service conducted at home by a member of the Scottish Kirk. Frances thus circumvented the need to agree to 'obey' as demanded in the Anglican marriage service. She also broke with convention in terms of class. Her husband was the son of a Scottish painter and decorator. George had left school aged twelve and been apprenticed to an engineer before serving in the navy. In 1868 he had begun studying medicine at the University of Edinburgh. As an anatomy demonstrator, he gave Sophia Jex-Blake and other female medical students their first class in practical anatomy. He also organised the escort protecting these young women when male medical students' rioted against women medics in November 1870.

In 1875 Frances became the second woman elected to the British Medical Association (BMA). Along with its first female member, Garrett Anderson, she addressed the BMA's annual meeting in Edinburgh. Frances' paper was on histological chemistry, so framed, she wrote, 'as not to shock even extraordinary susceptibilities'. Yet it still sparked antagonism. The *South Wales Daily News* ridiculed this response: 'female creatures' were deemed 'too delicate to discuss pathological subjects with men' or, rather, 'medical men were too delicate to discuss medicine with women'.[37]

Once again, the medical establishment appeared to be playing snakes and ladders with the women. A referendum was called to decide whether women should really be members. The result went against female membership, and at a special meeting in 1878 it was agreed that no female should be eligible for membership. Although Garrett Anderson was permitted to remain, Frances was expelled because, even though her name was on the Medical Register by 1877, this had not been the case at the time of her election.

An Enabling Act in 1876 had permitted all medical examining boards to examine women. The King's and Queen's College of Physicians of Ireland in Dublin was the first to do this, so Frances became a Licentiate of this College in 1877. Yet the 1878 retrospective ruling conveniently ignored this. Reporting on the BMA's decision, the *South Wales Daily News* speculated: might the Court of Queen's Bench rule as to whether Dr Hoggan could simply be turned out of the BMA on account of her sex? [38] Judicial action did not follow but there were lively exchanges in the *British Medical Journal*. Although the majority of those who had voted were clearly against women members, as Frances pointed out in a letter to the *BMJ*, fewer than half the members actually took part in the referendum and more than a quarter of those who did were in favour of women members.[39]

In 1880 Frances became a Member of the King's and Queen's College of Physicians of Ireland and thereby the first female Member of the British College of Physicians. During this period the Hoggans ran a joint practice, initially from Granville Place (George moved there after their marriage) and then Trevor Terrace in Knightsbridge. They each had a consulting room but worked to a common timetable and, interestingly, charged equal rates. Frances primarily dealt with women and children.

Specialists in microscopical pathological investigation, their papers appeared in scientific journals in English, French, German and Italian. They co-authored a number of papers on the anatomy of the lymphatic system.[40] When the Abstract of their joint paper for the *Transactions* of the Obstetrical Society appeared, Frances' name was omitted, an example of what she called 'this arrogance of sex'.[41] But in a paper in the *Journal of Anatomy and Physiology* in 1884 on 'New forms of nerve terminations in mammalian skin', George identified three different nerve endings, naming one after Frances: 'in honour of my ever-helpful co-worker and wife, without whose aid I should have done nothing in biological research'.[42] By this time they were both researching the nervous system.

In this same year Frances penned an essay on 'Women in Medicine' for the book *The Woman Question in Europe*.[43] She told the story of women's struggles to become medics. George, described as 'a staunch supporter of the equal rights of women', contributed the middle section. Writing in the third person for the remainder of the essay, Frances included her own experiences but used initialled footnotes to emphasise points. She protested against the exclusion in 1879 of women from membership of the Association of German Naturalists and Doctors. Both Frances and the pioneer Dutch doctor Aletta Jacobs[44] had been members of this Association and active in former congresses. The English Committee of the International Medical Congress then excluded women from all but social and ceremonial events. Frances conceded, however, that public attitudes towards women in medicine had improved greatly in recent years, and she ended on an upbeat note.

In another publication in 1884 Frances focused on the position of the mother in the family.[45] This had been her address in Birmingham to the annual peripatetic congress of the National Association for the Promotion of Social Science. The first British middle class forum to welcome the public voice of women, it promoted the language of family in its five-day events modelled on the British Association for the Advancement of Science.[46]

Frances painted a picture of the ideal situation as she saw it, with the mother as the 'pivot of the family and the home'. 'Happy is the child' she wrote, 'who has had a strong, wise, loving mother, and sad is the lot of those who have missed that priceless blessing'. Such words seem especially poignant if we recognise Elise as her unacknowledged daughter.

She reviewed the legal position of the mother since antiquity, as well as scientific factors. Frances' purpose was reform of the law of the custody and guardianship of children, hence her stark claim that 'the legal position of the English wife and mother of to-day [sic] differs but little from that of the Roman matron'. Thanks to the exertions of Caroline Norton, the Custody of Infants Act had been passed in 1839, but this and subsequent legislation in 1873, remained limited. Frances conceded that married women's property rights had improved due to legislation in 1882, but she stressed their lack of rights over their children. The legal position of the mother in the family was 'almost a fiction'. She was considered in all respects as 'secondary, supplementary, subservient' to her husband.

A number of feminists had, for some time, criticised marriage, focusing mainly on injustices, rather than attacking it as an institution.[47] They exposed unequal laws and the assumption of a husband's ownership of his wife. Some felt, as did Frances, that it was wrong for single women to have more rights than married women. The ideal for her remained a family in which married men and women had equality in law, yet with the bearing *and* rearing of children the responsibility of the mother 'by natural right'. In contrast, four years later more radical criticisms of marriage were voiced, geared around the writings of Mona Caird and the 'Is Marriage a Failure?' debate in the press, followed by the New Woman writers of the 1890s.[48]

Nevertheless, although Frances' critique urged reform at the expense of a more fundamental examination of the role of marriage in society, her purpose had been to help the case for altering the laws on the custody and guardianship of infants (though the modern reader might be surprised at how little infants featured in her analysis, the focus being primarily on the mother). She did achieve her aim. The Guardianship of Infants Act (1886) not only enabled a widow to be sole or joint guardian (depending on what the father had stipulated), but also – significantly – granted courts the power to override a father's common law rights of custody. It would be 1925, though, before recognition in law of the more modern concept that the welfare of the child should be paramount, and it was not until 1973 that mothers became entitled to full equal rights in guardianship cases. [49]

The Hoggans had no children of their own. They appear to have enjoyed what feminists of the time sought: a companionate marriage. However, we lack the first-hand sources that could shed light on domestic arrangements within the household or provide insight into Frances' and George's attitudes and emotions as well as the role of Elise in the family. The Hoggans were comfortably off and we know from the census of 1881 that the household, at that frozen snapshot in time, included not only a cook and maid but also Elise. She was then a student aged nineteen and described as George's sister-in-law.

Nevertheless, we can glimpse something of the their public life and commitment to causes. So busy were they that relaxing evenings at home must have been few and far between. They were part of the minority of medical figures who embraced liberal and controversial social issues. One was cremation. The Cremation Society was established in 1874 but cremation remained illegal until a decade later when Dr William Price, ex-Chartist, medical man (a works surgeon in Pontypridd) and fervent follower of Druidism, illegally cremated on the South Wales hillside the body of his baby son Jesus Christ Price whom he had fathered aged eighty-three.[50] He was tried and his victory in court legalised cremation in the United Kingdom.

The month after this victory, Frances seconded a motion in favour of cremation at a lecture on the subject.[51] The first official cremation took place at St John's Crematorium, Woking, in 1885. When George died in France six years later he was cremated at Père Lachaise cemetery in Paris and his ashes were buried in Woking. Frances would eventually be cremated there, her ashes interred in her husband's grave.

The Hoggans challenged the status quo and actively upheld the rights of the individual. They were members of the Personal Rights Association. It was formed in 1871.[52] Her article on 'American Negro Women During Their First Fifty Years of Freedom' was published in 1913 in their paper *The Individualist*. The organisation was anti-statist and championed equal treatment in law.

The couple championed animal as well as human rights. In the 1860s George had worked in Paris in the laboratory of the eminent physiologist Claude Bernard. George's graphic account of four months of experiments on animals – with dogs licking the hands that were about to sacrifice them – was published in the *Morning Post* nine months after he married Frances and was guaranteed a sympathetic public response in Britain, especially since he had first-hand experience and had seen the error of his ways. His letter has been described as marking 'the beginning of an organised nineteenth- century anti-vivisection movement'.[53]

The first legislation to protect animals from cruelty had been passed in 1822, followed two years later by the creation of the Society for the Prevention of Cruelty to Animals (it became the RSPCA in 1840) to help implement the legislation. Advances in physiology and the adoption of anaesthesia meant that vivisection grew apace: George saw the use of anaesthetics as 'the greatest curse to vivisectible animals'.[54]

Ironically, it was a Royal Commission on how to regulate experiments on animals, followed by the Cruelty to Animals Act of 1876, that prompted action. The legislation began a system of licensing and inspection but vivisection was exempt from prosecution for deliberate cruelty to animals. By 1878 three times as many vivisectors were licensed as were practising in 1875.[55]

The first specifically anti-vivisection society was the Victoria Street Society (its formal name was the Society for the Protection of Animals Liable to Vivisection). The prominent Anglo-Irish feminist, Frances Power Cobbe founded the society with George Hoggan. In her autobiography Cobbe credits him with suggesting and naming it.[56] Its first meeting took place at the Hoggan home in December 1875. George became its secretary and Frances (Hoggan) a member of its executive committee. Frances also became Cobbe's 'much-valued friend and lady-Doctor'.[57] The Victoria Street Society sought to expose the secrecy surrounding vivisection, and supported a strengthening of the 1876 Act. It attracted artistic figures including John Ruskin. Christina Rossetti described vivisection as 'cruelty of revolting magnitude'.[58] Over seventy per cent of its members were women.[59]

For Frances and George, commitment to clinical observation and microscopical research provided the acceptable approach to scientific research. Yet as Hilda Kean has shown, the early women doctors were divided in their attitudes. Garrett Anderson supported vivisection though

Blackwell was opposed to it.[60] There were also differences within the society and it split into two in 1878. The British Union for the Abolition of Vivisection, the branch spearheaded by Cobbe, adopted a policy of total abolition of all animal experimentation (rather than just objecting to painful experiments). The Hoggans were not members of its committee, but Cobbe's autobiography shows that they continued to speak at meetings.[61]

In 1882 a letter simply signed 'MD' appeared in the journal *Zoophilist* (and was reprinted as a pamphlet called 'The Scientist at the Bedside').[62] Its contents suggest that Frances most probably wrote it. Describing the experience of qualifying as a doctor abroad in 1870, the letter criticised vivisection as 'the quick way to honour and success' for medics. It went far further than a critique of vivisection as a practice, arguing that it helped to create an atmosphere in which neither animals nor humans received due respect. It suggested that the very ethos and ethics of medical training were problematic, encouraging students to focus on 'interesting' cases. 'The habit of looking on sentient creatures as if they were only so much teaching material' destroyed, it was argued, the essential tenderness and sympathy with the weak and suffering that should exist. It reflected badly on the profession and did a disservice to the public, especially women of the poorer classes who tended not to receive the respect they deserved.

In the 1890s Frances defended her late husband's views on vivisection in letters to the press and at the same time extended the link between the practice and treatment of human patients, arguing that a connection could and should be made between operations on animals and surgeons operating unnecessarily on humans, acts she deplored as 'surgical crime'.[63]

Frances and George were also vice-presidents of the London Society for the Abolition of Compulsory Vaccination. Legislation to make vaccination compulsory had been inaugurated in 1853, and was extended in an act of 1867, prompting some organised opposition. A smallpox pandemic in 1871-4 resulted in further legislation to secure compliance. In a long, joint letter of 1883 to the society's paper, the *Vaccination Inquirer*, the Hoggans explained their ambivalence about the presumed efficacy of vaccination, stressing that there was at present no scientific evidence in its favour and also a lack of reliable statistical evidence.

They were, however, not so much hostile to vaccination per se as to compulsion. Their belief in the rights of the individual meant that they were prepared to offer 'uncompromising opposition' to legislation.[64] Meanwhile the *Lancet* endorsed compulsory vaccination as 'a most beneficient use of the authority of the State and we exceedingly regret that any member of our profession should give any sanction to the crotchety people who oppose it'.[65]

In a letter of May 1884 (read out at the society's AGM), Frances reaffirmed her belief in resisting enforcement but carefully extended her message to embrace women's enfranchisement:

> If only the friends of liberty are earnest and united, the time is not far distant when the tyranny of compulsory vaccination will be swept away and parents left free to

> choose between conflicting medical opinions, and to decide for themselves whether their children shall be infected with disease as a means of maintaining health ... soon may women join with men in voting in one common accord for the return of Members of Parliament who will strenuously exert themselves for ... all personal rights and liberties, inclusive of the right to accept or to refuse vaccination.[66]

Seven months later the third Reform Act confirmed that not a single woman would gain the right to vote in national elections. In 1889 a Royal Commission was set up, which eventually led to further vaccination legislation in 1898. Its inclusion of a conscience clause was the first real step in modifying compulsion.

Unlike many active in the campaigns against vivisection and vaccination, Frances also made links between them and vegetarianism. She was a member of the Executive Committee of the Food Reform Society and contributed to its magazine. She suggested that, had monkeys been as cheap and available as stray cats and dogs, 'we should probably have heard much more about the processes of digestion of nuts, grains and fruit'.[67]

In the early 1880s she addressed Vegetarian Society meetings from Manchester to Norwich on issues such as how a vegetarian diet could prevent seasickness, and the exclusion of meat from prison and workhouses diets.[68] Her 1883 pamphlet 'On the Advantages of a Vegetarian Diet in Workhouses and Prisons',[69] pointed out that many Scots peasants ate very little meat yet were strong.

Although allying herself once more with those challenging accepted wisdom and practices, her views on this subject seem closer to the concept of 'Less Eligibility'[70] evident in the Poor Law Amendment Act of 1834, than to more progressive notions of prison and workhouse reform fifty years later. She insisted that inmates of prisons and paupers should not be better off than those outside these institutions, and stressed that many paupers were not hard workers, so not entitled to sympathy. She characterised the habitual pauper as 'usually self-indulgent', arguing for the exclusion of meat and alcohol more, it would seem, from the perspective of providing a deterrent and cutting costs, than from a desire for progress based on scientific research and arguments.

Frances was a busy woman, addressing societies and writing papers on a wide range of subjects for many years. In the 1870s and early 1880s she was occupied with the running of her medical practice and she was a London-based social reformer, part of the network of mid-Victorian respectable ladies who were seeking, through involvement in a series of voluntary societies, to improve opportunities for other women. They saw it as their duty to abolish the double standard in morality. This was most clearly spelt out in the Contagious Diseases Acts that from the late 1860s forced women in garrison towns and ports to undergo medical examinations if they were even suspected of being prostitutes. This gender-specific legislation exculpated male clients from any responsibility, and circumscribed women's freedom in public places. Frances supported the successful repeal campaign headed by Josephine Butler. Like many of the women who espoused a range of moral causes, Frances believed in what Philippa Levine has called a 'feminised humanism'.[71]

Historians have noted that the mid-Victorian women campaigners tended not to restrict themselves to one cause. Judy Walkowitz's work on the Ladies' National Association that galvanised opposition to the Contagious Diseases Acts, demonstrates well the overlapping concerns of campaigners. Examining the thirty-two executive board members of the 1860s and 70s, she shows that they were active in a range of causes. Seventeen were involved in suffrage activities, ten were part of the Social Science Association, eight active in higher education for women and sixteen in what she called medical reform (including anti-vivisection, anti-vaccination, rational dress and medical education for women).[72]

Brian Harrison's examination of fourteen moral reform organisations at work in 1884[73] shows that although not formally coordinated, they were all connected indirectly as pressure groups and there was considerable overlap in personnel. They could be loosely grouped into six areas of involvement: Sunday observance, personal liberty, sexual purity, women's rights, animal cruelty and temperance. Frances' interests straddled all but the first and last, and she was active in a number of the societies identified by Harrison.

Frances was in a highly unusual position as one of a small number of experienced female medical practitioners. She was therefore able to add scientific and medical knowledge and weight to the causes she supported as well as demonstrating how professional women could make a difference.

She also helped to bridge the gap between the 'mysteries' of medicine and science and the public. In the

1870s she gave Drawing Room lectures for ladies on human psychology. 1884 was an especially busy year for her, yet she also visited the Middle East during that same period to see how lepers were treated, offering help and advice.[74] In 1880 and 1883 the Hoggans had published research on leprosy. Frances later wrote an article for the *Journal of Hellenic Studies*.[75] Here she described seeing amongst a collection of ancient terracotta figures at the Polytechnic in Athens the figure of a leper. Frances contrasted this representation – a cruel caricature – with her own knowledge, recalling a leper she had met in an Athens hospital as well as a patient of her husband's whom she used to visit.[76] He died aged twenty-nine after gradually losing most of his physical senses and shrinking from six to four feet tall. But, Frances stressed, he maintained throughout an intelligent interest in world affairs.

Her linking of the arts and science was evident when she delivered a paper in Birmingham at the first annual congress on domestic economy in connection with the Society of Arts.[77] Her subject was the teaching of scientific subjects in the education of girls. She also wrote in the *Englishwoman's Review* on how the microscope could give women both employment and recreation, and provided hints for beginners.[78] These beginners were, however, presumed to be comfortably off ladies of voluntary or enforced leisure, since she suggested sixteen items worth purchasing in order to become amateur microscopists. They included a good microscope (likely to cost £4), histological rings for stretching membranes, forceps, glycerine and chloroform. Interestingly, despite her opposition to vivisection, she suggested experimenting on the skin of a mouse, which could be painlessly killed with chloroform.

Frances was passionate about health education. Like Elizabeth Garrett Anderson, she supported the physical education of girls. In 1879 she addressed the annual meeting of the Froebel Society on the subject. She stressed, as she did elsewhere, that 'able, cultured, and efficiently trained women' were central to the success of Froebel's Kindergarten system[79] (a Kindergarten Training College had recently been started in London). Her audience was overwhelmingly female.

At the nursery stage, Frances explained, boys and girls exercised and played together. But subsequently only boys were encouraged to enjoy vigorous play. Perhaps surprisingly, given her belief in intelligent, educated women, she argued that the development of the physical prowess of girls should take precedence over their intellectual development. Up to adolescence, physical and moral training should be paramount for both girls and boys.

She advocated major changes in attitudes towards dress. She was a member of the Rational Dress Society established in 1881[80] with its opposition to tight corsets, heavy skirts and high heels. But several years before its formation, Frances was declaring that 'Girls' dress cries imperiously for reform'. She was disparaging about those we call teenagers wearing skimpy clothes. It would, she claimed, be better to teach girls of all classes how and what to wear than the 'names and dates of all our bloody battles, or the exact order of succession of our English kings'. Stressing physiological differences between the sexes, it was, she declared, ludicrous that girls, whose chests were less capacious than those of boys, should have to wear corsets.

Her comments were not restricted to the middle class. Heavy skirts weighed down working class girls, as did carrying baby brothers and sisters. Frances warned that cheap corsets could affect breastfeeding adversely later in life. Delicate girls working as nursemaids risked curvature of the spine. Needlework, she argued was far from conducive to good health. Knitting was preferable, and she liked the idea of it being taught to boys as well as girls. She did, however, acknowledge that School Boards were delivering little girls from 'the thraldom of the baby' (school replacing the role of child-minder).

Some of Frances' remarks have a modern ring. It was not enough for mothers to tell their daughters that high-heeled boots were bad from them. She wanted to cast aside 'those trammels to free and healthy development of the body which fashion and the folly of mothers have devised', and to enable adolescent girls to learn and think for themselves what was beneficial for them.

Her advice included exercise. Middle class girls, she suggested, were worse off than their working class counterparts and all boys. They were often more conscientious than boys, and parents and guardians placed too much emphasis on studying at school which was then expected to set girls up for life. She suggested that 'Over-active brains in feeble bodies' meant that health might suffer later in life. This could also discredit the movement for the higher education of women. The training of the muscular system through exercise should be developed for all girls. The *Englishwoman's Review* urged that 'All mothers of girls should read this pamphlet'.[81]

Some of her recommendations would only be recognised

as valid much later. She understood, for example, that adolescents need a lot of sleep. Her advice that left-handed children should not be forced to use their right hands was often ignored, even as late as the 1950s. Yet not all her opinions and remedies are easily reconciled with what modern society sees as progressive. Social Darwinist overtones were evident (though the term was not yet widely used). Frances' rational system of physical education was predicated upon a belief that making girls physically strong from a young age 'will make them the strong mothers of a strong race'. She did, admittedly, see their becoming wives and mothers as a right but she went on to add that making young women strong enabled them to perform 'their special womanly duties'. Having said this, Frances tended to choose her words carefully and may well have couched her language knowingly so that she did not alienate from the outset those who needed convincing.

In 1882 Frances took a post at North London Collegiate School (NLCS). The twenty-three year old Frances Mary Buss had established this prestigious girls' day school in Camden Town in 1850. Frances Hoggan's putative daughter Elise (now living with Mrs Morgan in Wembley) was a pupil between 1873 and 1877.

Buss, who remained headmistress until 1918, recognised that the health of her charges was of prime importance. She was far-sighted in the promotion of preventive health education and advocated that 'mental work must be counterbalanced by bodily exercise'[82] for girls as well as boys. Health and hygiene featured in the curriculum. Calisthenics (exercises designed to enhance both gracefulness and strength) featured almost from the outset,

German drill was practised, and NLCS became the first girls' school to have a gymnasium.

Buss also developed a unique programme of medical inspection by a school doctor. Dr Emily Bovell-Sturge (who had qualified in Paris after studying in Edinburgh) was the first. Like Frances, she had an enlightened physician husband and they too set up a joint medical practice. Ill health led her to resign her NLCS post and practice, and the couple moved to the south of France, (as would the Hoggans). Dr Bovell-Sturge died there three years later. Frances succeeded her at NLCS. Ironically, in that same year, 1885, Frances had to resign her post due to George's ill health.

Frances examined each girl on entry. She assessed their fitness. Although she did not prescribe medication, she suggested what exercise might be most beneficial. Both Frances' private notes on her pupils over three years and the formal medical records of these individuals – the latter read by Miss Buss – have fortunately survived. They show that the gym became not just a literal site for the remedial exercise programmes she devised but also a means by which the doctor could exercise real control and authority. She, rather than the gym mistress, determined what was deemed most efficacious for the girls.

The gym was enlarged whilst Frances was the school doctor. Every pupil now spent half an hour there twice weekly. There were dumb bells, balls, a horse, a ladder, parallel and horizontal bars as well as the giant stride. It consisted of four light poles from which girls would swing. Frances' private notes on Mary Perch state that she 'had too much of the giant stride'. Although nothing was dislocated or broken, Frances declared: 'No giant stride for this term, and then only arm exercises and without apparatus'. Another girl was using dumb bells that were too heavy for her, to which Frances added: 'I spoke to the teacher about it'. Her recommendations for appropriate and strengthening exercises were linked to size rather than age.

Criticism and advice extended to the home: Octavia Poole had gained in strength so might return to the gym but should rest for five minutes after exercising. At home she should 'hang from a pole by both hands'. Lilian Haydon's slight goitre had not been noticed at home: 'It had better be pointed out'. A letter was duly dispatched to her family. Alice Clapton, who had a delicate chest as a result of bad posture, should do daily arm exercises at home as well as work in the gym four times weekly. Beatrice Eadie needed 'a good deal of motherly supervision and care', her eyesight was not good and she was (from the way she sat to write) in danger of curvature of the spine. These accounts of defective eyesight, curvature and even rickets seem more reminiscent of overworked needlewomen than of privileged middle class adolescents.

Frances continued her assault on high heels and corsetry. Thyrza Reed's dorsal curvature she attributed partly to her doctor's advice to wear tight stays and she informed Harriet Newbold's mother that her daughter's corset was restrictive. Over time she was able to discern some improvements in posture and health due to gentle, appropriate exercise.

Once again she spoke out about her beliefs. In response to a letter in the *Standard* newspaper in 1883 about the deleterious effect of the gymnasium on girls' health, Frances argued that many town-dwellers tended to stoop until they discovered the gym.[83] A valuable corrective to long hours at desks, it relieved congestion and helped eyesight in her view. She recognised that great care was needed for growing girls, and advocated 'competent medical women as advisers to gymnasia' (precisely what she was providing), with the physical capacity of every girl tested on the spot before entering the gym, followed by proper supervision of well-regulated, suitable exercises. Both here and at the Denbigh Eisteddfod,[84] she stressed that qualified and efficient female teachers were far more appropriate for adolescent girls than male instructors.

In her lecture to the Froebel Society in 1879 Frances had genuflected to traditional concerns about the possible effect of gymnastics on future mothers, stating that exercises for girls 'must be less violent, perhaps more frequent, but certainly less prolonged, than those designed for boys'.[85] She also had some reservations about girls rowing and skating. She voiced no such gender distinction three years later at NLCS.

Girls at the school had been encouraged to swim at St Pancras swimming baths from the early 1870s. Swimming for girls and young women was becoming increasingly popular, and there were even some female professional swimmers.[86] Elizabeth Garrett Anderson endorsed the benefits of swimming. Frances followed suit, addressing the London Women's Union Swimming Club in 1879 on 'Swimming and its relation to the Health of Women'.[87]

This club had been formed in the wake of a fatal accident on board the Princess Alice steamer where many non-swimmers lost their lives. Frances stressed that swimming liberated women from tight clothing, let them use their muscles naturally and provided 'lung gymnastics'. She stressed its value for those doing repetitive sedentary jobs as well as desk-bound schoolgirls. She attacked those vestries[88] where swimming baths were for men only or only occasionally open to women, suggesting that women should be appointed to vestries to help ensure decent public provision for girls and women to swim.

The *Women's Union Journal*, the organ of the Women's Protective and Provident League, forerunner of the Women's Trade Union League, printed Frances' lecture. The Women's Printing Society published it as a leaflet. Frances sat on the League's council from its formation in 1875. Middle class women and men sought to work with skilled trade unionists to build up trade societies of female dressmakers, printers and others.

At its inaugural meeting its founder and president Emilia Patterson (a former bookbinder's apprentice) stressed that this cooperative association existed not only for the protection of workers but also to foster self-reliance and independence rather than charity. Frances, seconding a speech by Cobbe, used the example of the famous scientist Mary Somerville to demonstrate that women might attain 'intellectual eminence without any sacrifice of womanly grace or gentleness'.[89] Frances' words were, like the initial title of the society, cautious and apparently modest. Whether she deployed this tone from expediency rather than natural inclination, was left to those in the know to discern.

Many of Frances' interventions focused on practical

matters. She tended to provide perspectives that would either have gone unnoticed by most men or would have been considered indelicate and thus not articulated. For example, in an article on 'Sanitary Conveniences for Women' in 1880 she wrote about the urgent need for 'water closet accommodation' for women. She established her credentials by stressing that she was a medical adviser of women 'of all classes' with many years' experience. She also indicated (albeit euphemistically) that menstruation increased the need for such conveniences when women were away from home.[90] She stressed that poorer women in London were worse off than previously, many now having to work some distance from home. She once again appealed to vestries. London ratepayers paid for men's urinals. Female ratepayers would suffer an injustice if vestries did not provide free public conveniences for women with female waged attendants. They needed to catch up with cities like Paris and Berlin.

Frances' work in this area can be traced back to the quaintly named Ladies Association for the Diffusion of Sanitary Knowledge (which became the Ladies Sanitary Association), established in the 1850s to spread via tracts, lectures and libraries understanding of sanitary knowledge amongst the poor. Frances was a member in the 1880s. By 1887 it had produced over 1,400,000 leaflets.[91] Branches were set up across the country, as were cooking and sewing classes and home visits to families. In 1891 the Health Visiting Service began, making this provision professional. The first public toilets for women in London were erected two years later.[92]

Frances was, along with Elizabeth Garrett's sister Agnes

and cousin Rhoda, a founder member of the all-female Somerville Club, established in central London in 1878 as 'a meeting place for solitary workers'. It too recognised the needs of women beyond the home. It was aimed at single women living in lodgings, and it had a modest subscription fee.[93] Its qualifications for entry were unusual: 'Personal respectability, and interest in social and political questions'.[94]

Frances also concerned herself with women rather further afield, advocating medical opportunities in India in the 1880s. At this time ideas about supplying women doctors to India abounded. Despite its distance, imperial India was never far from the thoughts of many Victorians. Frances also had a personal link: her paternal great grandfather Captain Thomas Morgan had worked for the East India Company. However, she does not seem to have worked in India herself.[95]

Frances' first public plea came in an article in the *Contemporary Review* in August 1882.[96] Here and in a well-attended meeting of the Indian National Association [97] held at the Medical Society of London that November, chaired by the Surgeon General, she argued that the existing medical service in India was a failure because it reached only 'the merest fringe' of the native population. Culture and religion militated against many women seeking medical treatment from male doctors (though recent research indicates that there seems to have been less opposition to the latter at the time than presumed).[98] Frances drew on India Office statistics. It is likely that she also consulted Dr Sarah Heckford (née Goff) with whom she had worked in London early in her career. Heckford was employed by the Zenana[99] Missions Charity in India between 1876-8, and had relayed to Elizabeth Manning (who ran the Indian National Association) her concern about the lack of medical care provided for high caste Indian women living in Zenanas.

Although Frances was passionate about extending women's opportunities in India – at this stage at least – the doctors were to be British rather than indigenous Indian women. Such schemes were likely to receive the blessing of the profession at home and helped to justify the need for more women medics.[100] It was also easier to accept the criticisms of the Indian system of medical care that Frances and colleagues outlined, than to question practices within western culture.[101]

Frances' language is interesting. She presented her appeal as coming 'from the womanhood of India to the womanhood and manhood of England', stressing that medical women were urgently needed in India, not only for their professional knowledge and skill but also as 'the most powerful agents for raising the tone and lives of women in that great empire'. Government should make provision for the study of medicine by women. Far from challenging empire, the reforms that she and others suggested would reinforce the civilising imperial ideal.

Yet whereas students trained at the London School of Medicine for Women gained a licence of Medicine, Surgery and Midwifery to work in dispensaries and Zenanas in India, Frances' plan was to open medical schools in India itself. What was needed, she argued, was a new medical department, part of the public service in India, managed by women and working in harmony with, but not subordinate to, the existing civil service. By making provision for the study of medicine by women, the lives of 'great multitudes' would be saved.

Frances was ambitious, seeking a fully-fledged women's medical service *in* India rather than simply training. She had not been involved in the development of the London School of Medicine for Women and had declined an invitation to join their Board of Governors when it opened in 1874. As Mary Ann Elston has intimated, Frances' different tack from them over India caused some tension, since they were raising funds for scholarships for women to train at the London School before practising there.[102]

After reading Frances' article, George Kittredge, an American businessman based in Bombay (Mumbai) and the Bengali, Sorabji Shapurji, along with Pestonjee Cama, built the Cama Hospital there, staffed by and for women. In 1883 the Countess of Dufferin accompanied her husband the Viceroy to India, tasked by Queen Victoria, Empress of India, to improve medical conditions for Indian women. Two years later, in 1885, the Dufferin Fund[103] was established.

In that year Frances addressed the exhibition of women's industries in Bristol,[104] criticising British missionaries who studied for medical degrees at home and then returned to India. She admitted that several missionaries currently in India were former pupils of hers. In her view missionaries were only really interested in imparting their religious beliefs. She argued that 'the social uplifting of Indian women must be a natural growth, developing out of the history and ancient institutions of the country' and she urged that medical training be 'disconnected from any proselytising or sectarian agencies'.

Frances made it clear that those who thought medical women in India required less knowledge and skill were completely mistaken. She outlined the thorough medical training she deemed essential for this work, alongside qualities such as sympathy and sensitivity. She also acknowledged the need – in time – for 'native growth', recognising that Indian women 'must take this matter in hand themselves, and not be content to see it taken in hand for them'. Referring to older traditions of independence, she stated that they must take up medicine and 'the right of medical practice amongst their own sex'.

Frances had also, for some years, understood that women's influence was needed in political life at home. She was a moderate suffragist. She joined the early suffrage society, the Central Committee of the National Society for Women's Suffrage in the 1870s (where she first met Cobbe). She also organised a petition to remove the electoral disabilities of women that was presented to the House of Commons in June 1882. Two years later Frances and George supported Henrietta Muller when she refused to pay her taxes on the basis of 'No taxation without Representation' and had her goods distrained (only to be snapped up by her supporters when sold at public auction).[105]

Although she had not signed the 1866 Women's Suffrage Petition, Frances was one of a number of medical women, along with headmistresses, female poor law guardians, school board members and others (including Elspeth Rhŷs, the mother of Myvanwy and Olwen Rhŷs) who signed a 'Letter from Ladies' to the 'House of Peers' in 1885. They emphasised their public standing in order to point up the injustice of the continued exclusion of any women from the vote now that many more men were enfranchised.[106] Frances also held Drawing Room meetings in support of the vote at her Trevor Terrace home.[107] In 1889, when she and George were living in France in a bid to recover his health (he had been unwell since 1884), they became corresponding members of the new Women's Franchise League founded by Elizabeth Wolstenholme Elmy, the first suffrage organisation to expressly include the married women's franchise. It unequivocally supported married, single and widowed women enjoying 'equal civil and political rights with men'.

In 1891, the year that George died, Elmy formed the Women's Emancipation Union ('An Association of Workers to Secure the Political, Social, and Economic Independence of Woman'). Frances addressed its conference on the industrial and social position of women at Westminster Hall in 1893. She spoke about Greece, suggesting, not altogether convincingly, that wives there enjoyed greater advantages than their British counterparts since an endowment by a father or brother was considered an essential prerequisite to marriage.[108]

Although the past two decades had seen Frances active in an energetic metropolitan women's movement alongside her professional work, she had also been involved in the development of female education in her native Wales. Part of the impetus for this appears to have been her own early experience of being despatched by her widowed mother to England because of the lack of decent educational opportunities for girls in Wales, but it was her standing as a professional that resulted in her opinions being sought about the future of education in the Principality.

The 1847 enquiry into education in Wales created in many ways more problems than it solved for Welsh people, with its indictment of educational and moral standards[109] and failure to recognise the importance of the Welsh language. Consideration of the role and responsibilities of women – and of wives in particular – was highlighted in discussions about recasting Welsh society in the wake of the infamous Blue Book, and formed a backdrop to subsequent legislation.

Frances' main contribution to the debates on the future of education in Wales came in November 1880, when she gave evidence in London to the committee appointed by the Liberal government to enquire into the condition of intermediate (secondary) and higher education in Wales, chaired by Lord Aberdare.[110] She had done her homework, arriving armed with letters from schoolmistresses in Wales to demonstrate the desire for girls' education, and accounts of Welsh female students in secondary and higher education in England, as well as her own scheme for supporting girls' schools via two kinds of scholarships, and suggestions as to how endowments should operate.[111] She answered 93 questions, many in great detail, demonstrating with facts and figures that she was well acquainted with different parts of her native land. It was only fifteen years since women had been included as expert witnesses for Royal Commissions.

Although she had not lived in Wales full-time since the age of ten (and would not do so again),[112] Frances carefully pointed out that she had been born in Brecon, that her father hailed from Pembrokeshire, her mother from Carmarthenshire, and that she had been brought up in Glamorgan. Most of her family still lived in Wales – her mother was now settled in Pembrokeshire – and Frances claimed that she had made 'long stays' there since leaving Wales. The Hoggans enjoyed summer holidays in locations in North Wales such as Towyn. When addressing English and international audiences, Frances tended to identify herself as English but with Welsh audiences she emphasised her Welsh heritage. In her letters to the Welsh press on education she carefully inserted the words 'born Morgan' beneath her married name.

Frances included the Aberdare Report's recommendations for the education of girls and an abridged version of her own evidence in a pamphlet entitled *Education For Girls In Wales*. She described the Aberdare Report as 'so valuable, so full of useful facts, so suggestive, so liberal, and so thoroughly democratic in its tendencies'[113] that it should 'be in the hands of all Welsh men and women who value education, and who desire to see Wales taking its proper place, side by side with England, Scotland and Ireland' in equipping young people with the educational advantages essential for them to succeed in life.

Her pamphlet was dedicated to 'Welsh Mothers, by their country woman' and the *North Wales Express* declared that it 'deserves to be read and digested by all of them'.[114] Here and in four detailed letters to the Welsh press (also included in her pamphlet), Frances spelt out her views on female intermediate and higher education. Aware of the low participation of Welsh women in the formal economy,[115] Frances labelled the provision of education for girls in Wales 'a miserable failure' in a letter to the *South Wales Daily News* in 1882.[116]

The focus in both her oral evidence to the Aberdare enquiry and her written accounts was on middle class girls. This largely reflected the line of questioning in the enquiry but it also accorded with Frances' belief that 'one class can never, even with the best intentions and most liberal views fully enter into the feelings of another class'.[117] Yet, although well aware of this problem when medical men 'endeavoured to represent the feelings of medical women and the desires and wants of medical women', she chose not to reflect on how the perspectives of working class Welsh women might actually get heard. She maintained – without examining it any further – that the Elementary Education Act of 1870 had solved the problem of education for the working class. A network of Board and Voluntary Schools provided 'a substantial' elementary education 'fitting', she argued, for boys and girls 'to make a fair start in life'.[118] The urgent task, she felt, was to do something about the 'lamentably deficient' education of the middle class.[119]

However, this daughter of a clergyman's widow – though, crucially, a widow of independent means – did not advocate state aid for secondary schools even though she was aware that France had recently decided to fund such education for girls. Sounding like a politician aware of the need for retrenchment and mindful of Smilesian principles, she suggested that since funding university for both sexes would be costly:

> It would at any rate be wise not to make exorbitant demands on the imperial exchequer, and to prove, by patriotic exertions and sacrifices, that a strong desire exists in Wales for sound intermediate education, and that parents are prepared to do what in them lies to obtain it for their sons and daughters.[120]

She supported public subscriptions and envisaged the State supporting two kinds of scholarships. Elementary school pupils could compete for scholarships at successful secondary schools and those at the latter could apply for funding for technical or higher education.[121] Despite the fact that she had studied and worked in a field seen as the preserve of men, Frances' concept of technical education for girls emphasised domestic economy along gendered lines. In order to achieve her overall goal she opted for a gentle rocking of the boat.

Although Frances' emphasis was on developing opportunities for middle class girls, she maintained that by competing in Board and other schools for scholarships or exhibitions, the clever children of less affluent parents could progress beyond elementary education. In the press she suggested that in industrial districts higher Board Schools or advanced Elementary Schools could be the answer.[122]

Frances was critical of the use of endowments in Welsh education. She made her views clear in her evidence and in the third of her letters to the *South Wales Daily News,* although the paper chose not to publish this lengthy account. The core of her concern was that endowments, once intended to include both sexes, now excluded girls. Endowments, supported by local funds, should, she argued, be used to establish girls' day schools with low fees in larger towns. Technical schools for women[123] and existing efficient schools should also be endowed.

She supported what amounted to positive discrimination in favour of girls being 'now, and for a long time to come, considered before boys', as they had been disadvantaged for so long. Unafraid of ruffling feathers, she attacked what she saw as a flagrant misapplication of endowments in the two Howell's Schools for girls. Her concerns were reflected in the Report's recommendations.[124]

It is hardly surprising that Frances championed female members of governing bodies, but this daughter of an Anglican priest also stated categorically that all education should be entirely unsectarian, with provision for 'the adequate representation of Nonconformists in the management of all endowed or publicly assisted places of education'.[125] She stressed that the fact that the majority of Welsh people were Nonconformists should be recognised in educational policy.

The committee did not focus much on the Welsh language, but Frances nevertheless paid attention to it. W. Gareth Evans suggests that her concern here was less with the promotion of the language for its own sake than with how Welsh-speaking teachers might help in the learning of English for native Welsh speakers.[126] But this was only the third reason she cited for the use of Welsh. The first was that schoolmasters and mistresses ought to be required to understand the language 'in order that they may be in sympathy with the people among whom they labour'.[127] It would also help them to explain clearly how *both* languages worked.

Frances argued that Welsh should be given the same status as French, German and Latin in secondary schools. It would therefore not be compulsory but could be selected as the chosen modern language. She stated categorically that 'in all schools established in the Welsh-speaking parts of Wales the wants of the Welsh-speaking children require to be specially considered, which they have not been so far, either in the case of boys or girls'.[128] In 1883 she stated that she would like to see 'good spelling and correct writing of the Welsh language common in every school'. She also suggested that a good phonetic system in elementary classes might be of value in a bilingual country like Wales.[129] This was an enlightened approach for the time from a non-Welsh speaker based in England for most of her life.

Her views on curricula at university level were also progressive. She warned against slavishly following the older universities, and urged incorporating 'the exigencies of modern life' with due attention given to the sciences and modern languages including Welsh. Unsurprisingly, Frances supported a degree-awarding Welsh university for women and men, and the need for qualified women teachers. Opportunities to obtain degrees within Wales would, she felt, raise the status of such teachers. Here and elsewhere she lamented the existence of what would later be called 'the brain drain' of bright young women.

Unlike some women educators, Frances was keen to urge the benefits of university co-education. She stressed her credentials: 'I believe that I am the only Welsh woman who is able to speak from practical experience of co-education at a university'.[130] In the first of her letters in the

South Wales Daily News she cited examples of co-education in the United States, Switzerland (where she had first-hand knowledge), Holland, France and England.

Frances had already intervened in the debates about the future of her father's alma mater, Jesus College, Oxford, which had been founded in 1571 for Welsh students. In 1878, due to a lack of applicants for scholarships by Welsh men, it was proposed that its endowments be opened up to all male students, regardless of their place of birth. In response Frances penned a letter to the *Western Mail* arguing instead that some of the scholarship should be diverted to Welsh female students.[131] She thus appealed to both a sense of national entitlement and to the Welsh women whose educational needs she felt had been so badly neglected. She later claimed to have been the first 'to make a public protest in favour of university education for my countrywomen'.[132]

Frances raised the issue again when giving evidence to the Aberdare enquiry. Ironically, this was during her questioning by Professor John Rhŷs, Oxford University's first professor of Celtic and a Fellow of Jesus College. Fifteen years later he would become its Principal. Frances declared that 'very strong doubts arise as to whether Jesus College is really useful to Wales in its present form or not'. As the essay on his daughters Olwen and Myvanwy demonstrates, Rhŷs supported women's equality and Frances' responses to the questions he asked her at the Aberdare Committee raised the possibility of funds from Jesus being used to support young women in school in Wales, as well as at the new Oxford Colleges for women.[133]

Frances was more familiar with the workings of English

girls' schools than those in Wales. She was especially keen on the successful Girls' Public Day School Trust Schools and the possibilities for extending them to Wales. Her intervention could be read as part of a civilising mission to bring decent education for girls to a benighted Wales with the sense of cultural superiority (and knowing what is best) that this implies.[134] However, Frances *was* Welsh, and had been raised in Wales. Moreover, she argued that Wales had once been a significant seat of learning. What she sought was that its 'former glory' could be captured and harnessed alongside new and vital equal opportunities for girls.[135]

Moreover, Frances' intervention as an expert witness and Welsh woman was both sought and appreciated.[136] John Gibson, the influential Liberal owner and editor of the *Cambrian News* also gave evidence to the committee, and he underscored Frances' stress on the provision of schools for girls as paramount and admired her work.[137]

Frances' immersion in the workings of the system in Wales in the early 1880s was evident. The Aberdare Report's positive recommendations proved to be a catalyst for change. Although critical of some witnesses and a few lost opportunities, W. Gareth Evans recognised its overarching achievements and described Frances' evidence as 'particularly impressive'.[138]

Frances' pamphlet ended with a flourish. Using words evocative of the Chartists and of Italian republican nationalist Mazzini, but also reflecting her parallel life in England defending personal rights and liberty, she appealed to 'Patriots, republicans, friends of the people,[139] and all who deeply care for the welfare of the Principality' to recognise that only by having a solid educational system encompassing both sexes could 'the full measure of national prosperity, of national happiness and usefulness, and of national growth' be realised.

In August 1882 she spoke at the National Eisteddfod, described by the *Manchester Guardian* that year as 'One of the most venerated institutions in Great Britain'.[140] This speech at Denbigh was for a section organised by the powerful Honourable Society of Cymmrodorion, founded in the eighteenth century. Elspeth Rhŷs (Myvanwy and Olwen's mother) presided and gave the opening address. Frances painted a picture of a Wales at a crucial stage in educational and national development, needing to create different forms of higher education but lacking an extant indigenous model: 'Other nations have to remodel', she stated, 'we have to model and to make'.[141]

Her title was 'Co-education at Different Ages'. She urged this as a practical way forward at all levels. Yet she also emphasised difference, pointing to women's 'intuitive sympathy with children' and a perception of their needs which, when harnessed to higher education, would provide the female teachers she felt Wales so badly needed. Doubtless bearing in mind the education report of 1847, she warned against women being held responsible for the present state of society.

In 1883 Frances spoke again at the Cymmrodorion Section of the Eisteddfod. It was held in Cardiff that year, not very far from her childhood home in Cowbridge. Her speech addressed 'The Past and Future of the Education of Girls'.[142] The Liberal *South Wales Daily News* described her as a 'pleasing looking lady' but did at least praise her eloquence and criticise the fact that no time had been set aside to debate such an important topic. Frances' own frustration was expressed in her comments that nothing seemed to have changed since 1880. Where were the Welsh patriots? Why was there no sign of the schools that were so badly needed? She pointed out that organising ability and business capacity were not lacking in Wales and, as she knew only too well, there were plenty of Welsh teachers in England who could fill posts.

In the same year Frances achieved the distinction of being one of fifteen (and the sole woman) elected as a member of the Cymmrodorion Society in London.[143] She was the first woman to dine with the Society. She responded to the Toast of the evening, on behalf of 'lady members', taking the opportunity to appeal for funding for scholarships for female students at Cardiff. Accompanied by George, she was present at a number of their meetings over the next year or so. She also maintained her association with the National Eisteddfod. In 1885 when it was held in Aberdare she was, along with Cranogwen[144] and Evan Jones, an adjudicator for the Essay competition. The subject was 'The Work and Mission of a Woman in the Family and Sick Room'.[145]

That summer Frances was one of the London Welsh educators invited by the Teachers' Guild of Great Britain[146] to join Frances Buss, Dilys Davies and others to discuss the Welsh Intermediate and Technical Education Bill in London. She was not, however, active in the Association for Promoting the Education of Girls in Wales, founded the following year. This organisation was influential in stepping up pressure for change.[147] Its leading lights were

Dilys Davies and Elizabeth Price Hughes.[148] Like Frances, the latter had written a paper on Welsh education and girls for the Cardiff Eisteddfod (though Hughes had not delivered hers in person). Both Davies and Hughes were educational campaigners in England as well as Wales. The former taught at North London Collegiate and Hughes became the first Principal of Cambridge Training College, the forerunner of Cambridge University's eponymous Hughes Hall.

Frances' absence from the Association was, it seems, due to George's ill health. In mid-January 1886 John Gibson's *Cambrian News* appealed for subscriptions for a presentation to Frances as a token of sympathy since she had interrupted her professional work to join her ailing husband in the south of France.[149] When Davies spoke about girls' education at Caernarfon that September, a letter from Frances was read out supporting the Association.

The 1889 Welsh Intermediate and Technical Education Act of 1889 provided equal educational provision for girls and boys in Intermediate (Secondary) schools, giving girls advantages over their counterparts in England. Frances had long applauded the quality of Welsh teachers in England but lamented the fact that so many left Wales. Now a greater number of young Welsh women had the opportunity to train and remain there. Women accounted for one third of University of Wales students by 1888, a remarkable and rapid achievement. The Charter of the new University of Wales in 1893 stated that women were to be eligible equally with men for admittance to any of its degrees. Frances had played a significant part in helping to make this pyramid of opportunities possible for girls and women in Wales.

When the University College of South Wales and Monmouthshire (later Cardiff University) was founded in 1883, its first elected president was Lord Aberdare. That September, as it was about to become fully operative, its Council met in Cardiff's town hall. A letter from Frances to Lord Aberdare was forwarded by him to the Council and read out at this meeting.[150] Here she explained that due to the ill health of the Council member Lewis Morris (who had sat on the Aberdare Committee and questioned Frances), he could not champion his proposal that women be admitted as members. In her speech at the Cardiff Eisteddfod the previous month, Frances had expressed her disappointment that this Council did not include any women.

So she now used her letter as an opportunity to get a female voice heard at the Council. In it she stressed that the most successful American mixed colleges included women on their Councils. It was, she stressed, undesirable that the conduct of female students should be the responsibility of men alone. She pointed out the good that women did on School Boards (created in the wake of the 1870 Education Act, they had produced able female members such as Rose Crawshay) and she emphasised that, being a new institution, it was all the more necessary for the University College to lead the way.

Council instructed the Registrar to reply, acknowledging that Frances' letter had aroused 'a considerable amount of interest' but making it clear that at present it was impossible to adopt her suggestions since the constitution of the College had been agreed. When, in 1950, Lady Rhondda became the first female president of the University College (and of any Welsh College), its principal argued that her election was 'in the best tradition of no sex discrimination in the college'.[151] Frances' treatment by the Council slightly undermines that claim.

In her letter of 1882 on university co-education[152] Frances had described higher education in Wales as a burning question. She had also discussed residential accommodation, suggesting that, for young country students faced for the first time with 'the seductions and temptations of a large town,' a hall of residence was desirable and especially necessary for young women (she worried lest their parents be deterred from letting their daughters study). She was well aware that this was a delicate subject and, as the experience of Myvanwy Rhŷs at Bangor would demonstrate in the following decade,[153] it was also divisive. Frances recognised, however, that although separate halls for men and women were needed, some families would opt for students to live out.

Her belief in co-education saw her support some male representation on the management of women's colleges and halls (as in England). Frances felt that men's experience could be valuable. She anyway believed that harmonious co-operation between the sexes was desirable amongst those who advocated women's equality. Nevertheless, 'a large infusion of womanly thought and watchfulness' was essential in a woman's hall and its managing committee needed 'experienced, capable, large minded women'.

Frances was one such woman. She briefly chaired the

governing body of the hall established for women students at Cardiff. Aberdare Hall was named after Lady Aberdare, who had worked hard to establish it. Accommodation for seven students was provided at Keswick House from 1885 with the distinctive brick and terracotta Aberdare Hall in the Gothic Revival style opening a decade later. At its AGM in 1896 (with Frances in the chair) it was announced that the number of women residents had risen to forty.[154] Students were now able to study for degrees of the University of Wales (created in 1893 with three constituent Colleges) rather than external London degrees. The colliery heiress Caroline Williams provided £1,000 for scholarships for female students to reside at Aberdare Hall, and Frances donated thirty volumes of books. It is still a women's hall of residence for Cardiff University.

Frances wrote about some Glamorgan and Pembrokeshire customs for the journal *Folklore* in 1893[155] but Welsh affairs seem to have ceased to be a priority for her after the 1880s. George died in Nice in May 1891 of a cerebral tumour and this presaged a further shift in Frances' lifestyle and concerns. Although she then returned to Britain, she does not seem to have resumed medical practice.

For the rest of her life Frances would write and speak at home and abroad on issues of gender and race.[156] She spent almost a year in the USA in 1907, returning in 1911 (her brother Thomas Herbert had emigrated there. His daughter and Frances' niece Georgiana – known as Georgia – Bullock became the first female judge in California).[157] Frances also spent the best part of a year in South Africa prior to the Universal Races Congress, visiting a cousin and joining an expedition to inspect native villages.[158]

When Frances met Du Bois in Atlanta in 1907, it was the start of a long friendship and mutual respect, evidenced in meetings, correspondence over many years and her contributions to *The Crisis*, the monthly journal he edited from 1910, published by the National Association for the Advancement of Colored People. Frances' writings for this journal looked at the lives of black men as well as women.[159]

Frances was based in north London during the First World War, but when she died on 5 February 1927 aged eighty-three she had been living in Brighton for five years. She retained her health and interest in her profession until the final three months of her life. She left Du Bois fifty pounds in her Will and the Colored Women's Club of Los Angeles received twenty pounds.

Over the course of a long and extremely active life, Frances had combined her career with an admirable energy and commitment to a range of causes. The focus of this essay on a specific period in her life, the fifteen years from 1870-1885 showed Frances in her thirties and early forties championing educational reform in Wales and England, as well as transnational medical opportunities for women, health education, a raft of humanitarian and personal rights issues, and much else. Evident throughout was a desire to improve women's lives and opportunities, especially those of the middle class, and concern to enlighten people about her chosen vocation. The year after Frances died, British women over twenty-one were enfranchised.

Putting her writings under the microscope she so treasured suggests a brave, highly intelligent and articulate woman who could be at one and the same time remarkably prescient and progressive as well as inevitably hidebound by some of the Victorian strictures that helped to shape her. As this essay has demonstrated, Frances was prepared to be outspoken and critical when she felt the need, but she also appreciated the art of subtle persuasion. This pioneering Welsh feminist and internationalist might – through no fault of her own – have been prevented from speaking out at the Universal Races Congress in 1911, but little, it seems, could have kept the irrepressible Frances Hoggan quiet for long.

Notes

[1] *The Times* 28 July 1911.

[2] Ulysses G. Weatherly, 'The First Universal Races Congress', *American Journal of Sociology*, 17/3, 1911, p. 318.

[3] See the Forum 'New Historical Perspectives on the First Universal Races Congress', *Radical History Review*, 92/ spring 2015, pp. 99-102.

[4] Daniel Williams, *Black Skin, Blue Books: African Americans and Wales 1845-1945*, University of Wales Press, 2012, Introduction. Williams sees Frances as giving Du Bois' views a feminist twist. Idem, 'Feminism, Imperialism and Uplift: Frances Hoggan and the Contradictions of Empire' in Huw V. Bowen (ed.) *Wales and the British Overseas Empire*, Vol 2, Manchester University Press, forthcoming. I am grateful to have read a draft version of this article.

[5] G. Spiller (ed.), *Papers on Inter-racial problems communicated to the First Universal Races Congress*, P.S. King & Son, 1911, p. 364.

[6] *Manchester Guardian* 29 July 1911.

[7] See Susan D. Pennybacker, 'The Universal Races Congress, London. Political Culture and Imperial Dissent, 1900-1939' in *Radical History Review*, Forum, pp. 103-115 where she discusses the British contributors (though not Frances Hoggan), suggesting that speakers roughly divided into older anti-slavery and colonial reformers and younger activists with more radical anti-racist ideologies.

[8] Frances Elizabeth Hoggan, MD, 'Women in Medicine' in *The Woman Question in Europe*, Theodore Stanton (ed.) Sampson, Low, Marston, Searle, and Rivington, 1884, p. 71. Fifty years earlier James Miranda Barry had obtained an MD at Edinburgh University. This Irish medic also qualified as a surgeon in

London and later held the highest medical rank in the British army as well as being the first person in the British Empire to carry out a successful Caesarian section. Posthumously it was revealed that Barry had been born Margaret Ann Bulkley. See Ann Heilmann, *Neo/Victorian Biographilia and James Miranda Barry: Studies in Transgender and Transgenre*, forthcoming for representations of Barry as transgender or as a cross-dressing woman. Frances Hoggan, however, remains the first British woman, recognised as female, to gain an MD in Europe. The English woman Elizabeth Blackwell had gained her MD in the USA in 1849.

[9] Onfel Thomas, *Frances Elizabeth Hoggan 1843-1927*, R. H. Johns, 1970.

[10] Emyr Wyn Jones, 'A Citadel Stormed: The Saga of Three Welsh Pioneers', *Transactions of the Honourable Society of Cymmrodorion for 1984*, 1985, p.367.

[11] See Neil McIntyre, 'Britain's first medical marriage: Frances Morgan (1843-1927), George Hoggan (1837-1891) and the mysterious "Elsie"', *Journal of Medical Biography*, 2004, p. 112 (the source of references below); *Transactions of the Honourable Society of Cymmrodorion for 2006*, 2007, pp. 160-175; Idem, 'Frances Hoggan - Doctor of Medicine, Pioneer Physician, Patriot and Philanthropist', *Brycheiniog*, xxxix, 2007, pp. 127-145.

[12] W. Gareth Evans, *Education and Female Emancipation: The Welsh Experience 1847-1914*, University of Wales Press, 1990, p. 100.

[13] Williams, 'Feminism, Imperialism and Uplift'; Idem, *Black Skin, Blue Books*.

[14] Dame Jean Thomas FLSW FMedSci FRS was its first recipient.

[15] Leaflet of the LSW; http://www.learnedsociety.wales/medals/hoggan-medal/frances_hoggan/; Western Mail (WM) 21 January 2016.

See too Alexandra Jones in *WM* 16 January 2017; *ODNB* (M.A. Elston) and *Dictionary of Welsh Biography* (Beth Jenkins). See too Beth Jenkins, 'Women's Professional Employment in Wales 1880-1939', Cardiff University, PhD, 2016.

[16] Presented by Ffion Hague for S4C, 27 March 2016.

[17] Benjamin Heath Malkin, *The Scenery, Antiquities and Biography of South Wales*, vol. 2, London, 1807, p. 514. The living and vicarage were in the gift of Griffith Llewellyn of Baglan Hall.

[18] Report of her speech to the Cymmrodorion section of the National Eisteddfod in 1883 in *Cardiff Times* 11 August 1883.

[19] Thomas, *Frances Elizabeth Hoggan*, p. 8.

[20] According to the Medical Women's Federation Archives. Little Biographies 6, Frances Elizabeth Morgan, SA/MWF/C, Archives and Manuscripts, The Wellcome Library, London.

[21] Thomas, *Frances Elizabeth Hoggan*, p. 8.

[22] McIntyre, 'Britain's first medical marriage'.

[23] Prys Morgan, 'The Port Talbot District and the Blue Books of 1847', *Transactions of the Port Talbot Historical Society*, 111/3, 1984, p. 88.

[24] This section draws on Neil McIntyre's articles and unpublished work (for which I am grateful) and Elizabeth Crawford, *Enterprising Women: The Garretts and their Circle*, Francis Boutle, 2002, p.50.

[25] *The Times* 2 February 1867.

[26] Hoggan, 'Women in Medicine', p. 70.

[27] It had accepted women students since 1864.

[28] Auguste Forel, *Out of My Life and Work*, translated by Bernard Miall, George Allen & Unwin, 1937 edition, pp. 56, 67; T.N. Bonner, *To the Ends of the Earth: Women's Search for Education in Medicine*, Harvard University Press, 1992, p. 38.

[29] Quoted in Bonner, *To the Ends of the Earth*, p.38.

[30] Ibid, p. 39.

[31] Thomas, *Frances Elizabeth Hoggan*, p. 13.

[32] Quoted in P. Hollis, *Women in Public: The Women's Movement 1850-1900*, George Allen & Unwin, 1979, p. 101.

[33] *The Modern Review,* April 1881, p. 300.

[34] See Crawford, *Enterprising Women*, p. 312 and Jo Manton, *Elizabeth Garrett Anderson*, Methuen, 1965, p. 229. Possibly there were also differences of opinion about status. Frances described the New Hospital as having been 'under the medical care of Dr. Garrett-Anderson, [sic] and Dr. Frances Hoggan', implying joint control. Hoggan, 'Women in Medicine', p. 78.

[35] Quoted in Claire Brock, 'Surgical Controversy at the New Hospital for Women, 1872-1892' in *Social History of Medicine,* 24/3, 2011, pp.17-18.

[36] She was a member of its General Committee between 1877-81.

[37] *South Wales Daily News* (SWDN) 9 September 1878.

[38] *Ibid, Cambrian,* 16 August 1878 noted that objections were made to her rejection.

[39] *BMJ,* 23 February 1878.

[40] For example, they co-authored a number of papers for the *Journal of Anatomy and Physiology* as well as writing in *Zoology*, the *BMJ*, the *Proceedings of the Royal Society of London,* and the *Journal of the Royal Microscopical Society.*

[41] Hoggan, 'Women in Medicine', p. 84.

[42] Quoted in McIntyre, 'Britain's first medical marriage', p. 109.

[43] Hoggan, 'The Woman Question in Europe', pp. 63-89.

[44] Like Frances, she received university training in the early 1870s. She became the first female medical doctor in the Netherlands and a suffrage activist.

[45] Frances Elizabeth Hoggan, MD, 'The Position of the Mother in the Family: Its Legal and Scientific Aspects', A. Ireland & Co, 1884.

[46] Eileen Janes Yeo, *The Contest for Social Science: Relations and Representations of Gender and Class*, Rivers Oram Press, 1996, pp. 121, 129, 135, 148.

[47] Lucy Bland, *Banishing the Beast: English Feminism and Sexual Morality 1885-1914*, Penguin, 1995, pp. 124-5.

[48] See Ibid, pp. 126-185.

[49] See Lee Holcombe, *Wives and Property*, Martin Robertson, 1993, pp. 53-4.

[50] Brian Davies, 'Empire and Identity: the "Case" of Dr. William Price' in David Smith (ed.), *A People and A Proletariat: Essays in the History of Wales 1780-1980,* Pluto Press, 1980, pp. 72-93.

[51] *WM* 1 April 1884.

[52] The Vigilance Association for the Defence of Personal Rights and for the Amendment of the Law where it is Injurious to Women (the latter part of the title was dropped in 1881). From 1886 it was called the National Association for the Defence of Personal Rights but better known as the Personal Rights Association.

[53] Susan Hamilton (ed.), *Animal Welfare and Anti-Vivisection 1870-1910*, vol. 1, Routledge, 2004, p. lxi. See too Coral Lansbury, *The Old Brown Dog: Women, Workers, and Vivisection in Edwardian England,* University of Wisconsin Press, 1985, pp. 163, 171.

[54] Quoted in Richard D. French, *Antivivisection and Medical Science in Victorian Society*, Princeton University Press, 1975, p. 68.

[55] Hilda Kean, *Animal Rights. Political and Social Change in Britain since 1800*, Reaktion Books, 1998, p. 105.

[56] Frances Cobbe, *Life of Frances Power Cobbe: As Told by Herself,* Swan Sonnenschein & Co, 1904 edition, pp. 644, 649.

[57] *Ibid*, p. 468. Cobbe spent her later years in North Wales living with Mary Lloyd (with whom she was buried in 2004). A codicil to Cobbe's Will directed that Frances or other medics sever the main arteries of her head to prevent any revival in the grave. *Cambrian News* 26 August 1904.

[58] Quoted in Frances Thomas, *Christina Rossetti: A Biography,* Virago, 1996 edition, p. 344.

[59] M.A. Elston, 'Women and Anti-Vivisection in Victorian England 1870-1900' in Nicolaas A. Rupke (ed.), *Vivisection in Historical Perspective*, Croom Helm, 1987, p. 289.

[60] Kean, *Animal Rights*, p. 107.

[61] Cobbe, *Life of Frances Power Cobbe*, p. 264.

[62] *Zoophilist,* 1 April 1882.

[63] See *Ibid* 1 April 1893 for her three signed letters to newspapers.

[64] *Vaccination Inquirer,* November 1883. For the campaign see Stanley Williams, *The Vaccination Controversy,* Liverpool University Press, 2007.

[65] *Lancet,* 12 June 1869.

[66] *Vaccination Inquirer,* June 1884.

[67] Quoted in Kean, *Animal Rights*, p. 107.

[68] *Manchester Guardian* 23 May, 9 December 1881.

[69] Frances Elizabeth Hoggan MD, 'On the Advantages of a Vegetarian Diet in Workhouses and Prisons', Conference of the Vegetarian Society at Norwich, 1883.

[70] This was the principle whereby conditions within a workhouse were to be harsher than those outside, thereby acting as a deterrent so that the workhouse became the last resort for those in need.

[71] Philippa Levine, *Feminist Lives in Victorian England*, Basil Blackwell, 1996, p. 96.

[72] Judith R. Walkowitz, *Prostitution and Victorian Society: Women, Class, and the State*, Cambridge University Press, 1980, Chapter 6.

[73] Brian Harrison, 'State Intervention and Moral Reform in Nineteenth Century England' in Patricia Hollis (ed.), *Pressure from Without in Early Victorian England*, Edward Arnold, 1974, Chapter 12, especially the diagram on p. 319.

[74] Thomas, *Frances Elizabeth Hoggan*, p.17.

[75] Frances E. Hoggan, 'The Leper Terra-cotta [sic] of Athens', *Journal of Hellenic Studies*, 13, 1892-3, pp. 101-2.

[76] George worked at St. John's Hospital for Diseases of the Skin between 1877-9.

[77] *Wrexham and Denbighshire Advertiser* 13 June 1874; *SWDN* 19 July 1877.

[78] *Englishwoman's Review* 15 May 1879, also published in pamphlet form.

[79] Her talk was published as a pamphlet and the following section quotes from it. Frances Elizabeth Hoggan, MD 'The Physical Education of Girls', W. Swan. Sonnenschein & Allen, 1880.

[80] She sat on its Reference Committee and an article on 'Girls' Dress' based on her pamphlet was published in the society's *Gazette*.

[81] *Englishwoman's Review* 15 March 1880.

[82] *North London Collegiate School Magazine*, 'Our Gymnasium', March 1885 p. 27. For this section see Medical Records: Mrs Hoggan; Mrs Hoggan's Notes in North London Collegiate School Library, also Margaret A. Claydon, 'How Strong the Girls Grow', University of London, MSc, 1982.

[83] Reproduced in the *Cambrian* 29 September 1883.

[84] Reported in the *SWDN* 23 August 1882.

[85] Hoggan, 'The Physical Education of Girls', p. 24.

[86] Dave Day, '"What Girl will now remain ignorant of swimming?" Agnes Beckwith, Aquatic Entertainer and Victorian Role Model', *Women's History Review*, 21/3, 2012, pp. 419-446.

[87] Medical Tracts 1851-86. No. 4, British Library.

[88] Civil administrative bodies managing local affairs in London.

[89] *Aberdare Times* 6 February 1875.

[90] *Sanitary Record,* 15 December 1880; *Modern Review,* April 1881, pp. 322-5.

[91] Peter Gordon and David Doughan, *Dictionary of British Women's Organisations 1825-1960*, Woburn Press, 2001, p.78.

[92] Sue Cavanagh and Vron Ware, 'Less Convenient for Women', *Built Environment,* 16/4, 1990, p. 282.

[93] Elizabeth Crawford, *The Women's Suffrage Movement: A Reference Guide 1866-1928*, UCL Press, 1999, p. 128.

[94] In Sally Mitchell, *Frances Power Cobbe: Victorian Feminist, Journalist, Reformer*, University of Virginia Press, 2004, p. 285.

[95] Antoinette Burton suggests that she had practised there. There seems no definite evidence that this was so, despite Frances' talks and articles, which sounded knowledgeable. Antoinette Burton, *The Burdens of History: British Feminists, Indian Women, and Imperial Culture 1865-1915*, University of North Carolina Press, 1994, p. 112.

[96] Frances Elizabeth Hoggan, MD 'Medical Women for India', *Contemporary Review,* xlii, August 1882, pp. 267-275.

[97] Founded by Mary Carpenter in 1870 after her visit to India, it promoted female education in India. Frances' paper

was reported in the Welsh press, for example, *Aberystwyth Observer* 9 December 1882.

[98] A. Burton, 'Contesting the Zenana: The Mission to Make "Lady Doctors for India" 1874-1885', *Journal of British Studies,* 35/3, 1996, p. 389; Maneesha Lal, 'The Politics of Gender and Medicine in Colonial India: The Countess of Dufferin's Fund 1885-1888', *Bulletin of the History of Medicine*, 68, March 1994.

[99] This was the part of the house reserved for women in families of high caste.

[100] Dr Jex-Blake spelt it out: over 1,000 English medical women were urgently needed for India in 1880. Just 54 women were registered medics in 1887, hence the pressing need for the medical education of women. Sophia Jex-Blake, *Medical Women: A Ten Years' Retrospect*, National Association for Promoting the Medical Education of Women, 1888, p. 13. See too, Burton, *The Burdens of History,* pp. 112-3.

[101] Catriona Blake, *The Charge of the Parasols: Women's Entry to the Medical Profession*, Women's Press, 1990, p. 177.

[102] M.A. Elston, http://www.oxforddnb.com/articles/46/46422-nav.html. McIntyre also points out that Frances refused to join the Association of Registered Medical Women because it was restricted to women on the Medical Register. Elizabeth Garrett Anderson was Dean of the London School from 1883. Early in her career Frances had been suggested as a teacher of midwifery at the latter but was not employed since she was not registered. Neil McIntyre, *How British Women Became Doctors: The Story of the Royal Free Hospital and its Medical School*, Wenrowave Press, 2014, pp.52, 116; Crawford, *Enterprising Women*, pp.76-90

[103] It paid particular attention to training Indian midwives. It also funded some women with diplomas from Indian medical

schools to study medicine in the UK.

[104] Printed in the *Englishwoman's Review,* cxvliv, April 1885, pp. 145-i58; cxlv, May 1885, pp. 193-200.

[105] *The Times* 23 June 1882; *Aberystwyth Observer* 5 July 1884; *Flintshire Observer* 5 February 1885.

[106] *Women's Suffrage Journal,* 1 June 1885.

[107] Crawford, *Enterprising Women*, p. 249 which places her at a 'national Demonstration' for suffrage in May 1880.

[108] *Manchester Guardian* 16 March 1893.

[109] Ironically, Frances' father had been outspoken in his condemnation of morals, parental responsibility and the intelligence of workers. Morgan, 'The Port Talbot District', pp. 84-96.

[110] Henry Austin Bruce, 1st Baron Aberdare, Trustee of Dowlais Iron Company and former Liberal MP for Merthyr Tydfil, Home Secretary.

[111] PP. 1881, C3047, p. xxix.

[112] She used 'Heatherland', her mother's new home at Llanteg, Pembrokeshire as her corresponding address in 1892, but it is not known whether she stayed there for long. She spent much of this period travelling.

[113] Frances Elizabeth Hoggan, *Education for Girls in Wales*, Women's Printing Society, 1882, p. 1.

[114] *North Wales Express* 10 November 1882.

[115] See, for example, Sian Rhiannon Williams, 'The True "Cymraes": Images of Women in Women's Nineteenth Century Welsh Periodicals' in Angela V. John (ed.), *Our Mothers' Land: Chapters in Welsh Women's History, 1830-1939*, University of Wales Press, 2011 edition, pp. 73-94.

[116] In Hoggan, *Education for Girls*, p. 17.

[117] PP. 1881, C3047, p. 346.

[118] Hoggan, *Education for Girls*, p. 11.

[119] *Cardiff Times* 11 August 1883.

[120] Hoggan, *Education for Girls*, p.19.

[121] When pressed, she also conceded that there could be instances where a government building grant might be desirable.

[122] Hoggan, *Education for Girls*, p. 17.

[123] Here Frances adhered to the idea of gender specific education for girls such as nursing and dairy schools.

[124] Hoggan, *Education for Girls,* pp. 3-4, 20-23; PP. 1881, C3047, 344-5, 349.

[125] PP. 1881, C3047, p. 344.

[126] Evans, *Education and Female Emancipation*, p. 114.

[127] Hoggan, *Education for Girls*, pp. 51-2. Supplementary evidence.

[128] PP. 1881, C3047, p. 348-9.

[129] Reported in the *SWDN* on 7 August 1883.

[130] PP. 1881, C3047, p. 346.

[131] In Hoggan, *Education for Girls*, pp. 58-9.

[132] *Ibid*, p. 12.

[133] PP. 1881, C3047, p.349. See Essay 4 below.

[134] See Williams, 'Feminism, Imperialism and Uplift'. Williams sees her approach to education in Wales with its commitment to 'uplift' the position of women via education prefiguring her endeavours in India, America and Africa. Williams, 'Feminism, Imperialism and Uplift'.

[135] In her speech at the 1883 Eisteddfod reported in the *SWDN* 7 August 1883.

[136] For example, the *Aberystwyth Observer* 18 November 1882 praised the 1882 pamphlet by 'Mrs. Doctor Hoggan'.

[137] The author of the 1891 booklet, *The Emancipation of*

Women, he was the first journalist to be knighted in Wales. See *Cambrian News* 15 January 1886.

[138] W. Gareth Evans, 'The Aberdare Report and Education in Wales, 1881', *Welsh History Review*, 11/2, 1982, p. 186.

[139] *The Friend of the People* was a short-lived Chartist journal established by George Julian Harney in the early 1850s.

[140] *Manchester Guardian* 23 August 1882.

[141] *SWDN* 23 August 1882.

[142] *Ibid* and *Cardiff Times* 11 August 1883.

[143] *SWDN* 10 February 1883.

[144] The remarkable Sarah Jane Rees, editor of *Y Frythones* and teacher of navigation and mathematics.

[145] *SWDN* 26 August 1885.

[146] Founded in 1883 as a professional association to promote the welfare and independence of teachers. *SWDN* 6 June 1885; *Weekly Mail* 13 June 1885.

[147] See Jane Aaron, *Nineteenth-Century Women's Writing in Wales*, University of Wales Press, 2007, pp.165-6. In 1888 John Rhŷs chaired a seminal Cymmrodorion conference at Shrewsbury on the future development of Welsh education. It passed a motion for equal educational opportunities. A delegation presented the conference's resolutions to parliament.

[148] See Pam Hirsch, Mark McBeth, *Teacher Training at Cambridge: The Initiatives of Oscar Browning and Elizabeth Hughes*, Woburn Press, 2004, chapters 7-14, also W. Gareth Evans, 'The Welsh Intermediate and Technical Education Act 1889 and the Education of Girls', *Llafur*, 15/1, 1990, pp. 84-92; Idem, 'Equal Educational Opportunities for Girls and Women in Victorian Wales: The Contribution of the London Welsh', *Transactions of the Honourable Society of Cymmrodorion 1995*, ns 2, 1996, pp. 123-140, and Idem, 'Addysgu mwy na

hanner y genedl': Yr ymgyrch i hyrwyddo addysg y ferch yng nghymru oes Fictoria', *Cof Cenedl* IV, 1989, pp. 93-119 for the broader picture.

[149] *Cambrian News* 15 January 1886.

[150] *Ibid* 28 September 1883; *Cardiff Times* 29 September 1883.

[151] *WM* 17 November 1950.

[152] In Hoggan, *Education for Girls,* p. 12.

[153] See Essay 4 below.

[154] *Cardiff Times* 17 October 1896.

[155] She explained that she remembered well how, in her 'young days', Cowbridge youths went from house to house before Christmas. One was dressed as a horse to elicit coins. Frances called this the White Horse. It is better known as the Mari Lwyd. (*Llwyd* means grey in Welsh). She told how a man who had worked on her grandfather's Pembrokeshire farm as a lad remembered the distribution of loaves of bread on what she called the old New Year's Day (12th January in the old calendar, *Yr Hen Galan*), and a third custom in south Pembrokeshire involving the last ears of corn at harvest time. Frances raised possible links to other cultures, suggesting for example that the Pembrokeshire loaves might be an unconscious survival of offerings to Ceres and other mother goddesses. Frances Hoggan, 'Notes on Welsh Folk-Lore', *Folklore*, 4/1,1893, pp. 122-3.

[156] See Williams, 'Feminism, Imperialism and Uplift' and McIntyre's articles for her later life.

[157] She was also the first woman member of the Los Angeles Bar Association and its first female Police Judge. www.genealogy.com/forum/surnames/topics/bullock/2778/

[158] *BMJ,* 19 February 1927. However, McIntyre has pointed out that no other evidence has been found to substantiate this.

For Frances' writings on race, see Williams, 'Feminism, Imperialism and Uplift'.

[159] For example, Dr. Frances Hoggan, 'A Black Statesman of the Last Century', *The Crisis*, January 1911, pp. 26-27 about Moshesh, chief of the African Basutos. The correspondence between Frances and Du Bois is in the Du Bois Library at the University of Massachusetts Amherst.

2

Gender and National Identity Margaret Wynne Nevinson

The old lady climbed Parliament Hill with the swift foot of one accustomed to steep ascents. The east wind blew keen and fresh, and she breathed in deep draughts as one half perishing for air ...

The sun was setting red in the west, and the old lady sighed as she thought how the rocks of Cader Idris would glow in the rosy light. A great home-sickness had fallen upon her.[1]

This expression of romantic nostalgia occurs in a short story published in 1922 but set during the First World War. The old lady is staying in London to look after her pregnant English daughter-in-law. She discovers that her son, Gwilym Jones of the 1st Welsh Fusiliers, has been killed in action. The longing for the Welsh landscape – and the *hiraeth* is expressed in words suggestive of a translation from Welsh – is partly assuaged when a London omnibus conductor addresses Mrs Jones in Welsh. He hails from her native Dolgellau and they chat as she travels to her Welsh chapel.

The author of this story was Margaret Wynne Nevinson, born Margaret Wynne Jones (1858-1932).[2] She spent most of her adult life in Hampstead, living close to Parliament Hill. Her life story suggests at first sight a well-travelled, middle class English woman with little in common with the fictional Mrs Jones. Born in 1858 in Leicester, she had been educated at home, and in Oxford, Paris and Germany. Returning to Britain she spent four years teaching classics at South Hampstead High School, recently established by the Girls' Public Day School Trust. She left in 1884 on marrying the aspiring writer Henry W. Nevinson, whom she had known since childhood. They spent their first year as a married couple in Germany, where Henry Nevinson was a postgraduate student at the University of Jena. Here Margaret gave private tuition in English.

The Nevinsons lived for several years in workers' dwellings (at Brunswick Buildings East in Goulston Street, Whitechapel) in east London. From their six rooms these 'slummers' helped with the newly established Toynbee Hall settlement just round the corner from them. Margaret taught modern language classes there, helped run a girls' club and was, along with Beatrice Potter (later Beatrice Webb), a rent-collector. She also spent twenty-five years as a school manager for the London School Board and subsequently the London County Council, initially in the East End and later in Hampstead (where she lived from the late 1880s).[3]

For many years Margaret was also a poor law guardian for the Kilburn ward of the Hampstead Board of Guardians. In June 1920 she became a magistrate on the Hampstead Bench and the first woman in London to adjudicate at Criminal Petty Sessions.[4] She was one of three women who sat on the Lord Chancellor's advisory committee for the appointment of justices of the peace in London.[5] She also visited the United States to study the American probationary system.

Margaret sat on the committee of the Society of Women Journalists and published not only newspaper articles but also two volumes of short stories and an autobiography. Yet despite a life lived largely in London among the intelligentsia of Hampstead and with numerous international links, Margaret can be viewed as part of the Welsh diaspora. She chose to identify herself as a Welsh woman. She was conscious of her nationality as well as her gender in the shaping of her sense of identity. She surrounded herself with symbols of Welshness, carefully insinuated them into her stories – albeit sometimes more akin to perceived stereotypes than to 'lived experience' – and unequivocally defined herself as a feminist. Why was this so, and what might her life story suggest about how Welsh history and biography are constructed?

Margaret's assumption of both a Welsh and a feminist identity can partly be traced to her parents. Her mother Mary was half-Welsh and her father Timothy was a Welsh-speaking Welsh man from Lampeter. Margaret adored him and adult life never seems to have quite lived up to her childhood or at least the way she chose to remember that time. Timothy Jones was a High Church Anglican in charge of a poor parish in the centre of Leicester. There were five sons and Margaret was the sole daughter. She helped her father in the parish and from the age of nine ran a Sunday school class. Her brothers' names, for example, Meredydd and Lloyd (he became canon of Peterborough) genuflected to Welsh roots. Family holidays were spent in Wales with Welsh-speaking relatives.[6]

Timothy Jones was a classical scholar. He taught Margaret Latin and Greek from the age of seven. Such an enlightened approach was not unknown. The educationalist Emily Davies also studied classics with a clergyman father. Margaret later used her classical training to debate contemporary issues, by applying (slightly tongue-in-cheek) modern beliefs to ancient thinkers. In an article in the *Fortnightly Review* she satirised Juvenal's reactionary tendencies. Here and in an article on 'Ancient Suffragettes', St Paul emerges as a misogynist who would have joined Juvenal and Mr Asquith in their hatred of suffragettes. In contrast, Plato is described as the original founder of the Men's League for Women's Suffrage.[7]

Her father's early death and her mother's traditional beliefs – Mary Jones feared that nobody would want to marry a girl who read Greek – helped to shape Margaret's determination to resist the traditional destiny of middle class daughters.

But the cost of educating her brothers meant that her hopes of reaching Cambridge University necessarily receded. Instead 'marriage was dinned into me from morning till night ... until I hated the very sound of the word'.[8]

Carving out her own career, Margaret took several posts as a governess and saved enough money to travel to Germany. Intelligent and adventurous, she became a pupil-teacher in Cologne, where she gained a diploma in German language and literature. Later, when teaching in London (a path trodden by many London-Welsh women) she undertook a part-time degree, a form of early distance learning imaginatively provided by Scotland's University of St Andrews. In 1883 she was one of sixty-three women who gained an LLA (Lady Literate in Arts) after studying Education, German and Latin.[9]

Margaret's early years had therefore given her some sense of a Welsh heritage and an awareness of how much gender mattered. Her marriage helped to cement further her sense of being defined by a dominant culture that was not quite her own, and her recognition of the need to assert her own rights and those of other women. Margaret and Henry Nevinson shared a childhood in Leicester (where his father was a solicitor), a love of Greek and German literature, and fascination with the work of writers such as Thomas Carlyle, but their year in Germany immediately after their marriage was not simply due to intellectual tastes. Although neither mentioned it in their writings, Margaret was pregnant when they married and their escape avoided scandal. Their eldest child Philippa was born in Germany. The marriage produced resentment and regret on both sides.[10]

Henry Nevinson became a famous war correspondent and writer of essays and fiction as well as a noted campaigner for causes at home and abroad. Although he took some time to establish his reputation, from the end of the nineteenth century until his death in 1941 he was an eminent journalist and radical. He championed numerous political campaigns from exposing slavery in Portuguese Angola to self-determination in Georgia. He was usually to be found in the right place at the right time (for a journalist). Thus he was in Ladysmith when the siege began, in Russia in late 1905 and in Gallipoli in 1915. He was even present at the Place-Royal in Mons when the Armistice was declared on 11 November 1918.

He worked at night as a literary editor – their son recalled that he was rarely home before 3 or 4 am – or abroad for months at a time covering wars. One of Margaret's stories called 'After the Wedding' was a bitter account of the lot of wives of journalists and other creative men.[11] Henry had several serious extra-marital relationships. Margaret was a deeply committed Anglo-Catholic and the couple did not divorce. Instead they inhabited separate spaces within their house in Downside Crescent, Hampstead, and led independent public lives. They never even achieved a companionate marriage in later life. Less than a year after Margaret died, Henry married the children's writer, journalist, former suffragette and pacifist, Evelyn Sharp with whom he had been involved for thirty years. They shared many interests and beliefs.

Margaret had not found motherhood easy. When her son was born in August 1889 she contracted puerperal fever and nearly died. She found the constant demands of small children both trying and debilitating. Indeed, in her autobiography she baldly stated that 'it is a terrible thing to be a mother'.[12] She was also keen to stress that in comparison 'all other work and vocations are as child's play'. Yet in the eyes of the law and the census, wives and mothers were 'unoccupied'. As Margaret neatly put it: 'Man, carpenter, ten children, wife, no occupation'.[13]

Margaret clearly adored 'my boy', the future talented artist C.R.W. Nevinson, and the two spent many holidays together. But he was obsessed with self and fame and, although he praised his mother's European outlook and modernity in his autobiography, he never really credited either parent with the support they both provided in their own ways. He told a fellow art student that 'if my mother does happen to be in for a meal she is so engrossed in other things that she hardly hears & certainly never takes in a word I say'.[14]

Clearly, Margaret's recourse to her Welsh background and feminism cannot simply be explained in terms of her upbringing and personal disillusionment with marriage. Yet they were important factors. Her published writings do not disguise her bitterness. The first story in her collection, *Fragments of Life*, debated the advantages and disadvantages of divorce. 'An Everyday Tragedy' suggests that a woman remains married because of her son, but can never forgive her husband's betrayals. Two other stories, evincing more polemic than narrative, stress that 'the wives of literary men must get used to being forgotten'.[15] The first few years of married life were the hardest and if a woman survived them without divorce or turning to drink or drugs, she would have learned indifference and have turned to 'philosophy or work or religion as an anodyne to despair'.

The four stories that Margaret published in a Women's Freedom League (WFL) penny pamphlet focus upon the double standard – differing expectations of morality and behaviour for men and women – and the effects on women's lives of an unfaithful husband. Two have titles that are quotations from the marriage service.[16]

Margaret's autobiography reinforces the image of a troubled soul. It is entitled *Life's Fitful Fever*, a quotation from Shakespeare's *Macbeth*. Duncan is in his grave, treason has done its worst and nothing, not even 'Malice domestic', can touch him. Like her husband's triple-decker memoirs, also published in the 1920s, Margaret's account refers only sparingly to a spouse and then with detachment.[17]

Those who did not know the Nevinsons well called them 'do gooders'. In a novel by Gilbert Cannan entitled *Mendel*, they were parodied as the Mitchells who had 'a platform manner of speaking' and 'seemed to have their fingers in innumerable reforms'. Cannan presents them as denouncers of sham Liberalism who, between them, would ensure that:

> Women would have votes, the slums would be pulled down, maternity would be endowed, prostitutes would be saved, prisons would be reformed, capital punishment abolished, the working classes would be properly housed...[18]

Yet the Nevinsons were not of one view. Throughout her married life Margaret held and articulated opinions distinct from those of her husband. She marked out her own space through the women's movement, and it was here that she gained the comradeship and respect that she lacked at home. This became most evident in the Edwardian years when Henry was at his busiest. Margaret's incipient feminism was now channelled through women's suffrage. She recognised how vital it was for women to extend on to the national stage the influence they could exert at local government level.[19] She emerged as a witty speaker (the adjective used most frequently in reports of her speeches), but confessed to the 'dizzy sickness of terror' when she first stood up in a cart to address south London gas workers on the subject of suffrage.[20] She sat on the committee of the Hampstead branch of Mrs Fawcett's constitutionalist National Union of Women's Suffrage Societies (NUWSS), then joined Mrs Pankhurst's Women's Social and Political Union (WSPU) soon after its formation.

When the WSPU split in 1907 Margaret became a founder member of the new WFL, chairing Hampstead's first meeting of 'the baby League' in the Town Hall. In 1909 she participated in a WFL deputation to the House of Commons to protest against the omission of votes for women from the King's Speech. She was caught up in the police charge, narrowly avoiding being trampled upon by their horses. Fifty-six women were imprisoned. Margaret gave evidence at one of the subsequent trials.[21]

The WFL had active branches throughout Britain (including Aberdare, Barry, Cardiff, Carmarthen, Montgomery and Swansea), and it became renowned for its commitment to passive resistance. Margaret embraced such tactics. She was a tax resister and took part in a suffrage vigil outside

Parliament in 1909.[22] In 1911 when the WFL was involved in census resistance, the Nevinson family was neatly divided by gender when it came to compliance. Henry Nevinson and son provided information about themselves before Nevinson Senior departed to spend the night skating and dining with Evelyn Sharp and other resisters. Details were also supplied about the two female servants but neither Margaret nor Philippa feature in the census schedule. There were, however, a number of unrecorded women in the house. The enumerator noted on the form that 'they refused consent to the Census on the ground that Women have no representation in this Country's Government'.[23]

Margaret became a skilled speaker. At a debate organised by the Belsize Park branch of the Conservative and Unionist Women's Franchise Association, she won a motion 'that the parliamentary vote should be given to qualified women'. The WFL's paper *The Vote* praised her speech for its 'racy vigour and strong good sense, pointed by some admirable arguments and illustrations'.[24] Margaret penned a number of WFL pamphlets, including *Five Years' Struggle for Freedom: A History of the Suffrage Movement from 1908-12*. A branch treasurer for the WFL and national treasurer of the Women Writers' Suffrage League for nearly a decade, she was also active in the Hampstead branch of the Church League for Women's Suffrage.

Margaret's gender politics and sense of Welshness coalesced in the Cymric Suffrage Union (CSU). Its origins lay in the Suffrage Coronation Procession of 1911. This involved at least 40,000 people and provided a superb opportunity for suffrage as spectacle. It was the one demonstration in which suffrage societies espousing different perspectives participated. It included a Welsh contingent of women in homemade national Welsh costume. But in place of red, black and white they wore costumes in the WSPU colours of purple, white and green. A Welsh socialist and suffragette, Edith Mansell Moullin (née Thomas) had orchestrated this.[25] Encouraged by the Welsh display, she promptly founded the CSU and became a vice-president. The president was Sybil Thomas, the mother of Lady Rhondda.

Founded in London, this was the only independent Welsh suffrage organisation. Early suffrage societies within Wales had been subsumed under titles such as the Bristol and West of England Suffrage National Society. Subsequent societies were branches of, or affiliated to, the WSPU, WFL or, most commonly, the NUWSS, as Ryland Wallace has shown.[26] The motto of the CSU was 'O Iesu n'ad Gamwaith' (Oh Jesus do not allow Unfairness) and its badge was a red dragon. Yet it amounted to more than just another special interest suffrage society.[27] It provided a public and recreational forum and network for London-Welsh women at a time when they lacked the social and occupational opportunities open to their male counterparts. For Margaret, who was outside the well-established chapel culture, this was especially welcome.

Margaret had been present at the 1911 demonstration but, as the illustration shows, she had chosen to wear her graduation gown.[28] She marched with the contingent of women graduates. She also joined the new CSU based at the Mansell Moullin home in Wimpole Street (Charles Mansell Moullin was a surgeon at the London Hospital, a vice-president of the Men's League for Women's Suffrage, and performed the unsuccessful emergency operation on Emily Wilding Davison after she threw herself in front of the King's horse at the 1913 Derby). The CSU had a few branches in Wales, including one at Ogmore Vale in Glamorgan and a Penllyn and Edeyrnion branch in Merioneth, but was most active in London.

The majority of Welsh women living in London worked in what might be called the 'three Ds': the dairy trade, drapery (increasingly in the new department stores) and domestic service. It was felt worthwhile to approach the least deferential of these occupational groups. So milkmaids were canvassed and Mary E. Davies, the CSU secretary, organised visits to Welsh people living in her area of Fulham.

Margaret, Rachel Barrett (a Welsh-speaking Carmarthen-born graduate teacher and WSPU organiser in Wales), Fannie Margaret Thomas (an elementary school headmistress who founded the Ogmore Vale branch of the CSU) and Australian-born Muriel Matters (WFL organiser in Cardiff) all spoke for the CSU at the massive Hyde Park demonstration on 14 July 1912. This date was celebrated as Mrs Pankhurst's birthday. The WSPU leader had actually been born on 13 July but, ever alert to publicity, she had chosen to mark her birthday instead on the following day, Bastille Day.[29] Banners with Welsh slogans were evident. Once again Welshness (of the nineteenth century manufactured variety) was literally donned: the women wore Welsh national costume.

In her speech Margaret stressed that Welsh people loved the concept of 'Chwarae Teg' (Fair Play). She even suggested that women's suffrage had not made much headway there because Welsh women were better appreciated than their Saxon sisters.[30] Such generalised claims and romanticised rhetoric may have been well received at the CSU's Platform 18 in Hyde Park, but sidestepped the realities of daily life. Margaret had expressed similar sentiments at the CSU's first public meeting at London's Steinway Hall a few months earlier where belated St David's Day celebrations were linked to the advocacy of women's suffrage. The stewards wore Welsh costume and the secretary's speech was in Welsh. A resolution by the lawyer Walter Roch demanded votes for women and Margaret seconded it. This Pembrokeshire Liberal MP was a member of the all-party Conciliation Committee that sought (ultimately in vain) a compromise suffrage bill. Margaret invoked a number of stereotypes: 'the Welsh ought to make good suffragists because of the equality of the sexes, their love of democracy, and their power of speech'.[31] The meeting ended to the strains of 'Hen Wlad Fy Nhadau' ('Land Of My Fathers').

Margaret's platitudes were called into question just months later with the infamous attack on suffragettes at Llanystumdwy in Caernarfonshire. Lloyd George (as Chancellor of the Exchequer) had already 'torpedoed' the Conciliation Bill in November 1911. To add insult to injury, suffrage interrupters of his speech at the National Eisteddfod in Wrexham the following September were not only forcibly ejected and manhandled, but were also described as 'foolish people' by Lloyd George. The subsequent attack on suffragettes by local men during his speech at Llanystumdwy just a few weeks later signalled open season for verbal attacks on English suffragettes in the Welsh press and on Welshness and Liberalism by sections of the English press.

Margaret's claims and loyalties were being tested. She wrote in the *Clarion* that 'as a Welshwoman' she had read with 'horror and shame' of the way women had been attacked. It had taken five policemen to extricate from her assailants the suffragette who had interrupted Lloyd George. Others had been kicked, beaten and partially stripped, and narrowly escaped drowning in the River Dwyfor. Until now, Margaret warned, she had believed that her countrywomen were courteous and chivalrous people.[32]

Internal divisions over tactics in the CSU led to a regrouping. Reflecting a major split in the WSPU, the Forward Cymric Suffrage Union was formed in October 1912. Spearheaded by Edith Mansell Moullin, the new Welsh society established closer links with Sylvia Pankhurst and East End suffragettes. It carried on into the war but without Margaret. Unlike Edith Mansell Moullin, Margaret was not a pacifist.[33]

Before the First World War Margaret had attended classes and qualified as a certificated pioneer masseuse. In wartime she did some voluntary physiotherapy with wounded Belgian soldiers, then worked for the Almeric-Paget Massage Corps at Hampstead Military Hospital (based in the workhouse). Like other hospital jobs, this was demanding work physically.[34] When the war ended, she served on the committee of the Ex-Servicemen's Welfare Society, the forerunner of today's Combat Stress. This enlightened organisation was started by women concerned about ex-servicemen of all ranks with 'acute nervous and mental breakdown as would otherwise be sent to asylums'.[35]

Margaret also resumed her WFL work, and in the 1920s contributed to its paper *The Vote*. In these years she became involved in other feminist campaigns and was a vice-president of the Women's Peace Crusade. She championed the work of the League of Nations and travelled the country lecturing on subjects such as infant welfare and (before she became a JP) the necessity of appointing women magistrates. Sometimes her talks took her to Wales. In the summer of 1920 she addressed an open-air meeting on the Aberystwyth promenade, talking about both the League of Nations and equal pay for equal work.[36] She supported the True Temperance Association, arguing not along the familiar teetotaller lines but recognising that public houses fulfilled a potentially important place in communities and should be welcoming to all, just as gardens and cafés were in Europe. Prohibition, she believed, entailed a dangerous interference with the liberty of the individual. Education was the way forward and self-discipline and moderation the goal.[37]

Like her husband, Margaret was active for many years in a range of campaigns. Their interests seem at first sight to have complemented each other well, but they held independent views and perspectives. Even when they broadly supported the same causes, they carved out different niches within them.[38] Henry was also a key player in women's suffrage. He was a founder member of the Men's League for Women's Suffrage and chaired the more militant Men's Political Union for Women's Enfranchisement. He wrote many newspaper articles on women's suffrage, and famously resigned his post on the *Daily News* due to the paper's difficulty in accepting his stance on the subject. Between 1907 and 1912 Henry was much more in sympathy with the Pankhursts than was his wife. He found her WFL dull.

Whereas Margaret drew upon her sense of nationality and celebrated it with like-minded London-Welsh suffrage supporters, the English Henry aligned himself with Irish cultural nationalism (initially fostered by his intense affair with the Irish woman Nannie Dryhurst). In the 1890s he had been fascinated by the Irish cultural revival, reviewing the plays and poetry of Yeats and other Irish literary figures whose gatherings he attended in London. His friends included a number of Sinn Féiners and he published articles on Irish nationalism. Unlike Margaret, he stood by Roger Casement in 1916, played an important part in the doomed campaign for his reprieve after he had been convicted of treason, and wrote moving verses in his memory.

On a number of issues the couple held markedly different views. They disagreed about the South African War, Margaret opposing her husband's increasingly pro-Boer stance.[39] Her religious faith became more prominent as Henry emphatically rejected organised religion. She lamented the fact that 'the average husband of to-day has degenerated in his knowledge of things spiritual', and contrasted this with the eloquence and devotion of Welsh women during the 1904-5 religious revival.[40] In 1905 she heard its leader Evan Roberts preach near Merthyr Tydfil to an overflowing chapel congregation, and later devoted four pages of her autobiography to this experience.[41] A number of her short stories centre on the tensions and temptations facing men of the cloth or their parishioners.

The Nevinsons did not share party-political beliefs. Margaret had flirted with Fabianism in the 1890s. Although alienated by the opposition of the Liberal Prime Minister Asquith to women's suffrage, she nevertheless eventually became a Liberal. Newly enfranchised in 1918, and having just recovered from influenza, she travelled to Scarborough to support the election campaign of the poet and writer Osbert Sitwell who was standing as a Liberal. He found her 'an accomplished and convincing speaker'.[42] In contrast, having briefly been an early member of the Social Democratic Federation, Henry became a Liberal but after the First World War joined the Labour Party. He and Margaret turned down several requests to stand for Parliament.

They were both crusading journalists who also wrote fiction. Henry's volume of 'slum stories', *Neighbours of Ours*, [my emphasis] won critical praise in the mid-1890s.[43] Margaret claimed at one stage that she had written this book.[44] Although the style and Henry's own notes suggest that her husband was the author, the material for a number of these stories appears to have been based on Margaret's experiences as a rent-collector in two large blocks of artisans' dwellings, Lolesworth and Katharine Buildings in Whitechapel. Yet she received no acknowledgement in the publication. Margaret also undertook research at the British Museum for *Celebrities of the Century*, a vast biographical dictionary in seventeen parts. In the preface Henry Nevinson was named as the editor's 'right-hand man' but there was no reference to a 'right-hand' woman.[45]

Some of Margaret's short stories appear to have drawn directly on personal experience. 'The Story of a Lonely Woman' is about a Welsh high school teacher in London who, in order to avoid a nervous breakdown, escapes to a Caernarfonshire cottage which is haunted by a woman who had committed suicide after discovering that her husband had been living with another woman.[46] The narrator, like Mrs Jones in 'Killed in Action', prides herself on possessing second sight. So did Margaret, attributing it to her Celtic descent. Like her husband, she also published stories about working-class people on the margins of society.

Margaret's most influential writing was based on her experiences as a poor law guardian. Henry Nevinson largely operated on an international basis but Margaret dedicated herself to work in the local community from London's East End to Kilburn (which came under the Hampstead board). Women had been entitled to stand as poor law guardians since 1875 and Hampstead was one of the first boards in the country to include them. The Hampstead Minute Book reveals Margaret's exemplary record of dedication and attendance, from her appointment in the autumn of 1904 to the end of December 1921. She attended between fifty and sixty meetings annually, and in some years exceeded this. She chaired committees in areas such as nursing, schools and asylums and maternity, attended conferences, challenged what today we would call sexist language, and was not afraid to ask awkward questions or to champion women's rights whenever the opportunity arose.[47]

Such experiences equipped Margaret to speak and write about some of the difficulties facing working-class women. For example, members of the WFL heard some 'astonishing facts' when she addressed a drawing room meeting on the treatment of married women in workhouses.[48] One of her many articles in *The Vote* argued that prostitution should be perceived as an economic rather than a moral problem. Since women were forced into prostitution by low wages, recognising the value of a living wage was much more important than philanthropy, she argued. She also criticised the allocation of old-age pensions and fashioned powerful short stories about the casualties of the workhouse. She readily acknowledged that 'Many of the characters are life portraits ... in a true Boswellian spirit'.[49] These sketches were published in the *Westminster Gazette*, the *Daily News* and the *Daily Herald*.

In 1918 twenty-six stories appeared in one volume entitled *Workhouse Characters*. This was highly praised by the American suffrage leader Susan B. Anthony.[50] One story, set in a casual ward, was about an old Welsh sailor. Another was turned into a one-act play published by the International Suffrage Shop. The Kingsway Theatre, London staged *In the Workhouse* in 1911 with a female cast provided by the Pioneer Players (run by Ellen Terry's daughter, Edith Craig). It focused on the fact that a married man retained the legal right to decree that his wife be detained in a workhouse against her will. Margaret was unequivocal about her intentions, arguing that unenfranchised women faced legal hardships and discrimination. She explained that her play sought to illustrate 'some of the hardships of the law to an unrepresented sex' as well as 'the cruel punishment meted out to women, and to women only, for any breach of traditional morality'.[51]

Its subject matter and politics shocked and it was deemed offensive, eliciting a somewhat dubious coyness from the mainstream press, though it at least succeeded in getting them to attend. One critic described the men in the audience as 'suffused with blushes'.[52] The reviewer for *The Times* explained that 'we had walked in so innocently imagining that the Pioneering of the Pioneer Players was to be dramatic, not (if it may be pardoned the ugly word) feminist'.[53] By providing such a strong indictment of the antediluvian state of legislation relating to married women, Margaret's 'disgusting drama' was instrumental in changing the law two years later.[54]

Yet despite this achievement and her pioneering work in the 1920s as a woman magistrate, Margaret Nevinson has not been well remembered. It cannot be said that she was airbrushed out of Welsh history for she never entered it. Like many Celtic women and men living in England, her allegiances were complicated and not one-dimensional. More recently, Charlotte Williams, daughter of a black father from Guyana and a white Welsh mother, has explored the powerful need for identity that was allied to a sense of being defined by others. Growing up in North Wales, then travelling in Africa and the Caribbean, she experienced a need for both roots and wings. This was evident too in Margaret's search for what constituted home.[55] And although the category of London-Welsh appeared to provide some sense of belonging, Margaret did not qualify as one of the 27,000 or so Welsh-born Londoners recorded as living there in 1911.[56]

Apart from fleeting references to her work in London's East End, Margaret has not featured much in English historical accounts.[57] This is perhaps not surprising. Unlike her husband who courted fame, Margaret seemed to shun attention. How many other autobiographies can there be where the subject neither mentions the year of her birth nor includes a picture of herself? Indeed, much of *Life's Fitful Fever* deliberately conceals and confuses.[58] Published in 1926, it needs to be seen as a statement about a woman in her late sixties looking back at lost opportunities. It is best read contrapuntally as it provides an unspoken yet distinct challenge to Henry Nevinson's autobiography. Two of his three volumes had already appeared to great acclaim: *Changes and Chances* in 1923 and *More Changes: More Chances* in 1925. A one-volume abridged version entitled *Fire of Life* appeared in the mid-1930s after Margaret's death. This title genuflected to Margaret's autobiography but asserted a clear distinctiveness in tone.

Margaret's suffrage activities and writings on the gendered state of the law have, however, received some attention from historians working in the burgeoning area of modern suffrage studies.[59] Yet she mainly falls into the interstices of historical writing. This can partly be attributed to a lack of personal papers. Henry, in contrast, left very detailed diaries covering almost fifty years. Margaret is conspicuous by her absence from most of them and where she does feature, his comments are usually critical and dismissive. On the day she died in 1932 he even referred in his diary to their 'dismal marriage' in 1884 and how she was 'little suited to me' and 'always inclined to contradict me on every point & all occasions'.[60] He nevertheless conceded that she had a way with words. As he put it, she was 'eloquent in the Welsh manner' and 'humorous & full of observant stories'. Other members of the Nevinson family such as Henry's cousin John L. Nevinson seem to have perceived themselves to be socially superior to the Jones family and had little to do with Margaret over the years.[61]

Margaret's life story serves as a cautionary tale for historians about the availability of sources. Although great care has to be exercised in reading the texts of personal diaries, Henry's are rich and revealing. We do not have a matching source for Margaret. There is no parallax view. Knowledge of her opinions is restricted to Margaret's published writings, alongside those of her family. Accounts of her personal life are problematically refracted through her husband's perspectives in his voluminous diaries, and through the pronouncements of their well-known son, who delighted in shocking society and whose own autobiography is notoriously unreliable. Modern biographical studies might now pay more attention to the wives of famous men than used to be the case. However, navigating the divergent interests of Margaret and Henry Nevinson warns us of the dangers of assuming congruence in purposes and beliefs between couples who at first sight appear to have endorsed similar progressive agendas.

Margaret searched for an identity distinct from the traditional role of wife and mother. Not surprisingly, contemporaries portrayed her as challenging conventional expectations. Ernest Rhys – Celticist, poet, novelist, editor of Dent's Everyman's Library and a Hampstead neighbour

– described her as a 'formidable' woman who gaily regaled his ailing wife the novelist Grace Rhys, 'in a deep voice' with the 'mortal horrors' she had witnessed in a hospital ward.[62] That little word 'deep' hints at issues of sexual identity and helped to distinguish Margaret from the felicitously named and fragile Grace.

Nationality and feminism mattered to Margaret. Living in the shadow of her famous rebel husband and outspoken artistic son, she too rebelled. So far as we can tell, she does not seem to have to have been especially close to her only daughter Philippa, a talented musician who trained at the Royal Academy and Milan Conservatoire. Henry's diary gives the impression that both of Philippa's parents paid more attention to their son than to their daughter. Margaret did, however, approve of the fact that at Philippa's wedding to the architect Sidney Caulfield the word 'obey' was omitted from the marriage service.

Margaret eschewed the conventional married life of a woman of her class. Her Welsh roots formed a vital constituent of the self that she cultivated. Choosing not to be defined by the dominant English culture surrounding her, she joined a group of metropolitan women who could romanticise Wales partly because they did not live there.[63]

Margaret's rejection of 'otherness' saw its most sustained and articulate expression in her claims for citizenship for women. She found comradeship in the Women's Freedom League, spreading the suffrage word in imaginative ways in collaboration with other like-minded women. In 1908 she travelled round Kent with them in a caravan, delivering speeches to audiences that could be hostile but at least provided a challenge.

Her exposure and interpretation of the gender bias in the legal system was impressive. She spent long hours attending committees and courts, and used her experiences her writing. For example, drawing on her experience as a JP, Margaret published in 1923 a wide-ranging pamphlet entitled *The Legal Wrongs of Married Women.*[64] It addressed issues such as the plight of deserted wives and the fact that British women married to aliens were denied a pension.

Margaret's canvas was much more modest than that of her husband, but the contribution she made to society via the local community should not be underestimated. She was a school manager for a quarter of a century. For eighteen years she was a committed poor law guardian who worked for the dispossessed and for poor women in particular, unafraid of voicing her opinions or of being in the minority at meetings. She was also an assiduous justice of the peace and a member of the Magistrates' Association. This was at a time when women magistrates were a novelty as well as in a minority, and she helped to publicise their work by participating in early radio broadcasts on the subject.[65]

Margaret had to make the most of gendered assumptions about what was deemed 'fit' for women. In 1920 when she went to enquire at Hampstead Police Court about when she would be sworn in as a magistrate, she was told 'We don't have any ladies here'. She explained that she was one of the new JPs. The young policeman 'blushed crimson' and admitted that it would be very awkward for him: 'We have such dreadful cases here. I shan't know how to say what it is my duty to say, ma'am, with ladies present. Women are always made to leave the Court before these cases are taken, even the women police'.[66] Yet, as Anne Logan has shown, these pioneer women helped to change the magistracy and spearheaded new approaches to work on the bench.[67]

Margaret's imagined community was a Welsh nation, devout and anxious to dispense justice to men and women (though the events at Llanystumdwy forced some adjustment of this idealised picture). Her goal was a vote and equality for women. Yet although in her story of 1922 the North Walian Mrs Jones laughs at what Londoners call a hill, Parliament Hill was a steep climb. And in the meantime the London-Welsh woman Margaret Wynne Nevinson continued the unpaid, unsung and uphill task of working for a community in north London.

'Exiles' do not always fit easily into accounts of Welsh history. And there is a final irony, one familiar to historians of gender. The opposition of women like Margaret Nevinson to ascribed identities has not infrequently resulted in their actual achievements being sublimated and forgotten precisely because we do not always know how to read and appreciate the identities they constructed.

Notes

[1] Margaret W. Nevinson, 'Killed In Action', in Idem, *Fragments of Life*, London, G. Allen & Unwin, 1922, p.161.

[2] For further information about Margaret's life see Angela V. John, 'A Family at War: The Nevinson Family' in Michael J. K. Walsh (ed.), *A Dilemma of English Modernism: Visual and Verbal Politics in the Life and Work of C.R.W. Nevinson 1889-1946*, University of Delaware Press, 2007, pp. 23-35; Angela V. John, 'Nevinson, Margaret Wynne (1858-1932)', www.oxforddnb.com/view/article/45464.

[3] The Hampstead group included Fleet Road School, known as the best elementary school in London. Its headmaster was W.B. Adams, formerly of the Cyfarthfa Schools, Merthyr Tydfil. His wife Mary was a department head at Fleet Road. W. E. Marsden, *Educating the Respectable*, London, Woburn Press, 1991, p.182.

[4] The Sex Disqualification (Removal) Act enabled women to become magistrates. Margaret was one of 234 women named in July 1920 in the first sizeable appointment of female Justices of the Peace.

[5] Interestingly, the Lord Chancellor was Lord Birkenhead who, as the essay on Lady Rhondda in this volume demonstrates, was hostile to Lady Rhondda's claim for peeresses to sit in the House of Lords.

[6] In the early years of her marriage, Margaret spent holidays in North Wales. She also went on walking tours in Wales.

[7] Mrs H. W. Nevinson, 'Juvenal on latter-day problems; an unscholarly gossip', *Fortnightly Review*, 87, 1907, pp. 903-15; Idem, 'Ancient Suffragettes', Women's Freedom League, nd.

[8] Idem, *Life's Fitful Fever. A Volume of Memories*, A & C. Black, 1926, p. 44.

[9] R.N. Smart, 'Literate Ladies – A Fifty Year Experiment', *The Alumnus Chronicle*, University of St Andrews, 59, June 1968, pp. 20-1.

[10] For an exploration of this see Angela V. John, *War, Journalism and the Shaping of the Twentieth Century. The Life and Times of Henry W. Nevinson*, I.B.Tauris, 2006.

[11] Wynne Nevinson, *Fragments of Life*, pp. 131-9.

[12] Idem, *Life's Fitful Fever*, p. 113.

[13] *Ibid*, p. 114.

[14] From a letter to the art student Dora Carrington, quoted in Michael J.K. Walsh, *C. R. W. Nevinson. This Cult of Violence*, Yale University Press, 2000, p. 4; C.R.W. Nevinson, *Paint and Prejudice*, Methuen, 1937, Chapter 1.

[15] Wynne Nevinson, *Fragments of Life*, p. 119.

[16] Idem, 'The Spoilt Child of the Law', Women's Freedom League, nd.

[17] Evelyn Sharp features rather more prominently in Henry Nevinson's autobiography than does Margaret. See Wendell Harris, 'H.W. Nevinson, Margaret Wynne Nevinson, Evelyn Sharp: Little-Known Writers and Crusaders', *English Literature in Transition* 45/3, 2002, p. 291.

[18] Gilbert Cannan, *Mendel: A Story of Youth*, Fisher Unwin, 1916, pp.186-7. See too Pat Barker's representation of the Nevinson family in her modern novel based loosely on C.R.W. Nevinson and fellow art students at the Slade, Pat Barker, *Life Class*, Hamish Hamilton, 2007, p. 41.

[19] See Patricia Hollis, *Ladies Elect: Women in English Local Government 1865-1914*, Oxford University Press, 1987.

[20] Wynne Nevinson, *Life's Fitful Fever*, p. 212.

[21] HO. 144, 1033/175.878, National Archives, Kew.

[22] As Margaret explained in the journal *Church League for*

Women's Suffrage in May 1913, this also led to the founding of the eponymous Anglican suffrage society.

[23] See Jill Liddington, *Vanishing for the Vote. Suffrage Citizenship and the Battle for the Census*, Manchester University Press, 2014, Chapter 12.

[24] *The Vote* 10 February 1912.

[25] Edith Mansell Moullin was a member of the WSPU (imprisoned in 1911) and treasurer of the Church Socialist League. Letters from Edith Mansell Moullin to Edith How Martyn, 1930-1935, 57.116/76-9. Suffragette Fellowship Collection, Museum of London; Angela V. John, 'Moullin, Edith Ruth Mansell (1858/9-1941), www.oxforddnb.com/view/article/63876.

[26] Ryland Wallace, *'Organise! Organise! Organise!': A Study of Reform Agitations in Wales 1840-86*, University of Wales Press, 1991, Chapter 11 and Idem, *The Women's Suffrage Movement in Wales 1866-1928*, University of Wales Press, 2009.

[27] Angela V. John, '"A Draft of Fresh Air": Women's Suffrage, The Welsh and London', *Transactions of the Honourable Society of Cymmrodorion*, new series, 1, 1995, pp. 81-93; Idem, '"Run Like Blazes": The Suffragettes and Welshness', *Llafur: Journal of Welsh Labour History* 6/3, 1994, pp. 28-43._

[28] The Irish feminist, nationalist and teacher, Hanna Sheehy (also a linguist) and bridegroom Francis Skeffington, wore their graduation gowns at their wedding in 1903. Margaret Ward, *Hanna Sheehy Skeffington: A Life*, Attic Press, 1997, p. 27.

[29] Paula Bartley, *Emmeline Pankhurst*, Routledge, 2002, p. 15.

[30] *South Wales Daily News* 15 July 1912. See too Kay Cook and Neil Evans, '"The Petty Antics of the Bell-Ringing Boisterous Band"? The Women's Suffrage Movement in Wales, 1890-1939', in Angela V. John (ed.), *Our Mothers' Land: Chapters in Welsh Women's History 1830-1939*, University of Wales Press, 2011 edition, pp. 157-85.

[31] *Votes for Women* 23 March 2012.

[32] *Clarion* 4 October 1912.

[33] She did, however, lecture on the importance of peace in the 1920s.

[34] The Cambridge MP Almeric Paget and his American wife Pauline initially organised and funded this, but from 1916 the Corps received a government grant. It employed more than 2,000 by the end of the war.

[35] See Margaret Millman, 'In the Shadow of War: Continuities and Discontinuities in the Construction of the Masculine Identities of British Soldiers, 1914-1924', University of Greenwich PhD, 2002, pp. 222-3.

[36] *The Vote* 13 August 1920.

[37] Margaret Wynne Nevinson, 'Self-Control versus Legislation', *The Woman's View*, January 1927, pp. 3-7, written for the Women's True Temperance Committee.

[38] Conversely their friends Henrietta and Samuel Barnett used marriage as a firm springboard from which to conduct social challenges. Yet Henrietta Barnett has, until recently, been effectively written out of this political partnership. See Seth Koven, 'Henrietta Barnett 1851- 1936: The (Auto)biography of a Late Victorian Marriage', in Susan Pedersen and Peter Mandler (eds.), *After the Victorians: Private Conscience and Public Duty in Modern Britain: Essays in Memory of John Clive*, Routledge, 1994, pp. 31-53.

[39] See her letter to John Lea, MSS RP2679 (ii), 10 April 1900, British Library, for her reaction to Canon Scott Holland's pro-Boer sermon at St Paul's Cathedral.

[40] Nevinson, 'Juvenal on Latter-Day Problems', p. 913.

[41] Idem, pp. 173-7.

[42] Osbert Sitwell, *Laughter in the Next Room*, Macmillan, 1950 edition, p. 108.

[43] See Angela V. John, 'Henry W. Nevinson, *Neighbours of Ours* (1895)' in Andrew Whitehead and Jerry White (eds.), *London Fictions*, Five Leaves, 2013, pp. 43-50.

[44] Nevinson Diaries, e611/1, 23 January 1901, H.W. Nevinson Papers, Bodleian Libraries, University of Oxford.

[45] Lloyd C. Sanders (ed.), *Celebrities of the Century*, London, Cassell, 1887, p. vi.

[46] In Wynne Nevinson, *Fire of Life*, pp. 24-43.

[47] Hampstead Minute Book, Hp B.G. vols.30-40, Greater London Record Office. For an account of women poor law guardians in Wales see Catherine Preston, '"To do good and useful work": Welsh Women Poor Law Guardians 1894-1914', *Llafur*, 10/3, 2010, pp. 87-102.

[48] *The Vote* 5 March 1910.

[49] Margaret Wynne Nevinson, *Workhouse Characters*, G. Allen & Unwin, 1918, p. 9.

[50] Nevinson Diaries, e622/3.

[51] Margaret Wynne Nevinson, *In The Workhouse*, New Era Booklets 2, The International Suffrage Shop, 1911, p. 21.

[52] Wynne Nevinson, *Life's Fitful Fever*, pp. 224-5.

[53] Quoted in Lis Whitelaw, *The Life and Rebellious Times of Cicely Hamilton*, The Women's Press, 1990, p. 125.

[54] Wynne Nevinson, *Workhouse Characters*, pp. 9-10.

[55] Charlotte Williams, *Sugar and Slate*, Planet, 2002. See too the life and work of the novelist, journalist and socialist Lily Tobias, born in Swansea in 1887, daughter of Polish-Jewish immigrant parents. She grew up in the mining community of Ystalyfera. A Zionist from her teenage years, she and her husband moved to Palestine in 1936, where he was killed. Her first novel *My Mother's House* (1931, reprinted by Honno Press, 2015) centres on a Welsh-Jewish working class boy

seeking to reject his dual heritage and culture in order to better himself but eventually reconciling his conflicting loyalties. Jasmine Donahaye, *The Greatest Need: The Creative Life and Troubled Times of Lily Tobias, a Welsh Jew in Palestine*, Honno Press, 2015.

[56] See Emrys Jones (ed.), *The Welsh in London: 1500-2000*, University of Wales Press, 2001.

[57] See Rosemary O'Day, 'How Families Lived then: Katharine Buildings, East Smithfield, 1885-1890', in Ruth Finnegan and Michael Drake (eds.), *From Family Tree to Family History*, Cambridge University Press, 1994, pp. 129-66; Ellen Ross (ed.), *Slum Travellers Ladies and London Poverty, 1860-1920*, University of California Press, 2007, pp. 172-7. See too Michael J.K. Walsh, *Hanging a Rebel: The Life of C.R.W. Nevinson*, The Lutterworth Press, 2008 as well as Idem (ed.), *A Dilemma of English Modernism* and *This Cult of Violence.*

[58] See Roy Foster's assessment of the Anglo-Irish writer Elizabeth Bowen, who also dealt with the complexities of national identity and belonging: 'Elizabeth Bowen and the Landscape of Childhood' in Foster, *The Irish Story: Telling Tales and Making it up in Ireland*, Penguin Books, 2002 edition, pp. 148-63.

[59] For example, Claire Eustance, 'Daring to be Free: The Evolution of Women's Political Identities in the Women's Freedom League 1907-1930', University of York, DPhil, 1993; Sheila Stowell, *A Stage of Their Own: Feminist Playwrights of the Suffrage Era*, Manchester University Press, 1992; Maroula Joannou and June Purvis (eds.), *The Women's Suffrage Movement: New Feminist Perspectives*, Manchester University Press, 1998; Elizabeth Crawford, *The Women's Suffrage Movement: A Reference Guide 1866-1928*, Routledge, 2001 edition, pp. 445-6.

[60] Nevinson Diaries, e625/4, 8 June 1932.

[61] See the diaries of John L. Nevinson, vol.3, 15 September 1924, The Society of Antiquaries of London, Burlington House.

[62] Ernest Rhys, *Wales England Wed: An Autobiography*, J.M. Dent, 1940, pp. 158-9.

[63] Kenneth O. Morgan has noted how David Lloyd George drew upon Welsh life when it was expedient. Kenneth O. Morgan, 'Writing Political Biography' in Eric Homberger and John Charmley (eds.), *The Troubled Face of Biography*, Macmillan, 1988, pp. 44-5.

[64] Published by the Women's Freedom League as a threepenny pamphlet in 1923.

[65] For example, in a BBC radio broadcast on 22 April 1924.

[66] *The Vote* 30 July 1920.

[67] Anne Logan, 'Making Women Magistrates: Feminism, Citizenship and Justice in England and Wales 1918-1950', University of Greenwich, PhD, 2002.

3

The Good Life of Edith Picton-Turbervill

The autobiography of Edith Picton-Turbervill, Labour MP, social reformer and champion of women's rights, is called *Life is Good.*[1] It's a title that many would not have contemplated for their memoirs, either considering it inappropriate or a little anodyne, and maybe even smug. Yet it does seem to have been heartfelt and to reflect its author's approach to life, even though, at first glance, this Welsh woman's early experiences appear to challenge her claim.

Edith was born in 1872, but her parents were largely conspicuous by their absence. During her childhood in England, they lived thousands of miles away. She was moved from place to place and, after a fractured education, was eventually sent away to school. There were tragedies: a three-year-old brother perished when his baby brother got hold of matches and caused a fatal fire, then Edith's mother died when she was fourteen. Two years later she gained a stepmother. It might all have been a recipe for a troubled young woman.

Yet in her autobiography Edith insists that her upbringing was a very happy one. And despite later experiencing, at first hand, harrowing scenes such as the servitude of young girls in the Far East, her adult life was both rewarding and remarkable. Much of the explanation for her equanimity can be found in her faith, which provides a key to her politics and perspectives. She already possessed a confidence that emanated from her background though, as a woman who seemed to many to be trespassing in a man's world, especially when it came to parliamentary politics and preaching, she needed to draw upon many resources.

Edith Picton-Turbervill came from a Conservative, well-connected background. Even her identical twin sister Beatrice, to whom she was devoted, was a lifelong 'arch Conservative'.[2] Their father's family had been in Glamorgan since the late eleventh century. Their great-grandmother narrowly missed being guillotined in revolutionary France.

The best known of Edith's forbears was Sir Thomas Picton, her 'great-grand-uncle'. *Life Is Good* opens with an account of the final, illustrious period of his life. He became an MP, was knighted, and thanked seven times in

Parliament for services rendered to his country in the Peninsula War. Best remembered is his heroic death (after being wounded from an earlier battle) at Waterloo in 1815. Picton has been celebrated as Wellington's greatest General. He was the first Welsh person to be buried in St Paul's Cathedral, and gained an imposing public monument in Carmarthen.

Yet Edith's account omits the distinctly murky side of Picton's career. A rather different picture emerges if the middle period of his life is examined.[3] Picton had been a boy soldier who then furthered his military career in the Caribbean. He became the first British Governor of Trinidad after the island was captured from the Spanish in 1797. Since it was expected to revert to Spanish control after the Peninsular War ended, he felt he could, for the time being, exercise military rule under Spanish law, free from the constraints of the British legal system. Keen to build up the sugar trade, the number of slaves was doubled to close to 20,000 – Picton was himself a slave owner – and he sanctioned torture. The Trinidadian historian Claudius Fergus stresses that the name of Picton evokes images of terror and tyranny in modern Trinidad.[4] Eventually, in 1803, Picton was forced to resign. He was censored in Britain for illiberal administration of the law, facing thirty-six minor charges. He was tried in London for having permitted the illegal torture of a woman, found guilty but eventually won his appeal. Had he died just after the start of the nineteenth century, his legacy would be far from that of the heroic warrior.

Edith was not unaware of the Trinidad years and court case,[5] but chose not to mention Picton's blemished earlier record in her autobiography, proudly casting her ancestor instead as a heroic adventurer. Her connection to Picton and the way she chose to present him is worth noting, not least because she too would be involved in slavery issues, albeit in a markedly different context, and with infinitely more humane intentions than those of her flawed ancestor.

Edith's maternal grandfather Sir Grenville Temple Temple, [sic] 10th Baronet of Stowe, was another relative whose dashing life she admired.[6] He was in the 15th Hussars and spent much of his time travelling in the Middle East in 'Eastern dress'. He spoke Arabic, and Edith, who never knew her grandparents, observed that his sympathies 'seemed to be more with the Muslims than Christians' (one son was called Abdullah). His wife, Edith's grandmother, was a Baring. When she was widowed she lived in a Swiss castle, then, after losing her fortune, settled in a house on Lake Constance, where she made ends meet by becoming a governess. This was neither a provincial nor a run-of-the-mill family.

Edith's father was an army officer in India. In 1893, on the death of his elder brother, he inherited the Ewenny (Ewenni) Priory estate near Bridgend in South Wales, and became significantly more affluent (the Priory had passed through marriage to the family in the eighteenth century). It was where Sir Thomas Picton had spent his last night in Wales. It had been a cell of the Benedictine Abbey of St Peter, Gloucester and founded within the lordship of Ogmore in the early twelfth century. Unusually for a monastic house in Wales, it was a fortified stronghold (for the Normans against the Welsh).

Ewenny boasted battlement walls complete with towers, as well as a beautiful Romanesque church. In 1797 J.M.W. Turner displayed at the Royal Academy his watercolour of its south transept. In due course, a memorial plaque was erected to Edith there, alongside many of her family, but it simply refers to her as a 'Sometime Member of Parliament'.[7] Home was a Georgian house on the site of what had been the monastery.[8] There, E and B (as the twins were known) had their own three-room suite. The estate covered more than 3,000 acres.

Yet although Edith essentially defined herself as from Ewenny Priory, it was only when she was in her early twenties that she began to live there. Proud of her Welsh heritage, she chose to identify this place as 'my happy home for many years'. A substantial section of her 1946 book *In the Land of My Fathers* was devoted to the history of Ewenny.[9]

She had been born Edith Picton Warlow at Lower House, Fownhope in Herefordshire on 13 June 1872. She changed her surname, as did her parents and some siblings, after the family inherited Ewenny. During her early years she saw little of her parents, as Captain (later Colonel) John Picton Warlow and her mother, his second wife, Eleanor (née Temple), spent much of their time in India, leaving four of their children with their aunt Rosa in Brighton. By 1884 Edith was one of ten surviving children, including four boys under the age of six and, unusually, three sets of twins.[10] She and B were tall, had big brown eyes and dark brown hair.

Her father retired from the army in 1883 and for nine months the family lived in Bruges (the idea was to economise). Edith attended school there. But the following year they moved back to Britain, settling in the little village of Laleston, close to the market town of Bridgend in Glamorgan, and just three miles from Ewenny. Their home, an old stone building called Laleston House, is thought to have been a gift from Queen Elizabeth I to the Earl of Leicester, who used it as a hunting lodge. The family had a cook, a nurse and two housemaids.

Edith's account of her time here suggests that the children enjoyed considerable freedom. Boys outnumbered girls, and Edith joined them bird-nesting in nearby Bryntirion, riding bareback and fencing. She became a competent archer. They were part of the county set. When Edith's half-sister Daisy went to Rhyl to train as a children's nurse, the notion of this young lady taking up such a career apparently 'electrified the county'.[11]

In 1887, after surviving numerous pregnancies and childbirths, Edith's mother died of typhoid fever. Edith and her twin were sent away to the Royal School, Bath, catering for the daughters of army officers who might otherwise have been unable to afford such education. The teaching emphasised religious instruction. Edith later claimed that her headmistress Carrie Blake 'first fired me with the desire to be of some use in the world'.[12]

In the meantime their father married a Scot: Caroline (Cara) Frances Miller. This brave woman took on the entire rumbustious, close-knit family and they all appear to have coped remarkably well. Writing on 'Myself When Young' in a chapter for an eponymous collection of essays published in 1938, Edith's contribution (sandwiched between accounts by Sylvia Pankhurst and Maude

Royden), referred to these years at Ewenny as 'spacious happy days'.[13]

They involved a degree of social responsibility. Edith's mother and aunt had been Evangelicals, and regular attendance at the Priory church – next to the house – was the norm. Edith played the organ in church, (still Church of England: Welsh disestablishment was not until 1920). She also taught at Sunday School.

Prayers before breakfast included not only the family but also, as in other grand households, the hierarchy of servants, from butler to scullery maid. Cara was a 'Lady Bountiful'. She was active in temperance work, established Bands of Hope and Sunday Bible Classes and visited Bridgend Workhouse weekly.[14] Beatrice became president of the Bridgend branch of the British Women's Temperance Association.

Edith was, however, beginning to question her faith, fearing that church attendance had become mere convention. In 1893 she and her twin spent three months in Florence and Rome. At the end of the following year, Edith and her eldest brother Charles (an agricultural student) travelled to America to visit her half-sister Daisy, who was living in Florida. Edith sailed home some months later with a friend and a Colonel and Mrs Drury Lowe. The latter was the niece of Lord Radstock, a well-known Evangelical preacher. The Drury Lowes had been described to Edith as 'a psalm-singing couple who went about asking people if their souls were saved'.[15] Unhappy at the prospect of spending time in their company, she sought, unsuccessfully, to change ships. Once aboard, it was difficult to avoid them and their Bible readings. Having nothing better to do, Edith went along. She was impressed.

Back in London she heard Lord Radstock preach but was still not won over. However, soon afterwards she had her epiphany in a rather more prosaic – and unlikely – setting: a railway carriage on the London train. It was whilst travelling on the Paddington express due to arrive at Bridgend Station at 4.11pm on her twenty-third birthday, that Edith had the industrial equivalent of a 'Road to Damascus' experience. She later explained how, in that train, she experienced 'the supreme deciding moment' of her life. She was almost home and, as she put it: 'A new life opened before me that I felt to be full not only of joy but of power ... The world for me was changed'.[16]

Perhaps appropriately, given the location of her conversion, Edith now sought to share her sentiments with those more intimately connected with the railway but infinitely less privileged than herself: the navvies building the Vale of Glamorgan railway just two miles from her home. Her story of 'Ginger Joe'[17] the ganger, and the navvies' one-room accommodation in wooden huts (Edith raised the funds to get one built as a reading-room), reads a little like a Hannah More cautionary tale. Such well-intentioned accounts are inevitably one-sided. What, we might ask, did the navvies have to say after this imposing (five foot ten inches) daughter of the squire left them? Sunday after Sunday, she sought to persuade these men that 'they too could become sons of God'.[18]

Her relatives were sympathetic to Edith's religiosity but wary of how she expressed it. Noting her soiled dress, one brother remarked 'What can you expect when she is always kneeling with navvies in dirty huts!'[19] Sundays also involved early communion, evensong and a two-mile walk each way to a long mission service in Bridgend. Most evenings Beatrice was subjected to lengthy Bible readings from her twin. Edith studied the Bible whenever possible and, long before the Welsh religious revival of 1904-5, stuck gummed labels with biblical texts on trees and gates. She was, at this time, both pious and priggish.

She learned how to conduct a choir and trained volunteer singers in Bridgend to help in Temperance missions. In America she had met Emily Kinnaird whose mother, Lady Kinnaird, had founded the Young Women's Christian Association (YWCA),[20] and Emily came from London to spend a fortnight with Edith in the winter of 1896. They organised, with local assistance, a mission for the navvies in Barry Dock, and were rewarded with audiences of more than 400 men.[21]

Not content with evangelising at home, Edith wished to become a missionary. Her father, who had spent most of his adult life in India, was uneasy with the idea of his daughter – by now in her late twenties – leaving home to pursue a vocation. Seeing a newspaper advertisement for a London training school for missionaries, Edith visited the Principal. Discovering that it did not commit her to a foreign mission, she persuaded her father to let her become a student.

She spent a year at college, most probably at The Willows, the missionary arm of the network of Mildmay institutions in Islington's Mildmay Park. Her studies included theology and comparative religions.[22] The trainee missionaries accompanied Mildmay Deaconesses on district mission work in homes and hospitals.[23] More imbued with a desire to save souls than reform appalling living conditions, 'sweated' women match-workers in the slums of Shoreditch now replaced the railway navvies in Glamorgan as Edith's candidates for salvation.[24]

In late 1899 she went to India with the Young Women's Christian Association (YWCA). It had begun work there in 1875. Its Indian arm had recently affiliated to the YWCA World Movement[25] and was developing activities amongst Anglo-Indians and Indian students through 'Time and Talents', a programme of service that had been inaugurated by the YWCA in Britain.

Edith and her twin had 'heard the call to India' in the Lake District through the philanthropist Mary Morley.[26] First launched in 1875 'for the promotion of Practical Holiness', the interdenominational Keswick Convention had rapidly attracted thousands drawn to the prospect of attaining a 'higher life' in the world through being delivered from sin. Although Edith's autobiography makes no mention of it, the twins made a number of trips to Keswick. Beatrice later recalled how, leaving an evening meeting in 1898, Edith had confessed that Morley's call had gone 'straight to her heart'.[27]

As Antoinette Burton has demonstrated,[28] British culture was saturated with images of Indian women requiring the intervention of concerned Christian women reformers. Edith's family history was steeped in service to imperial India. Some of her siblings were born there. Her maternal uncle Algar Temple had been involved in the taking of Delhi during the Sepoy Rebellion of 1857, known in Britain as the Indian Mutiny. Having been thrilled as a child by stories of events such as the siege of Lucknow, Edith retained a romanticised notion of the Rebellion.

Her father had been awarded the 'Mutiny' Medal aged just nineteen for suppressing a concurrent rising in South India.

Yet the retired Colonel saw it as a very different matter for his daughter to contemplate living in India not as an army wife but as a single, working ,woman. In the past Edith had found him indulgent and broad-minded, but he now reacted 'almost violently against the idea of my working amongst the "natives"'.[29]

She sought to placate him by travelling with Marjorie Hobbs, an Irish Mildmay Deaconess. The young women went to the YWCA's National headquarters at Calcutta (Kolkata). Edith settled in a YWCA hostel mainly occupied by Anglo-Indian shop assistants and teachers. A pamphlet explained that 'Any girl in sorrow or trouble and who is in need of loving advice and sympathy' would find there 'a friend who will be to her both a mother and a sister'. But it also emphasised that its doors would be wide open to welcome 'those willing to live in a 'European way'.[30] The young YWCA women organised Bible-study, shorthand, dressmaking, and other 'improving' classes, using any opportunity to recruit. Edith lectured on English literature to Indian college students, but viewed this primarily as an opportunity to smuggle in teaching on Christianity.

Evangelising was paramount for this earnest young woman, and the conversion of British India was her impossible dream (just 1.02 per cent of its population was Christian by 1911).[31] From Calcutta she moved to Bombay (Mumbai), where she briefly shared a flat (built for three) with thirteen young women, mostly Anglo-Indians. She then went to work in the Settlement for University Women at Kamballa. Mary Dobson, music graduate, Gujarati scholar and daughter of the poet Austin Dobson, was in charge there. The aim was to win over the Parsi community to Christianity. Edith often went to the homes of these young women, ostensibly to teach English literature. But it was on condition that they listened to her reading from the New Testament for fifteen minutes before leaving.

In common with numerous women missionaries in British India, from the representatives of the London Missionary Society to the many Welsh Presbyterians, Edith was driven by the conviction that evangelising was what young women needed. Her work was primarily geared towards Anglo-Indians and the educated elite of Indian women. She did proudly record – though from a later vantage point – that she had attended social gatherings to which very few Europeans were invited.[32] And she stressed that she 'made many friends amongst the young Indian women students', most of whom were Brahmo Samaj, the monotheistic Hindu sect that drew on Christian faith and was active in social reform. Yet the chapter on India in her autobiography does not mention a single Indian woman by name.

Edith achieved in India some personal emancipation through the sense of purpose and authority she could command so far from home. In Britain she was unable to assume any real authority either within the church, or in her own family. At the very moment when women were demanding voting rights in Edwardian Britain, Edith was, with comrades of like mind, bicycling around crowded cities, buoyed up by a conviction that she was of use.

The 'Time and Talents' experiment in India did not,

however, achieve its aims, as Edith conceded at the YWCA conference at Lucknow in 1906. It then ceased to be a YWCA department.[33] She had enjoyed rather more success in another venture. In Simla (Shimla), the summer capital of British India since the 1860s, Edith, Mary Dobson and Marjorie Hobbs opened in May 1900 'The Yengherries', the YWCA's first Holiday Home. Shop workers and teachers travelled there to enjoy the temperate Himalayan climate, and after a couple of hours in the office each morning, Edith would call on these visitors: 'I must get to know some of the people', she told Emily Kinnaird.[34] She also ran an employment agency for those seeking nurses and governesses. Her weekly Bible class for shop workers was disappointingly small but she remained optimistic. The following year she attended the opening of the first Holiday Home in the south.

When the weather was bearable for her in the Bombay area, Edith worked in its University Settlement. There she fell dangerously ill with typhoid fever in 1904. It had killed her mother. Edith was far from home and, even when times were good, felt keenly the separation from her twin: they wrote weekly and, as Beatrice put it, they 'shared each other's' lives and interests as I think few sisters do'.[35] But her younger brother Ivor, who had, like most of the men in the family, joined the army, was stationed with the Gordon Highlanders in northern India, and he travelled down to see her. She recovered sufficiently to be taken back to Wales, accompanied by a nurse, in time for a family Christmas at Ewenny.

She spent the following year at home, witnessing the 1904-5 religious revival and, like Margaret Nevinson, listening to its leader Evan Roberts preach.[36] She then returned to India, to a new YWCA post based in Bangalore. She was now the first travelling District Secretary for the student department, covering the whole of southern India. The job involved visiting schools and colleges as well as established YWCA branches, and starting new branches. Edith also spoke, via an interpreter, to the long-established Syrian Christians of the Malabar Coast. The president of the National Committee praised her 'valuable reports' that 'more than justified this special use of her able and devoted labours'.[37]

In 1908, after almost three years back in India and a particularly severe bout of malaria in a remote area, the YWCA told Edith that she must leave the country for the sake of her health. So she returned home once more. Emily Kinnaird replaced her.

Conspicuous by its absence in Edith's later account of her life in India was any sense of the growing unrest of the time. There was, for example, no mention of the 1905 partition of Bengal and its effects, the *swadeshi* (buy Indian) movement, or the formation of the Muslim League.[38] Her only reference to the Viceroy Lord Curzon concerned his feud with the Lieutenant Governor of the Punjab. Edith noted that Curzon was sensitive to public opinion.

And although by the time she wrote this account Edith had been an MP, there was no mention of the Indian National Congress, of Moderates or Extremists. This period of her life was not one in which she saw herself as a political animal or questioned the tenets of the imperial venture. Instead, by her own admission, she focused on rather narrow religious beliefs. Although, like a number of British 'Maternal Imperialists' (for example, Mary Carpenter), Edith was involved in education in India, it was as a means to a religious end rather than as part of a feminist or fundamental social reform programme.[39]

India had, nevertheless (through the YWCA), given her a voice and revealed her ability as an organiser. By 1932 Edith was proud to report that it had eighteen hostels in Indian cities, a number of Holiday Homes and numerous cultural and educational institutions as well as ten employment agencies.[40]

The years in India also offered close female friendships, most notably with Mary Dobson. Mention of this friendship in Edith's autobiography of 1939 was followed by a confessional digression in which she admitted that she had never lost her heart to a man. And she celebrated 'Women's strong attachments' that, she argued, could be 'as deep, as beautiful, and as exhilarating as any human relationship'.[41] At the same time, she felt the need to add that such intimate and dear friendships, sustained by a shared commitment to spiritual values, did not mean that they were 'necessarily silly and unwholesome'. Like Lady Rhondda, she was well aware that, as a powerful single woman in the public eye, with a lifestyle and work that was essentially female-centred, it was only too easy to be judged severely.[42]

Although Eleanor Rathbone and other single British women went to India in the wake of involvement in women's suffrage, for Edith it was the reverse. She joined the moderate National Union of Women's Suffrage Societies (NUWSS) headed by Mrs Fawcett on her return to

Britain, and had the temerity to try to win over the anti-suffrage writer Mrs Humphrey Ward. In an even more futile exercise, in 1912 she urged Mrs Pankhurst to abandon militant methods. Quoting the Bible at the suffragette leader simply produced equally effective retorts from the same source.

Edith now worked for the YWCA as head of its new Foreign Department, living in London and sharing a home with Anna Smith, a retired missionary. She still spent as much time as possible at Ewenny. Her job involved travel at home and overseas. For example, early in 1914 she went to Egypt, where she helped to establish a YWCA hostel in Cairo and launch a fundraising campaign. There is also one tantalising reference to her visiting Jamaica.[43]

During this period she gradually became more tolerant and less bound by religious dogma, emerging as a leader of the progressive wing of the YWCA.[44] From 1914 to 1920 and again from 1922 to 1928 she was one of its national vice-presidents (there could be as many as six in any one year), and acting president for some months in 1923-4. She was keen to stress improvements in the treatment of those with social problems, citing, for example, the YWCA's sympathetic and 'profoundly more Christian' treatment by the 1920s of the unmarried mother.[45] Letters from Edith appeared in the national press, where she made jaunty, ambitious appeals for funds for holiday camps. 'Oh! For some cheques,' she wrote in *The Times*, anticipating that these summer camps would soon be filled with 'relays of happy girls'.[46]

After the outbreak of war, Edith chaired the committee to raise funds to house and feed munitions workers. She travelled across Britain fundraising as part of the appeal for £25,000 for canteens, rest homes and hostels, visiting factories and occasionally doing a night shift in a canteen. She wrote the Foreword to *The Second Picture of the War.* It told the story of YWCA war service, stressing that working conditions for women and girls should contribute to 'the uplifting of moral and spiritual life'.[47]

Her twin Beatrice ran, with her long-term partner Anne Macnaghten,[48] the Joan of Arc Hostel where Woolwich Arsenal workers were housed. Edith's sister Violet (Durand) was a controller with the Women's Army Auxiliary Corps (WAACs). Through the YWCA, Edith helped to raise funds for recreation rooms for the WAACs in France.[49] Two of her brothers lost their lives, and two others became prisoners of war. Edith received an OBE for her war work.

Shortly before war ended, Edith, Beatrice and a few other YWCA women, were invited to the United States to lecture on munitions welfare work and fundraise. Braving torpedoes, they sailed on the *Aquitania,* now converted into a troop ship. As in Wales and London, Edith's social life encompassed the well known and wealthy, and the first weekend was spent with the Rockefellers. She spent six weeks on the lecture tour, and was in Chicago when the Armistice was signed. Here she met, for the second time, one of her heroines: Jane Addams, who ran the Hull House Settlement.

Edith had been one of the 180 women keen to attend the Women's International Peace Congress held at The Hague in the spring of 1915, the first major transnational gathering since the outbreak of war. Its two fundamental principles were that international disputes should be settled by peaceful means and that the vote should be extended to women. The government, however, refused exit permits for the women to attend. Although a small number were finally permitted to travel, the escalation of naval conflict then closed the North Sea and English Channel to commercial travel.

Mrs Fawcett, leader of the NUWSS to which Edith belonged, did not endorse the Congress but with Jane Addams as its president, Edith was behind it. Like the suffragette and writer Evelyn Sharp, religious faith fuelled by wartime experiences, played a part in a commitment to peace. Both women joined the Women's International League[50] formed in the wake of the Congress that October. Within a couple of years, it had more than 3,500 members. Edith spoke at their meetings, stressing the danger of easy optimism, and the necessity of working for complete disarmament and all-in arbitration.[51]

The following year, at a League of Nations Union meeting, she voiced her fear that life was not necessarily good, stressing that war was endemic, and that if money were spent on arms another war would be inevitable.[52] In 1919 she had signed a memorandum for the release of Conscientious Objectors still in prison. In a letter to *The Times* in 1921, she quoted the Monmouthshire-born evolutionist Alfred Russel Wallace on the woman of the future as 'the regenerator of the race', and argued that women were essentially non-combatant.[53]

She supported a No More War demonstration and attended the 1926 Peacemakers' Pilgrimage Rally at Hyde Park, urging the settlement of international disputes by arbitration. Later, as an MP, she was asked what Parliamentary issues most interested her. She cited the impending disarmament conference and the Town Planning Bill. This member of a family steeped in the military declared that the priority should be to outlaw war. Her ideal was securing both world peace and cities of beauty.[54]

One of Edith's many friends was the pacifist, feminist and early woman barrister Chrystal Macmillan, who had been the first female science graduate from Edinburgh University. The two women owned tiny huts on Box Hill in Surrey where they enjoyed weekend visits and long rambles after the war. Edith's was named 'Chatsworth'. Lilian Baylis (of Old Vic fame) had one too, and the actress and writer Cicely Hamilton had a caravan close by. They called themselves 'the fellowship of the Hill'.[55]

On 24 May 1917 Edward Lee Hicks Bishop of Lincoln attended a meeting of bishops at Lambeth Palace. That evening he dined with a few friends. They included Edith and 'Miss Leaf who lives with her'. No such person features in Edith's autobiography. So who was she?

Emily Maud Leaf was part of the circle of suffragists and pacifists galvanised by the events surrounding The Hague Congress.[56] She was a couple of years younger than Edith, and grew up in south London. Her close family was very wealthy and remarkably similar in size to Edith's: she had seven brothers and three sisters. She spent two years at Newnham College, Cambridge, became secretary to the Women's Liberal Association and did social work in Bermondsey. By 1911 she was the press secretary for the NUWSS.

Leaf was one of five NUWSS women – Chrystal Macmillan was another – who travelled to The Hague for a planning meeting three months ahead of the Congress. Leaf was, however, like other British women, prevented from attending the event itself. She resigned her NUWSS post due to Mrs Fawcett's lack of support for the Congress. She became active in the Women's International League of Peace and Freedom and, like Edith, was at their Vienna Congress in 1921. In wartime she worked with the British Committee of the French Red Cross. Her friends included the Quaker sisters Alice and Hilda Clark, and she knew Olwen Rhŷs.[57]

It is not known when Emily Leaf met Edith, but their interests and friends clearly overlapped. She lived with her brother Henry in Barton Street, Victoria from 1905 until his marriage in 1915. From 1916 Edith rented a small Queen Anne House (owned by the London County Council and full of antique Welsh furniture) in Gayfere Street. It was just minutes away from Barton Street. We do not know how long the friendship lasted. Emily Leaf lived until 1941 but we lack Edith's own diary and there is no trace of the elusive Miss Leaf in Edith's other records. Her private life remained just that. Edith is more easily traced as a public figure.

Edith can be seen as part of the networking machinery of women's societies campaigning in the post-war years for issues such as the appointment of women police.[58] She was a member of the Executive of NUSEC, the National Union of Societies for Equal Citizenship (the successor to the NUWSS).[59] In the 1930s it branched off into two distinct organisations: the Townswomen's Guilds – Edith was their second president from 1938 – and the

National Council for Equal Citizenship. She also became the latter's president. Cheryl Law cites her as a 'sound illustration of the diverse nature' of participation in the women's movement at this time.[60]

Like many others in the wake of the First World War, Edith was initially naively optimistic about women's future prospects. In an article in the YWCA's *Our Own Gazette* in March 1922,[61] she stressed the importance of training for all girls so that they could earn their own livelihoods. Economic independence for young women was a moral duty. Current unemployment rates were likely to represent just 'a passing phase'. This would surely be replaced by 'a nobler social system' providing employment for all.

By the 1930s she was more realistic, but still committed to improving women's lives. She travelled widely. In 1932 she made a short visit to Russia where she spent an afternoon with the communist revolutionary Alexandra Kollontai, then the Soviet Ambassador to Sweden. Edith was also part of the British delegation to the International Woman Suffrage Alliance in Istanbul in April 1935, attended by three hundred women.[62] They stayed in a former harem. During her stay, Edith managed to preach in the Crimea Memorial Church in Istanbul. She was in Turkey at a seminal moment and she was one of the thirty women invited to Ankara, the republic's new capital, where she met its leader Mustafa Kemal. That week he had been proclaimed Atatürk (father of the Turks). In the 1880s Edith's father had been a military consul in Turkey, charged with reporting on Abdul Hamid's promised reforms.

After talking to Atatürk about women's opportunities,

Edith proudly described him in an article in the *Saturday Review* as 'the greatest of all feminists'.[63] There was, however, no reference to the modernising achievements of Turkish women, such as the remarkable Halide Edip [64] (who was then in exile and later became Istanbul University's first female professor). Despite praising Atatürk's faith in women, and their shift from wearing the veil to voting and sitting in Parliament, here and in her autobiography four years later, Edith was nevertheless careful to question his intention to dissolve the Turkish Women's Union. She emphasised his kindly appearance but noted his 'steel grey' eyes. Her article was pointedly entitled 'The New Turkey's Dictator'.

Yet although she had remarked on Atatürk's feminism in her article and autobiography, elsewhere in *Life is Good* Edith distanced herself from the word 'feminist'.[65] This partly reflects the point at which she was writing. By the late 1930s, affairs in Europe were concentrating minds on a different set of priorities from those of the early 1920s. Many concerned about threats to political freedom stressed the urgent need for women and men to work together. Edith had, however, always believed in cooperation. She expressed some reservations about the equalitarian language of feminists such as Lady Rhondda.

The YWCA saw women's citizenship as the way forward. As Catríona Beaumont argues, its lack of overt feminist statements should not prevent the organisation from being seen as part of a significant and wider women's movement.[66] Edith and the YWCA were challenging the status quo gently but effectively. Christian beliefs lay behind her ideas about social welfare, though in practice her primary concern was invariably for women, especially mothers. Edith might have committed to paper her dislike of the term 'feminist' but as with Menna Gallie later on, her writings and her actions belied her protestations about feminism.

Perhaps Edith's clearest endorsement of feminist principles came in her advocacy of women's right to preach in the Church of England and her support of women priests. Although the mid-nineteenth century had seen the revival of Anglican sisterhoods and deaconesses, women lacked an official recognised role in the Church. Some brave individuals such as Ursula Roberts were trying to effect change. The 'High Priestess' of the movement for the ordination of women was Maude Royden,[67] daughter of a Liverpool ship owner and MP. She and Edith shared many a platform over the years. They first met in about 1913 when Royden was editor of the suffragist monthly *Common Cause*, and it was Edith who wrote her friend's obituary for *The Times* in 1956.[68]

Royden was four years younger than Edith, and also from a large Tory family, but *she* went to Oxford University. She preached the first of many sermons in 1903 in Rutland, where she assisted the Rev. Hudson Shaw (eventually her husband) in his South Luffenham parish. But she spoke in the schoolroom, not the church. She later preached in Labour and Ethical Churches Her fame spread during the First World War. Seeking to revitalise the Church through a National Mission of Repentance and Hope, a small number of women were due to give addresses in Churches in wartime, but the Bishop of London retracted this invitation due to opposition from traditionalists within the Church.[69]

Although an Anglican, Royden began preaching in March 1917 at London's imposing Congregationalist City Temple, accompanied by her supporters, including Edith, who wrote to tell her that 'many angels will surround you'.[70] For the next three years Royden was a pulpit assistant there, attracting vast crowds. As Sue Morgan has shown, it was perfectly possible for figures like Maude Royden to be both law-abiding suffragists yet also ecclesiastical militants.[71] The same was true for Edith.

Hudson Shaw had become Rector of St Botolph's in nearby Bishopsgate. Royden sometimes read the lesson there, and even addressed its Thursday lunchtime service in the autumn of 1918. St Botolph's ran a series of addresses by women at which both Edith and her twin spoke. Dressed in a cassock, surplice and with a biretta on her head, Edith, who had obtained the Bishop of London's Certificate for Pastoral and Evangelical Work, gave four sermons to crowded congregations. But when Royden was asked to speak at the Three Hour service on Good Friday 1919, the Bishop of London intervened and she had to decamp to the parish room.

In recent years, the Church had been considering women's position.[72] When the Lambeth Conference (composed of Bishops from the Anglican Communion world-wide) met in July 1920, it reaffirmed the deaconess as the sole order of ministry for women with apostolic approval. It did, however, concede that women could, on occasion, be allowed to speak and unofficially lead prayers at non-statutory services. But decisions were actually made by Convocation. It concurred with the Lambeth Conference but made clear that sermons by women were normally intended for congregations of women and children.

The Bishop would not sanction Edith taking midday services in Holy Week or permit Royden the non-statutory Three Hour Service on Good Friday because the latter was 'a specially sacred service'.[73] The women went ahead regardless, addressing a congregation of more than 900 people at St Botolph's on Good Friday 1921, thus incensing the Church authorities even further. At the same time, the press, whether outraged like the *Church Times,* sensationalist or even progressively supportive, could not resist engaging with Royden's magnetic appeal from the pulpit and so gave the whole subject the wide airing it needed.[74]

Less well known is the fact that the first woman to preach at a *statutory* Church of England service was Edith.[75] This was on 22nd June 1919, when, clad in cassock and surplice, she read the lessons and preached sermons from the pulpit in the afternoon and evening Sunday services in the twelfth century St Mary's Church at North Somercotes, Lincolnshire. The church was crowded and Edith entered it with the vicar. She was participating not in a special service but in regular services with clergy and choir present. Prior agreement had been made with the churchwardens and sidesmen.

Why this location? It was because both Vicar and Bishop were supportive and progressive. The former was the Rev. Samuel Proudfoot, originally a Congregationalist from Carlisle. He became an Anglican curate to Hewlett Johnson, who would be known as 'The Red Dean'. Proudfoot was a socialist Tractarian who later encouraged Walter Greenwood to write *Love on the Dole.*

As we have seen, Edith already knew Edward Hicks, the Bishop of Lincoln. He had endorsed Edith's action the previous December. He was a champion of the unemployed, had been a vice-president of the Men's League for Women's Suffrage, and president of its Manchester branch as well as the first president of the Church League for Women's Suffrage (chaired by Maude Royden). This society had been founded in 1909 to secure the vote for women on the same terms as men, and advocated equal rights and opportunities between the sexes. It increasingly focused on women's ordination as a central goal. Hicks got on well with Proudfoot, and even offered to pay his son's school fees. Their interests overlapped in a number of ways, for example, Hicks was the president, and Proudfoot the secretary of the Lincolnshire Labourers' Temperance League.

Just how far Edith was rocking the boat here can be gauged from the fact that from 1897 until 1914 women had even been debarred from the Church of England's new parochial church councils, and only in the year of Edith's symbolic gesture did an Enabling Act permit them to serve on its higher councils.[76] For some, the idea of women preachers was anathema, raising even issues of uncleanliness. It was suggested to Proudfoot that he sprinkle his pulpit with holy water after Edith had preached.[77]

Edith's preaching at North Somercotes did not go unchallenged.[78] The Archdeacon of Stow, the Rev. J. Wakeford, hauled Proudfoot before the Archidiaconal Court. In letters to Edith, who was on holiday at Ewenny, Proudfoot told her how Wakeford had made a 'fierce assertion of the Church's determination to "stop the woman"'. Unfortunately, Bishop Hicks was by now seriously ill, and Wakeford saw this as an opportunity to argue that, had Hicks been in his 'normal health', he would not have granted 'conditional' permission for Edith to preach. He claimed that Hicks had written 'begging him' to extricate him from a 'painful position'.

Hicks did not advocate female ordination, but he had long supported women playing a much greater part in church services. In 1913 he had spent what he described in his diary as 'a pleasant evening' dining with Edith, where they talked about women reading Lessons in church. Proudfoot could not accept that Hicks would have undergone such a volte-face as to contradict his endorsement of Edith preaching, and told the Archidiaconal Court that he was incredulous. After being told of the pain he had caused 'good Church people', he was asked to apologise to the Court for his actions. He *'sternly'* refused and, in his words, was given a 'medieval monition' and described as 'a disorderly turbulent priest'.

Proudfoot was incandescent at his humiliation. He was eager to counteract 'our modern pharisees', and the farce of this 'burlesque Court'. Here, and in several other letters to Edith, he stressed that 'This Cause must be fought... The Crusade must go forward'. The defiant action of a woman preaching in a statutory Church of England service had ironically turned into a battle of words between two outspoken men of faith as a third lay dying.

Proudfoot told Edith that they must take united action. She wrote to Hicks for his support and received it. She and Proudfoot drew up the terms of a petition and a press release. The Archdeacon described an article in the *West-*

minster Gazette about the event as 'truculent, boastful' and 'unchristian'. Although one female parishioner (already at loggerheads with Proudfoot) lodged a protest about Edith's action, nobody in the parish of 1,300 inhabitants had uttered a word of disapproval to the Vicar's face.

Hicks died in August. This was a personal blow, and appeared to be a setback for the case. However, Hicks' daughter unexpectedly aided Edith and Proudfoot. She had discussed the subject often with her father. Most usefully, she been his amanuensis and had a copy of the letter he had sent the Archdeacon. It proved that, far from wishing to reverse his decision, the Bishop had merely been articulating his regret that the Archdeacon and Proudfoot were at loggerheads. He had reiterated his support for Proudfoot's endorsement of Edith's action, and stated: 'I am no less confident than I was of my own position'. Hicks had also instructed his daughter to write to Proudfoot and underline 'his perfect belief in the strength and justice of his case'.

Interestingly, although Edith's autobiography mentions that she frequently preached in nonconformist chapels in and beyond her parliamentary constituency, there was no reference to her appearance in the pulpit in North Somercotes and its repercussions. Her obituary in *The Times* did, however, mention this historic occasion.

Edith also spoke in a Dublin Church, and at an Anglican Church in Geneva during the Congress held in 1920 by the International Woman Suffrage Alliance.[79] She repeatedly argued that the barriers to women in the church implied that women were spiritually inferior and so were insulting to all women. She preached too at nonconformist chapels across the country. Winifred Coombe Tennant heard her at a Baptist chapel in North Wales that year. 'Dressed in a black plain dress and close fitting black cap', she noted that she 'gave us no more than glorified common sense'.[80] The next year the nonconformist minister, Rev. R.J. Campbell (formerly of City Temple) invited Edith to occupy his pulpit at Christ Church in London's Victoria. She spoke on 'The Spiritual Aspect of the Women's Movement'.[81] She also preached several times in a chapel near Ewenny.[82]

Edith was a vice-president of the successor to the Church League for Women's Suffrage. Its title – The League of the Church Militant – proclaimed a defiant stance and advocated the 'openness to women of the ministry of the Word and Sacraments'.[83]

So great was the demand for tickets for a meeting at Lady Brassey's on the ministry of women (chaired by Dick Sheppard and addressed by Edith) that a second meeting was held the following day.[84] In one public debate on the subject at Church House, Westminster, Edith towered above her opponent Canon Goudge, much to the amusement of her audience, who were assured by him that women lacked the physical strength to bear the strain of a clergyman's life.[85]

Her transgressive views were not restricted to those who heard her preach in pulpits or address NUSEC and other groups. Many would also have read Edith's books on the subject. Indeed, her writings helped to sharpen debates about whether and how women might play a more direct part in the Church, given the extra pressures on clergy due to war. Two lectures that Edith delivered in 1914 appeared in the journal *The Nineteenth Century and After* in the autumn of 1916, and formed the second and third chapters of *Woman and the Church*, a short book she co-authored with the Oxford academic Canon Streeter in 1917. The Bishop of Durham gave it a cautious welcome in his Foreword to the volume, suggesting that the arguments were at least worth an airing.

A brief Introduction by the two authors explained that it was a plea for an entire rethinking of the place of women in the Church. Streeter's two chapters were more conservative than Edith's. A moderniser, he argued for a more democratic form of church government as an essential prerequisite to further change. But in his view women's admission to the priesthood 'ought to be indefinitely postponed'.[86] Drawing on history, Edith argued in 'The Coming Order in the Church of Christ', that Christ and early Christian thinking had accorded women a very different place in the ministry of the church from their current position. In 'The Spirit and The Letter', she claimed that ordained women should occupy 'as wide a sphere of service as is open to men'.[87]

Copies of the book were sent to all the Bishops.[88] Predictably, the most enthusiastic was Hicks, who 'heartily' supported the whole scheme and argument. The Bishop of Ripon agreed with much of it. Some, including the Bishop of St Davids, sat on the fence by merely expressing thanks for the gift and saying they had not had time yet to read it. The Bishop of Norwich's message was plainer: he had nothing to say, since he had not looked at it. A few, such as the Bishops of Lichfield and Sheffield, voiced displeasure, the latter emphasising that many considered the employment and preaching of laymen in consecrated buildings to be illegal. He suggested that the book failed to acknowledge sufficiently the already increased involvement of women in the church. He stressed that they had always played a part in parochial life.

Edith's other books were also timely. *Christ and Woman's Power* appeared in 1919, soon after women over thirty had gained the vote. It was dedicated to Millicent Fawcett and Mary Morley. In the Foreword, Lady Frances Balfour called Edith 'a seer for the future of women'.[89] In thirteen short chapters – each prefaced by quotes as though they were texts for a sermon – Edith rehearsed the ways in which western women pioneers had recently gained power, providing cameos of achievers in areas such as education and medicine. Two chapters on social purity tell the story of Josephine Butler's moral crusade. Chapters on India and China were predicated upon an acceptance of western culture as the model, and predictably emphasised the role of missionaries.

Here and elsewhere, Edith stressed that what unified women was 'a great plea for the freedom of motherhood – and all it implies – of love and preservation of love in the world'.[90] In line with other so-called New Feminists, she emphasised women's difference and the potency of potential as well as actual motherhood. There existed, she believed, the basis for a new order of spiritual life helping to transform the world. But, Edith warned, the Church needed first to recognise the ministry of women.

In the same year she published a book dedicated to 'The Christian in the Street'. *Musings of a Laywoman on the Life of the Churches* was intended as a straightforward introduction to the state of the Church of England (despite the word 'Churches'), and the need for radical change. She argued boldly that theologians, bishops and priests failed to engage sufficiently with the spiritual needs of ordinary people. Confirmed laypeople should, if a clergyman were not available, be able to administer the sacrament. Clergy who were not good at addressing audiences should restrict themselves to parochial work. To exclude women from the ministry of the Church was, in Edith's view, contrary to the spirit and attitude of Christ. It was no good looking to the past for the solution to everything: if St. Paul's teachings were followed to the letter, there would be a largely celibate clergy. She sought to look forwards not backwards, and ended with a rallying cry for the laity 'to destroy, reform, rebuild'.[91]

Although entitled *Christ and International Life,* Edith's final book on religion was about women's potential power to transform the world.[92] Published in 1921 and dedicated to Jane Addams 'Master Builder', the influential Lord Robert Cecil, one of the architects of the League of Nations, wrote the Introduction.[93] Edith argued here that Christian morality must be the cornerstone of national policy. A new conception of national and international life – what amounted to a new internationalism – was essential to save civilisation.

How, it might be asked, would she later view such remarks in the light of subsequent events culminating in the Second World War? But in the aftermath of the destruction of the Great War, her hopes for a better future were understandable, and she placed women, who looked to a better world for children in the future, at the centre of this new order. Her plea to bring religion into the heart of politics, and her conception of the Sermon on the Mount as the essence of true statesmanship, would, she believed, bring a new sense of values to the nation.

And this conviction that moral questions – such as child labour – needed to be seen as part of a wider approach to society that fused religion and politics and advocated social justice, provided the bridge that led Edith to party politics. In January 1919, this woman from a staunchly Conservative family had joined the Labour Party. She had read and been impressed by Arthur Henderson's book *The Aims of Labour*. The Labour Party was not yet tried and tested by office. Unlike the Liberals, who had let women down over the vote before the war, Labour appeared to offer real change and, crucially, Edith felt that it was 'in harmony with Christian thought and ethics'.[94] She declared that she voted Labour because the party 'does its thinking in human terms'.[95]

The post-war era of Reconstruction appeared – at first at least – to offer new hope for all. Edith had finally gained the right to vote, and in the same year the Parliament (Qualification of Women) Act enabled women to become MPs: in fact they could stand for Parliament at a younger age than they could vote. Megan Lloyd George was selected as Liberal candidate for Anglesey aged twenty-six in 1928, before the Equal Franchise Act enfranchised women under thirty.[96]

Edith's high-profile position in the YWCA put her in touch with trade unionist activists at home and abroad. They included figures such as Margaret Dreier Robins, president of the American Women's Trade Union League, and Margaret Bondfield, a former shopworker and committed Roman Catholic who became Britain's first female cabinet minister. Edith also got to know Labour figures such as George Lansbury (with whom she discussed the aims of the labour movement) and her future leader, Ramsay MacDonald. Such individuals influenced her thinking and inclination towards Labour.

Edith's YWCA work had already given her an insight into the lives of those far removed from her own background. It had also acquainted her with issues of social purity and the inadequacy of much legislation. The age of consent had been raised to sixteen in 1885 but, before the war, pressure grew to extend it to eighteen and to tighten the law for streetwalkers and brothel keepers.

A Criminal Law Amendment Bill in 1912 had increased penalties against procurers and those living on the earnings of prostitution, and tightened the law concerning brothels. Edith had been appointed to the 'Pass the Bill' Committee and had made her first speech in the House of Commons (in a committee room). The YWCA's constitution stated that it should not take sides in party politics, but might support action on questions affecting the welfare of women and girls.[97] Edith was increasingly convinced of the need to take action.

During her visit to the United States in 1918, she had attended a conference of American, British, French and Canadian women on social hygiene and sat on its findings committee. It adopted eight principles, the first urging a single standard of morality for men and women. Other recommendations included not treating prostitutes as a class apart, the need to combat venereal disease, and the importance of sex education.

On her return, Edith wrote about America and prostitution in *The Nineteenth Century and After*. Here she praised what she had seen of the US War and Navy Department Commission on Training Camp Activities in, for example, publicising the problems of VD. But, just as Josephine Butler and others had campaigned against the double standard in the Victorian Contagious Diseases Acts, so Edith attacked the gendered nature of legislation in the States: 'So long as the man is not equally punished so long will the measures taken against the woman be of little value'.[98]

Back home in the 1920s Edith was still campaigning, protesting against a new Criminal Law Amendment Bill that permitted the detention of 'common prostitutes' for medical examination. Such gendered legislation seemed to put the clock back. She campaigned with feminists like the former actress and suffragette Elizabeth Robins, who had written a disturbing novel about a middle class girl and the White Slave trade, entitled *Where Are You Going To ... ?*[99]

In a letter to *The Times*, Edith, Lady Frances Balfour, Florence E. Booth and Eleanor Rathbone argued against the designation of 'common prostitute'.[100] They stressed that the law about soliciting was out of date: whereas a century earlier no respectable woman would be in the street alone at night unless on an errand, now that many women lived on their own they needed to use the streets after dark. Such an argument was in effect voicing concern about single middle class women, even implying that they were synonymous with respectability. But the point that soliciting was not just about one sex was an important one. They urged support for Viscountess Astor's bill about public places that would enable the arrest of those who annoyed or molested men and women.

Before long, Edith would be sitting with Astor in the House of Commons. In 1922 Hilda Caroline Miall-Smith, a former teacher and Labour activist who was standing for the Greater London Council in North Islington, asked Edith to stand as the Labour candidate for the constituency. She agreed and was adopted on her birthday that June. At her first meeting – described as 'overflowing' by the *Manchester Guardian* – the leader of the Labour Party, J.R. Clynes, spoke.[101]

However, Edith was suddenly taken ill, and when the date of the General Election was announced she was in a nursing home recovering from a major operation. There were just three weeks before polling day and she was in no position to do much canvassing. She wrote her election address from her bed. It addressed firstly unemployment, then housing and industrial reconstruction.[102] Edith declared too that she was anti-waste[103] and supported the League of Nations. She also stressed the importance of an equal franchise for men and women, mentioned widows' pensions and the need to ensure equal rights for women as citizens, voters and workers. Her election, she stated, would help to alter the fact that more than 600 men sat in the House of Commons but just two women.

Her friends rallied round. Emily Kinnaird patrolled the Holloway Road with a string of 'sandwich women' wearing placards and distributing leaflets. The Leeds socialist Isabella Ford went out daily in a decorated horse-drawn van, then held evening meetings. Maude Royden addressed a crowded meeting at a school. Lady Frances Balfour, president of the National Council of Women on whose executive Edith served, made an unprecedented appearance on a Labour Party platform.[104] Accompanied by a nurse and doctor, Edith attended a special women's meeting just before the final gathering. She also travelled round the constituency in a decorated car, distributing handbills.

The YWCA's monthly magazine, ignoring the fact that it was not meant to be partisan, declared that readers would look forward to having their first 'YWCA Candidate' in Parliament'.[105] Criticism of this claim forced it to backtrack and admit the following month that many would not sympathise with her Labour politics. Nevertheless, it stressed, all would sympathise with her aim 'of bringing Christian principles to bear on politics, even where we do not agree with her methods'. Edith was congratulated for being the first YWCA official to stand.[106]

But standing was not translated into sitting. The Conservative easily held onto his seat, though Edith beat the Liberal and increased the Labour share of the vote.[107] At the same time, the Labour Party made important gains nationally.

Undaunted by the defeat at North Islington, Edith stood again in the election of October 1924. Her father had recently died. She had learned the news whilst lecturing in America. The election came in the immediate wake of a 'Red scare' – the infamous Zinoviev letter[108] – that helped to defeat the first Labour government. Edith stood for an agricultural constituency this time: the Stroud Division of Gloucester. They had adopted her in the summer but, apart from the last couple of weeks of canvassing, when the novelty of a woman candidate clearly piqued the electors' interest, she found it hard work rallying support. She focused on housing and peace, but she and the Labour government led by Ramsay MacDonald were defeated.[109]

It was a case of third time lucky. In 1929 Edith was elected to the second Labour government, after the first election (known as the flapper election) in which all women over twenty-one had the right to vote. Women now constituted 53 per cent of the electorate. By this time Edith was well acquainted with Ramsay MacDonald, leader of the minority Labour government. She had campaigned for him in his constituency of Aberavon during the 1923 election. Labour's first short-lived period in office came early the following year.

Edith later recalled his campaign headquarters in the centre of the constituency at Port Talbot's Walnut Tree Hotel and how, wherever he appeared, vast audiences sang the rousing words written by his organiser Minnie Pallister to the tune of 'Men of Harlech'. Each verse ended with 'Ramsay is our Man'. Edith addressed crowds with MacDonald in Porthcawl, a place that was relatively affluent and so more challenging. But in poorer Briton Ferry and Aberavon itself, enthusiasm for MacDonald was 'beyond all words to describe'.[110]

It was in December 1925 that The Wrekin Division of Shropshire[111] selected Edith as their candidate. So effective was she that a prominent journalist admitted that he would have voted for her whatever her politics.[112] Her opportunity finally came in May 1929. Unlike most politicians, she admitted to dreading some meetings, but for the first time she was confident of winning. She polled 14,569 votes, beating the sitting Conservative by 2,862 votes.

Her maiden speech that December was on the second reading of the Coal Mines Bill (it reached the statute book in 1930). Edith's constituency was mainly agricultural but included some 4,000 miners. She had supported them and visited soup kitchens during the General Strike and was a signatory to the letter from the Women's Committee for the Relief of Miners' Wives and Children appealing for funds.[113] She also protested in a letter to *Time and Tide* (to the annoyance of its editor and proprietor, the coal owner Lady Rhondda), that it should be seen as a Lock Out.[114] That summer she wrote to *The Times* about her recent experience of visiting miners' homes and how 'deeply moved' she had been by 'the agonised distress' of some of the women compelled to live in antiquated, confined conditions.[115]

Her own links with miners were more tenuous and equivocal than she implied. Her father, who had died in 1924, had mining interests in the Llantrisant area, something she chose not to stress at this juncture. Edith came from the Vale of Glamorgan, closer to the sea than the valleys that were so famous for their coalmines. But there were some collieries nearby, and in this speech and her autobiography, she drew upon the Welsh mining tradition, recalling the impact of the disaster of August 1892. 112 men and boys, including a few men she knew from Laleston, were killed at the Parc Slip colliery at Aberkenfig.[116]

She also read to the House an account of a Rhondda collier's shift.

Sixty-nine women stood for Parliament in 1929. Betty Morgan from Barry stood for the Liberals at Sunderland. The youngest woman candidate, she possessed both a doctorate and what the *Manchester Guardian* called 'the national gift of fluent speech'.[117] Another woman defeated her: the Labour Party's woman organiser, Dr Marion Phillips.

Megan Lloyd George became the first woman to win a Welsh seat (Anglesey), but the novelist Grace Roberts could not turn Caerphilly Liberal. Neither could May Williams win Pontypridd for the Conservatives. As Deirdre Beddoe has noted, it was not only difficult for women to be selected but if they were, they tended to be contesting 'forlorn hopes' rather than safe seats.[118] Edith scored a triple victory: she was selected in preference to a trade union official,[119] stood in a seat that could be won, and regained it for Labour in a decisive victory.

The first three female Labour MPs had been elected in 1923, but now Edith was one of nine (out of thirty) such candidates elected.[120] She was not alone in being a Labour MP from a privileged background. Lady Cynthia Mosley, for example, was the daughter of Viscount Curzon and wife of Sir Oswald Mosley. Edith was one of several leading NUSEC member MPs. They included Eleanor Rathbone, NUSEC's president, elected as an Independent. But, unlike Edith, Rathbone (just a month older than Edith), Labour's Susan Lawrence and Ellen Wilkinson all had the benefit of a university education.

Although an MP for less than two years, seven of the

seventeen chapters of Edith's autobiography were devoted to her parliamentary aspirations and experience. 1929-31 was a time of drama and difficulties for a Labour government that had previously known just ten months in power. The Wall Street Crash in October 1929 famously heralded an era of economic depression and deprivation. But MacDonald's government was also an oasis of opportunity for women even though numbers were only swollen to fourteen (fifteen in 1931) out of a total of 615 MPs.[121]

Edith worked hard yet had no secretary, as most of her salary was ploughed back into her constituency and political work. She replied by hand to most of the many letters she received, though occasionally dictated them in Westminster Hall's typewriting office. She sat – and on at least one occasion lay down reading out of sight of the Speaker – through all-night debates. Lacking a majority (there were 288 Labour members but 260 Conservatives, 58 Liberals and 9 Independents), the Government had constantly to be on its toes. 'We lived', she wrote, 'in a state of acute apprehension', becoming 'a slave to the House' and not daring to take a day off.[122] Luckily, her Gayfere Street house was not only handy for getting to the Commons, it was also just off Smith Square, where the Labour Party had recently established its headquarters.

Edith proved to be an able debater, unafraid of asking difficult questions. Despite being a backbencher and a novice, whenever she rose to speak she was asked to go ahead. Here she was probably aided by her height and dignified demeanour (she was in her late fifties), as well as by the fact that her interventions were to the point and well informed. She later claimed that she had heard better speeches made at meetings of the Mothers' Union than many in the House.[123] She ensured that she raised issues pertinent to her constituency, such as improvements to the Oakengates Employment Exchange. However, most of her speeches concerned the plight of the poorer woman and her children.

The Labour women supported each other. During the second reading of the Nationality of Women Bill (moved by Ethel Bentham), allowing women to choose whether or not to take their husband's nationality, Edith deplored how: 'The moment a woman is married she is classified in nationality with minors and lunatics as without reason'.[124] She spoke on subjects such as widows' pensions, the school leaving age, nursery schools and the Children's Act.

Edith supported Eleanor Rathbone on the Family Maintenance Bill, welcoming its provision that a widow could not be left absolutely penniless. Neither woman married nor had children, but both were nevertheless especially concerned with child welfare. As Susan Pedersen's biography of Rathbone, suggests, they were also conscious how their privileged backgrounds set them apart from the working class mothers whose difficulties they both felt morally impelled to address.[125]

At times Edith spoke against the Tory Viscountess Astor (the American-born Nancy Astor had been the first woman to take her seat).[126] But she wisely refrained from engaging in verbal duels with her across the floor, aware that the veteran politician would not only have won in the repartee stakes but also provided the press with the sort of publicity they loved. Edith was president of the Westminster

Women's Housing Council, and a few years earlier – irony of ironies – they had met in Astor's sumptuous ballroom at Carlton House Terrace to discuss squalid housing conditions and urge the council to take action.[127]

Edith admired Astor's moral courage and when it came to issues such as women police, the two women were clearly united. Edith led a cross-party deputation on the subject to the Home Secretary in 1931, and brought together organisations such as the National Council of Women and fifty MPs at a meeting at the Palace of Westminster. Her long speech on 30 July demonstrated 'eloquently and persuasively'[128] the patchy and inadequate provision to date.

Edith espoused pink rather than the red politics of her colleague Ellen Wilkinson, but her claim during a debate on the Consumers' Council Bill in 1930 that 'Slowly, silently but surely, people are waking up to know that socialism spells common sense'[129] would have alarmed her relatives. She was not afraid to speak out. During a debate on Civil Estimates in 1930 for the Foreign Office (where she was the only female speaker alongside heavyweights such as Lloyd George and Churchill), she upheld the self-determination of small nations, and claimed that some of the opposition 'get so excited with their verbosity that they do not realise how little substance there has been today in their attacks on the Government'.[130]

In the debate on Civil Estimates for the India Office the following year, she ridiculed Churchill's claim that poor industrial conditions and troubles in India might be attributed to the recent move for Dominion Status, calling it 'fantastic, ludicrous, impudent'. She drew upon her experience in Bombay (Mumbai) twenty years earlier and demonstrated just how far she had moved politically from that time. She annoyed Sir Charles Oman by yoking the terms 'India' and 'Liberty' and stressing the complexity of different races within the country.[131]

As Mari Takayanagi has argued, women were disproportionately represented in relation to their numbers as members of standing committees scrutinising bills at the committee stage. They were more assiduous in attendance than their male counterparts. This was especially marked in 1930-1. Edith played her part on these committees in both sessions.[132] Here too she spoke out on behalf of women, stressing – for example, in debates on the Mental Treatment Bill – the need for female members on visiting committees.[133]

Edith was part of the Labour Anglican Group. Soon after first taking her seat, she became the first woman to sit on the Ecclesiastical Committee of the Lords and Commons. Since 1919 it had considered all measures passed by the Church Assembly (with its House of Bishops, House of Laity and House of Clergy) before a member presented them to parliament. For example, Edith presented the Pensions Measure for Royal Assent in 1930. The committee met bi-monthly in the House of Lords. She admitted in her diary to 'Great Awe' at the first meeting, but she made her mark. When the chairman suggested passing the Pluralities Measure without discussion, Edith, who always did her homework, suggested that it interfered with the right of appeal to the Privy Council. She was correct and it was not passed.

Her parliamentary moment of glory, however, came in 1931, when her own Private Members' bill reached the statute book. She was not the first woman to succeed here. Viscountess Astor's Intoxicating Liquors (Sales to Persons under 18) Act had been passed in 1923, piloted through the Lords by her husband. But Edith was the first Welsh woman as well as the first female Labour MP to introduce what became a successful private members' bill. She did this with the Sentence of Death (Expectant Mothers') Act. Seven years later, Ellen Wilkinson would be responsible for the second successful private members' bill introduced by a Labour woman, but not until the 1950s would any other Labour woman achieve this.[134]

The law already prohibited the execution of mothers found guilty of murder whilst they were pregnant. The practice was that they would later be reprieved and sentenced to life imprisonment. But despite this, at the point that the conviction for murder was announced, the judge still had to go through the macabre farce of pronouncing the death sentence. In a powerful ten-minute speech that was all the more effective as she had learned it by heart, Edith evoked the dreadful ceremony:

> The breathless waiting for the jury to return the verdict, the deathly silence, the putting on of the black cap, the terrible concentration of the whole Court on the words that are about to be uttered, and then the sentence: 'That you be hanged by the neck until you are dead'.[135]

She told how such words moved even strong men and women, suggesting how much more they must affect a poor, malnourished woman about to give birth. She argued that the law was antiquated and formulated before pre-natal science was understood. She cited the recent case of such a woman. Deserted by her lover and pregnant, in desperation after not being able to get into the workhouse on Christmas Eve, she gassed her nine-month baby. She was arrested for murder, found guilty and sentenced to death. Only then was she permitted to state that she was expecting another child.

Edith's bill provided that a woman should have the opportunity to state that she was pregnant *before* the death sentence was pronounced and, if her statement proved correct, this sentence could not then be given. She conveniently provided a precedent: since 1765, the death sentence had not been passed on a pregnant mother in Scotland. Her words produced silence in the Chamber. Her bill was not opposed and, after presenting it, she was cheered.

The *Sunday Times* stated that 'without exploiting any of the ordinary arts of oratorical persuasion', Edith Picton-Turbervill 'was able to thrill the House to a greater sense of corporate responsibility than it has experienced since Mr Baldwin's famous plea for 'Peace in our Time'. The *Yorkshire Post* declared her speech to be 'a thing of beauty'. It added:

> If in some heavenly court Members have to justify what they have said and done in the House, Miss Picton-Turbervill will have more grace shewn [sic] her because of that one speech, than many a famous and consummate Parliamentarian will for the speeches of his whole career.[136]

She followed up the successful first reading with appeals to the Prime Minister and Home Secretary as well as

Cabinet Ministers. Government starred the bill, the Lord Chancellor moved it in the House of Lords and it became law.

Economic instability and an inexorable rise in unemployment rates, as well as growing national expenditure, put increasing pressure on the minority government. The economic and political crises came to a head in August 1931.[137] Edith was enjoying a holiday in County Antrim when she heard on the radio that the Government had resigned and a new National Government had been formed: a coalition with the Conservatives and Liberals to pursue a policy of retrenchment and secure a balanced budget. Edith was especially incensed at the swingeing cuts to unemployment benefit.

For once, life did not seem good: well aware of what this would mean in a constituency that already included several distressed areas, she also felt a personal betrayal that was not alleviated by the letter that MacDonald sent her, suggesting that 'swift measures' were necessary to avert the crisis. She admitted in a note appended to this letter: 'I do not remember in all my life having so difficult and agitating a time when making a decision on this question'.

Parliament was recalled. Edith went first to Transport House for a meeting of the Parliamentary Labour Party. She agreed with Arthur Henderson that, although the budget needed balancing, this should not be at the expense of the unemployed. But she kept prevaricating. Most of her former colleagues were not prepared to continue supporting MacDonald.

When a vote of confidence was taken, she was one of

four Parliamentary Labour Party members who abstained. Used to consulting her conscience, Edith could not accept that she lacked *any* confidence in her erstwhile leader. As though to ward off harsh judgement of MacDonald, her autobiography (written a good seven years after the events) but drawing on her diary from the time, emphasises that he had been a tired man, looking 'harassed and worn' from the moment he became Prime Minister in 1929.

MacDonald held a long private meeting with Edith and the others, distressing her even further with his harrowing personal comments on the tragedy. But though 'My heart was with him; my head was not', she wrote, and 'I could not follow him'. Cuts followed and Britain came off the Gold Standard.[138] Edith resolved to stay in the Labour Party, a decision fortified by news of a General Election for a National Government. This was despite MacDonald's original claim that once the immediate crisis was over, the Labour Party would be 'left untrammelled as to its policy and programme'.

Edith's autobiography stresses that she was well aware from the outset that she and Labour stood little chance of success, especially since the media was weighted against them. The National Government was returned with a majority of more than 500 and an overwhelming number of Conservative MPs. All the Labour women lost their seats. Edith still managed to garner 14,162 votes, just 407 fewer than in 1929, but the Tory candidate received more than 22,000 votes. The Wrekin would remain Conservative until 1945.

Although she was no longer in Parliament, Edith's involvement in formulating government policy was not over.

In the mid-1930s, this descendant of Sir Thomas Picton was especially adroit in dealing with the subject of child servitude in Hong Kong and Malaya. She was appointed to a Royal Commission to investigate the system known as Mui Tsai (Little Sister in Cantonese) and not only authored a Minority Report but also had the satisfaction of seeing it, rather than the Majority Report, accepted.

So how did this come about? Edith had long been interested in colonial affairs. She had sat on a parliamentary committee pledged to secure Dominion Status for India.[139] She had also been part of an all-party committee in 1929-30, chaired by the Duchess of Atholl, to investigate 'the Protection of Coloured Women in the Crown Colonies'. This Committee of eleven included Eleanor Rathbone and R. A. Butler. It concentrated on Kenya and the long-established customs of clitoridectomy and of bridegrooms purchasing their brides by paying cattle. They heard evidence in London from a range of experts in East Africa, including Kenyatta. In 1933, determined to see social conditions for herself, Edith visited friends in Kenya.[140]

Concerned about prevarication and complacency on the part of the British authorities, Edith had been asking awkward questions in the Commons about Mui Tsai since the end of 1929. She stressed that Chinese girls from aged three or even younger, were still in effect slaves, being bought and sold for money, then working in domestic servitude without wages or the right to leave. They were sometimes treated with great cruelty, despite the system having been condemned in Hong Kong since the 1880s and forbidden by law since 1923 (Malaya followed suit a decade later).[141]

In the House of Commons in May 1931, during a powerful speech attacking the 'abominable' system, Sir John Simon held up a bill of sale for a nine-year-old child. Edith thanked him, but expressed disappointment that such a speech could still have been made after ten years of debate on the subject. The Female Domestic Service Ordinance of 1923 was a dead letter. An Ordinance six years later compelled the registration of Mui Tsai in Hong Kong. Although about 4,000 were registered, it was only open for six months, yet it was thought that about 10,000 Mui Tsai were in Hong Kong alone. Edith posed the basic questions: were Mui Tsai currently being sold or not? Did they or didn't they receive wages for their work?

Outside Parliament, humanitarians such as the Haslewoods (fervent anti-Mui Tsai campaigners) had long been protesting in Hong Kong and at home. So too had the YWCA and a number of progressive Chinese women. The Anti-Slavery Society was flexing its muscles, as were women's groups. Sir George Maxwell, an experienced Malayan administrator, was vice chairman at the League of Nations Slavery Committee. He put forward a new set of proposals. However, the Loseby Committee, appointed by the governor of Hong Kong, attacked them.

Aware that enquiries and ordinances were exacerbating tensions rather than solving the problem, J.H. Thomas, the Colonial Secretary, opted for a commission to investigate the situation properly within Hong Kong and Malaya. Thomas had a very different background from Edith, having worked on the railways since the age of twelve, later becoming general secretary of the National Union of Railwaymen and president of the TUC. But he was a fellow South Walian and the two had sat together as Labour MPs, although Thomas chose to serve in the National Government. He appointed Edith to the new commission in March 1936.

Sir Wilfred Woods, a former civil servant in Ceylon, chaired the commission. Its third member, nominated by the Anti-Slavery Society, was C.A. Willis, who had been in the civil service in the Sudan. When Eleanor Rathbone asked why, given the nature of the enquiry, two women had not been appointed alongside the two men, Jimmy Thomas replied: 'I think Miss Picton-Turbervill will be able to hold her own'. Laughter ensued, invoking Edith's reputation as 'formidable', that gendered term often used to describe, yet ridicule, capable women. This reaction conveniently circumvented the need to address the serious side of the question.

The brief was to investigate:

> The whole question of Mui Tsai in the Crown Colony of Hong Kong and Malaya and any surviving practices of transferring women and children for valuable consideration, whether on marriage or adoption, or in any other circumstances, and to report to the Secretary of State for the Colonies on any legislative or other action which the Commissioners may consider practicable and desirable in relation to these matters.

Before leaving for the Far East in April, the three commissioners met at the Colonial Office, where they talked to the Haselwoods (this meeting convinced Hugh Haselwood that Edith would be 'excellent') and to Sir George Maxwell.

They received a deputation of women from the British Commonwealth Society, along with representatives from women's organisations.

Arriving in Hong Kong in mid-May, the commissioners stayed in Government House for a month. Edith later described this as 'an unfortunate arrangement'. Evidence was taken in the council chamber from 43 witnesses, Chinese and British, government officials and private individuals, and they visited registered Mui Tsais. Edith recognised that they were not the ones they really needed to see. Those who were unregistered were now often sold under the pretence of being 'adopted daughters' and so not scrutinised. She also understood something of the difficulties for those who were questioned. Just as the sub-commissioners looking into the employment of children in coal mines in the early 1840s in Britain must have appeared intimidating to the women, girls and boys they interviewed, so young Chinese children, faced with powerful foreigners speaking an alien language, were 'terrified by our presence', especially since replies were given in front of their mistresses.

Edith, Woods and Willis then visited Singapore before crossing to the Malay mainland. As Rachel Loew has pointed out, concern about Mui Tsai at the time and since has been overwhelmingly focused on Hong Kong, rather than on the much larger territories known as British Malaya (including the Straits Settlements, four Federated and six Unfederated Malay States), even though there was less regulation there and, unlike Hong Kong, no law forbidding the employment of domestic servants under the age of ten.

The commissioners mostly stayed in hotels so were better placed than they had been in Hong Kong to meet non-government professionals such as doctors, health visitors and teachers. They travelled widely and found that although there were 3,000 Mui Tsai registered, a large number throughout the country remained unregistered. Domestic servitude was not just confined to the Chinese, and might, for example, involve Tamil girls. They also visited homes and refuges.

Edith's return voyage was via the Pacific and Canada. In Honolulu she heard that her beloved stepmother Cara had died. Returning home, she was immediately plunged into more work as she and her colleagues drafted their recommendations. It soon became apparent that Edith could neither accept the views of Woods and Willis nor persuade them to advocate new legislation. The result was a document of more than 300 pages, comprising a long Majority Report and a 34-page Minority Report by Edith.

The Majority Report was cautious, suggesting that disquiet was unjustified, with the system obsolescent in Hong Kong and decreasing in Malaya. Edith, in contrast, disagreed with the claims made by Woods and Willis of rapid progress towards abolition since 1930. The two men recognised that current legislation was inadequate as it stood, but they recommended strengthening administration rather than taking a more radical step that might offend powerful Chinese interests and thereby possibly jeopardise trading relations. Whilst Edith agreed that these administrative reforms were useful, she nevertheless boldly denounced them as totally inadequate to address, let alone solve, the fundamental problem.

Most official enquiries, then and now start with a straightforward definition of terms. Edith was conscious that defining Mui Tsai and their status actually lay at the heart of the difficulties. In her view, any transferred child was in a potentially perilous position. She heeded Sir George Maxwell's outline of an Ordinance for Female Child Protection and incorporated it into her recommendations.

Her report abandoned an attempt to define and legislate specifically for Mui Tsai, as this ran the risk of ignoring others who, although not labelled in this way, were in practice also in servitude. The machinery of protection should, in Edith's view, be applied to all girls below twelve, transferred for any reason from parents to persons other than relatives. They should be registered and given protective supervision. Without this, she insisted, a form of slavery would persist in British territories.

As one 'Chinese sympathiser' put it, the Majority Report prescribed mild treatment whereas the Minority Report plumped for a major operation. Edith's approach was an interesting one, turning what was unknowable – the impossibility of obtaining reliable statistics – into a reason *for* rather than against legislating. The style of her report was also refreshing. She admitted, for example that 'Perhaps I ought to have been prepared for it, but nothing took me aback more than the sight of a number of "prostitutes" in a Po Leung Kuk.[142] They looked like mere children'. Although her Christian beliefs would have influenced her thinking, they were not discernible in her report. She also avoided being sensationalist or suggesting that Hong Kong and Malaya had especially cruel practices, and she admitted that some evils were probably exaggerated.

Her focus was child centred. As Susan Pedersen points out, 'An issue that had been defined largely in terms of racial opposition or sexual exploitation thus became, in Picton-Turbervill's report, one of the appropriate treatment and care of children'.[143] This emphasis on the welfare of the young grew out of Edith's earlier YWCA work with its focus on the protection of girls. Her membership of various women's societies in the 1920s had also influenced her thinking on this subject. Her report refers to protective legislation to restrict the employment of children in factories and homes in Britain, a subject much debated by organisations such as NUSEC. The word 'protection' features prominently in her account.

Before her visit, Edith had indulged in some stereotypes about Chinese 'secrecy' when considering the difficulties of finding out what really went on in homes.[144] Yet after her return, she scorned generalisations such as the claim of Chinese inscrutability. She admitted that only a 'thoroughly experienced Chinese woman inspector' could really discover the true state of the children concerned. She also recognised that whilst Chinese feelings and customs should be understood and respected, customs did not remain static, and new ideas would circulate, so that to reject change on the grounds of it being contrary to a custom ran the risk of failing to appreciate the 'currents of socially progressive opinion amongst the Chinese as elsewhere'.

The reports were published on 1 March 1937. At first, the new colonial secretary William Ormsby-Gore (who had sat on the 1933 Committee on the Protection of Coloured Women with Edith) assumed that, if anything, the Majority Report would be adopted. Edith wrote a long memorandum to the Colonial Office. Newspapers such as the *Manchester Guardian* and *Observer* endorsed her advocacy of blanket reform, as did Hong Kong's social reformers. Edith addressed groups such as the National Council of Women and they in turn, along with organisations such as the Society of Friends and the Women's Freedom League, formed a delegation to the Colonial Secretary. The Archbishop of Hong Kong organised a petition, and the English Archbishops, familiar with Edith's utterances in a rather different capacity, endorsed this.

In September Sir Shenton Thomas – governor of the Straits Settlements – told the Colonial Office that they had decided to accept the Minority Report in principle and that he had no doubt that Edith was right. He urged the Malay States to follow their example. When this decision was announced in November, Edith admitted she felt like 'weeping for joy'.[145] Meanwhile, war between China and Japan saw large numbers of refugees entering Hong Kong. Alarmed at the implications, Edith wished that her recommendations had gone even further. In May 1938, Sir G.A. Northcote, the new Governor of Hong Kong, wrote Edith a very supportive letter. Hong Kong now made it compulsory to register all adopted girls.

Edith published a leaflet entitled 'The "Slave" Girls of Hong Kong' in 1939. She expressed her delight that all the governments concerned had accepted the spirit of the Minority Report. She stressed that the new law was already making a difference in Hong Kong. For example, the Lady Proctor (a post that had been urged by both reports) was revealing a considerable trade in young girls for enforced prostitution. They were being rescued and procurers prosecuted. Edith's leaflet appealed, as did her letters to the press and to former Hong Kong civil servants, for funds for schools and orphanages for rescued girls. She personally contributed £100.

Edith had dealt skillfully with officials without ruffling too many feathers. In his history of imperial Hong Kong, Norman Miners argues that the campaign to end the Mui Tsai system was 'the longest and most successful effort made between the First and Second World Wars to force the Colonial Office to change its policy'. Edith was one of the key players here. She was not, however, fundamentally challenging colonial control, but keen that what she saw as a blot on successful British administration should be removed.

The extent to which the sale of children was permanently changed by the legislation Edith helped to prompt is debatable: her rejoicing was in some ways premature. But the way in which she stood up for child welfare – in Malaya the new Ordinance embodying her report's recommendations became known as The Children's Charter – is impressive. Unafraid of taking on the colonial office, she articulated issues clearly and identified solutions.

After her work on the Mui Tsai, Edith wrote her autobiography. *Life is Good* was published in June 1939. Had it appeared a little later, she might well have used the past tense for her title. She was living at Berkeley Court in Baker Street in a flat belonging to the elderly Emily Kinnaird, who was based there in-between her trips abroad. But after the Second World War began, Edith left London for a safer location, installing herself in 1940 at the Prestbury Park Hotel in Cheltenham, then at Cleeve House. Her brother Ivor lived locally, and Beatrice also moved to the town with Anne Macnaghten.[146] In 1942 a bomb destroyed Edith's old home in Gayfere Street, Westminster.

Between 1941 and 1943 she was attached to the Ministry of Information. In the year that she turned seventy, she went to the Potteries, Cannock Chase and Chatham on Ministry of Information work – concerned, it would seem, with the wartime lives of working class women. She spoke on the need for female war workers at a large cinema in aid of the Russian Red Cross, addressed groups of women in Cheltenham, and gave radio talks on the subject entitled 'Calling All Women' and 'Calling the Home Front'.[147]

After the war, she stayed on in Cheltenham, living at Woodend, a pleasant house in the Charlton Kings area. It belonged to an elderly widow. Here, Edith occupied several rooms. She never returned to live in Wales. In 1922 Ewenny had passed to Edith's eldest brother Charlie, and soon afterwards his daughter inherited it.

But her interest in South Wales and History, especially where it intersected with her family, resulted in a number of radio broadcasts on the subject (mostly for the Western Region) between the 1930s and 1950s. Some of these romanticised and increasingly anachronistic accounts formed the basis of her 1946 book entitled *In the Land of My Fathers*. The title of its first chapter, 'The Romance of South Wales', sets the tone for somewhat idiosyncratic, fond meanderings centred on the Vale of Glamorgan and other parts of her home county, but also encompassing Carmarthenshire and Pembrokeshire.[148]

Edith had started broadcasting in 1930-1, with eight contributions to 'The Week in Westminster'. In its first few years these mid-morning talks about parliamentary proceedings were solely from the perspectives of women.[149] Over subsequent years she scripted and presented a number of talks, usually earning five guineas apiece. In 1929 on the 124th anniversary of the battle of Waterloo, her talk 'A Top-Hatted Hero of Waterloo' was about General Picton.[150]

Had she had her way, Edith would have done many more broadcasts. For several decades she wrote regularly to the BBC, offering subjects as diverse as Kenya, Lady Balfour, her meeting with Atatürk and the report of the Archbishop's Commission on the Ministry of Women. On at least three occasions she sought, unsuccessfully, to make a programme about the history of the frescoes at the Palace of Westminster.

Edith's public roles had boosted her confidence. She repeatedly assured the BBC that 'Everyone tells me that my voice is extraordinarily clear'.[151] She was undaunted by polite letters rejecting many of her suggestions. Internal BBC memos were less flattering. Doubts were voiced about her ability as a broadcaster, though it was her persistence and somewhat peremptory manner that really riled, especially since it was recognised that she was influential so couldn't be easily dismissed. Senior BBC women tended to view her more kindly than the men. Janet Quigley, for example, was concerned that Edith sometimes sounded as though she were delivering a sermon but defended her sincerity and ability to convey her feelings to the listener.[152]

Her final broadcast (one of her reminiscences about Glamorgan) was in September 1955. Two years earlier she had been a guest on BBC television's afternoon magazine series for women 'Leisure and Pleasure'. Never one to be idle, Edith kept busy in these final years. Reading gave her pleasure. So helpful did she find the librarians at Cheltenham public library during her weekly visits that she left them money in her will. On the centenary of the 1857 Sepoy Rebellion and three years before she died, she published the letters of her relative Algar Temple with an eight-page preface, describing him as 'one of the heroes of the mutiny'.[153]

She enjoyed listening to gramophone music, especially opera. She also played bridge and kept up to date with current affairs. There were letters to *The Times* on subjects such as the quality and frequency of sermons.[154] Edith maintained a keen interest in family, though younger relatives in particular were slightly in awe of this highly capable woman with a commanding presence and powerful voice who never quite understood the point of small talk.

Who's Who neatly encapsulated Edith's achievements with a lengthy entry under 'Work'. For 'Recreations', she baldly stated: 'Walking across country with a silent companion; swimming'.[155] Her particular sense of humour and fiercely independent perspectives and politics were at odds with conservative (with lower and upper case C) Cheltenham and her family. A relative once jokingly asked Edith to sign a petition against the nationalisation of the railways. This she did not find amusing and it was indignantly rejected.

She spoke daily on the telephone to Beatrice. The twins were devoted to each other, but although they were almost identical in appearance, they still maintained – and respected – different views. Her family remembered Beatrice as the more sophisticated of the two, despite Edith's public standing and travels across the globe.

Beatrice died in 1958. Edith lived on. According to her relatives, her hair never turned grey. Two years later, that mind which had served her so well finally failed her. Edith's long, good life ended in Barnwood House, a mental hospital in Gloucester where the eighty-eight year old spent her final weeks. She died on the last day of August 1960.

Notes

[1] Edith Picton-Turbervill, (EP-T), *Life is Good*, Frederick Muller, 1939. See too Ann Holt's entry for EP-T in Joyce M. Bellamy and John Saville, *Dictionary of Labour Biography*, IV, Macmillan, 1977, pp. 137-44.

[2] Observed by their nephew Wilfred. 8 SUF/B/174, Box 1, Disc 35, TWL, LSE. In the spring of 1910 the twins enjoyed an idyllic holiday together in Palestine.

[3] For another way of looking at Picton's life, see Robert Havard, 'Thomas Picton and Sir Thomas Picton: Two Welsh Soldiers in Spain', *Transactions of the Honourable Society of Cymmrodorion* ns. 7, 2001, pp. 169-170, and 'Dylan Ar Daith: O Benfro I Trinidad', Cwmni Unigryw, S4C, 19 September 2017. As a child, Edith was told stories about Picton by her aunt Elizabeth Warlow, who lived to be 96, and had been brought up by his sister.

[4] Interviewed in 'Dylan Ar Daith'. Fergus suggests that Picton's case played a pivotal role in the development of the abolitionist movement.

[5] Edith recounted the episode briefly in a chapter about the life and death of Picton in Idem, *Into the Land of My Fathers*, Western Mail & Echo, 1946, p.63. She stressed his innocence, and presented him as a gallant Welsh man.

[6] A.G.Temple, *The Story of Algar Temple and the Indian Mutiny*, Western Mail and Echo, 1957, pp. 10-14 of Edith's preface.

[7] This can still be seen. A photograph is reproduced in Sue Crampton, *A Head Above Others*, Perigord Press, 2013, p. 87.

[8] Part of it, at least, dates from 1833.

[9] Her father, like other members of the family before and since, was involved in restoration work (and wrote about this). In 1896 he restored the north aisle of the church and, during

the excavation, pre-Norman stones and Celtic crosses were discovered along with the tombstone of Dame Haweis de Londres, ancestor of Henry IV. Her second husband was, it seems, the 13c Henry de Turbervill, Lord of Ogmore.

[10] Her father had two children from his first marriage. One died as a young man.

[11] EP-T, *Life is Good*, p. 41.

[12] *Ibid*, p. 309.

[13] In Margot Oxford (ed.), *Myself When Young*, Frederick Muller, 1938, pp. 313-60. This account was almost identical to Chapters 2 to 5 of *Life is Good,* published the following year.

[14] Her Obituary in *The Times* 3 August 1936 was headed 'A Life of Service'.

[15] EP-T, *Life is Good*, p. 74.

[16] Ibid, p. 76.

[17] By 1946 she was, however, calling him 'Ganger Joe'. Perhaps she had earlier misread her old diary or her typesetter had done so with the manuscript of *Myself When Young*.

[18] EP-T, *Life is Good*, p. 78.

[19] *Ibid*.

[20] Its origins lay in two separate Christian women's societies, both started in 1855 (the YMCA dated from the previous decade) but integrated in 1877. It sought to provide, through prayer and bible study, a space for young working women to relax and learn, with middle class support. Restructured in the 1880s, one of its six arms covered Colonial and Missionary work. By 1900 it had 1700 branches across Britain.

[21] *Barry Dock News* 7 February 1896.

[22] The theological writings of Bishop Westcott had a marked impact on her, notably his *History of the New Testament Canon* and the edition of the New Testament that he co-edited.

[23] In 1856 the Rev. William Pennefather had held the first conference for interdenominational missionary work. The Mildmay missionary organisation began at Barnet and, four years later in 1860, an institution was created for training Deaconesses. See Jeffrey Cox, *The British Missionary Enterprise since 1700*, Routledge, 2008, Chapter 8.

[24] A letter Edith wrote in May 1901 from India indicated that she also visited navvies in the London area. Quoted in EP-T, *Life is Good*, p. 98.

[25] The World's YWCA had been formed in 1894. Representatives from twenty countries and each continent attended its first conference four years later.

[26] Emily Kinnaird, *Reminiscences*, John Murray, 1925, p. 129. Morley was one of the eight children of Liberal MP and philanthropist Samuel Morley. She ran a Girls' Club in East London. Edith met the Bryant & May match workers.

[27] Neither does Edith refer to the smaller version of this gathering in Llandrindod Wells. *Our Own Gazette* xvii, 1899, MSS. 243, Modern Records Centre, University of Warwick. See too D.W. Bebbington, *Evangelicalism in Modern Britain: A History from the 1730s to the 1980s*, Routledge, 1989, pp. 159, 174-5.

[28] Antoinette Burton, *Burdens of History: British Feminists, Indian Women, and Imperial Culture, 1865-1915*, University of North Carolina Press, 1994.

[29] EP-T, *Life is Good*, p. 88. Beatrice's recollection is slightly different, suggesting that Edith was 'generally supported by father', *Our Own Gazette* xvii, 1899.

[30] YWCA, MSS 243/13/6, MRC, University of Warwick.

[31] Judith M. Brown, *Modern India: The Origins of an Asian Democracy*, Oxford University Press, 1994, p. 154.

[32] EP-T, *Life is Good*, p. 93.

[33] *The Story of Fifty Years*, YWCA of India Records, New Delhi, India, p. 49.

[34] In Kinnaird, *Reminiscences*, p. 130.

[35] *Our Own Gazette* xvii, 1899.

[36] For the significance of the ex-collier Evan Roberts of Loughor, see M. Wynn Thomas, 'Evan Roberts: The Ghost Dance of Welsh Nonconformity' in Idem, *The Nations of Wales 1890-1914*, University of Wales Press, 2016, pp. 214-256. This essay also considers the impact of Jessie Penn-Lewis, a middle class woman from Neath who, inter alia, established YWCA branches in Glamorgan. Her international missionary activity included working in India.

[37] *The Story of Fifty Years*, p. 51.

[38] For a rather different British perspective on India at this time see Henry W. Nevinson, *The New Spirit in India*, Harper & Brothers, 1908.

[39] Compare, for example, her work in India with that of the five women examined by Barbara N. Ramusack in 'Cultural Missionaries, Maternal Imperialists, Feminist Allies: British Women Activists in India, 1865-1945' in N. Chaudhuri and M. Strobel, *Western Women and Imperialism,* Indiana University Press, 1992. See too Antoinette M. Burton, 'The White Woman's Burden: British Feminists and "The Indian Woman", 1865-1915' in Ibid.

[40] Appeal Letter from EP-T and Emily Kinnaird in *The Times* 13 December 1932.

[41] EP-T, *Life is Good,* pp. 93-4.

[42] For a thoughtful account of the relationship between Edith's contemporary and colleague Eleanor Rathbone and Elizabeth Macadam, see Susan Pedersen, *Eleanor Rathbone and the Politics of Conscience*, Yale University Press, 2004, especially p. 96. See too Angela V. John, *Turning the Tide: The Life of Lady Rhondda*, Parthian, 2013, Chapter 11.

[43] *Manchester Guardian (MG)* 9 November 1922.

[44] For developments in the YWCA see Susan Mumm, 'Women and philanthropic cultures' in Sue Morgan and Jacqueline de Vries, *Women, Gender and Religious Cultures in Britain, 1800-1940*, Routledge, 2010, Chapter 3.

[45] She stressed this in a speech at a Manchester maternity home. *MG* 29 April 1927.

[46] *The Times* 16 June 1919.

[47] J. Kennedy Maclean, T. Wilkinson Riddle, *The Second Picture of the War: The Story of the YWCA Service*, Marshall Brothers, 1918, p.7. For the YWCA during this period, see Jan Rutter, 'The YWCA of Great Britain 1900-1925. An Organisation of Change', University of Warwick, MA, 1986.

[48] The two women had previously run a finishing school in Wimbledon. After the war they became joint governors of Dr Barnardo's Girls' Village Home at Barkingside, Essex.

[49] See, for example, *The Times* 28 May 1920.

[50] It became WILPF – Women's International League for Peace and Freedom.

[51] *MG* 24 June 1930.

[52] *Ibid* 21 March 1931. The YWCA had been actively involved with the League of Nations since 1920. Edith was the YWCA representative on its Women's Advisory Committee.

[53] *The Times* 2 September 1921.

[54] *Labour Woman* May 1931.

[55] EP-T, *Life is Good*, p. 151.

[56] www.wilpf.org.uk/wp-content/uploads/2015/07/these-dangerous-women-wilpf-bo.pdf

[57] See Essay 4.

[58] Although in 1921 she was one of 45 applicants to become one of the early women magistrates (nominated by the

Women's Section of the Westminster branch of the Labour Party), she did not become a JP. Greater London Record Office, LTGY/86. For the YWCA and groups such as women police, see Catríona Beaumont, 'Fighting for the "Privileges of Citizenship': the Young Women's Christian Association (YWCA), feminism and the women's movement, 1928-1945', *Women's History Review,* 23/3, 2014, pp. 474-5.

[59] She was a member of the drafting committee of the Consultative Committee of Women's Organisations and sat on the National Council of Women.

[60] Cheryl Law, *Suffrage and Power: The Women's Movement 1918-1928*, I.B. Tauris, 2000 edition, p. 7. At the same time, women such as Gertrude Horton (who worked for NUSEC then the Townswomen's Guilds), did not find it easy to square Edith's religious beliefs with their perspectives, especially since she held strong views. The Women's Library Collection (TWL), LSE Library, Brian Harrison interview in 8 SUF, 1977, Box 1, Disc 27.

[61] *Our Own Gazette* 40/3, March 1922.

[62] She also attended their Copenhagen Conference.

[63] *Saturday Review* June 1935; EP-T, *Life is Good*, p. 293.

[64] For an account of her achievements, see Charles King, *Midnight at the Pera Palace: The Birth of Modern Istanbul,* W.W. Norton, 2014, pp. 206-216.

[65] *Life is Good*, p. 173.

[66] Catríona Beaumont, 'Citizens not Feminists: the boundary negotiated between citizenship and feminism by mainstream women's organisations in England 1928-39', *Women's History Review*, 9/2, 2000, pp. 411-20.

[67] Sheila Fletcher, *Maude Royden: A Life*, Basil Blackwell, 1989, p.144 and Sue Morgan, 'A "Feminist Conspiracy": Maude Royden: Women's Ministry and the British Press 1916-1921', *Women's History Review*, 22/15, 2013.

[68] *The Times* 3 August 1956.

[69] For this see Morgan, 'A "Feminist Conspiracy"', p. 787.

[70] 7 AMR/1/24. Maude Royden Letters, TWL, LSE.

[71] Morgan, 'A "Feminist Conspiracy"', p. 795.

[72] See Jacqueline de Vries, 'Transforming the Pulpit: Preaching and Prophecy in the British Women's Suffrage Movement' in Beverly Mayne Kienzle and Pamela J. Walker, *Women Preachers and Prophets through two millennia of Christianity*, University of California Press, 1998, and Morgan and de Vries, *Women, Gender, and Religious Cultures*. See too Jessica Thurlow,'"The Great Offender": Feminists and the Campaign for Women's Ordination', *Women's History Review,* 23/3, 2014.

[73] Maude Royden, *A Threefold Cord*, Victor Gollancz, 1947, p. 61. See too Effie Shaw's cartoon on p. 60 ridiculing the situation and naming a sermon by Edith called 'The Coming Clergywoman'. In May 1925 Edith spoke from the pulpit at St Botolph's on 'Women of Today and Yesterday'.

[74] Morgan, 'A "Feminist Conspiracy"', pp. 793-4.

[75] *The Times* 3 August 1956.

[76] Brian Heeney, 'The Beginnings of Church Feminism: Women and the Councils of the Church of England 1897-1919' in Gail Malmgreen, *Religion in the Lives of English Women 1760-1930*, Croom Helm, 1986.

[77] Fletcher, *Maude Royden*, p.198.

[78] For this incident, see 'Women in Church' Letter Collection TWL, LSE, Microform 6.1 Box 3, Letters of 2, 8, 14, 20 August 1919, Proudfoot to EP-T, and 18 September 1919 Christina Knox to EP-T; Graham Neville (ed.), *The Diaries of Edward Lee Hicks 1917-1919*, Lincoln Record Society 82/1993, The Boydell Press, pp. 87, 106, 177 and 219; *Westminster Gazette* 24 June 1919.

[79] Law, *Suffrage and Power*, p. 8.

[80] A suffragist and first female delegate to the League of Nations, she was a noted patron of Welsh art. Peter Lord (ed.), *Between Two Worlds: The Diary of Winifred Coombe Tennant,* National Library of Wales, 2011, 22 August 1920, p. 296.

[81] A socialist, he had also been a member of the Men's League for Women's Suffrage, and had authored a pro-suffrage tract. He had sent an open letter of protest to the Prime Minister about the forcible feeding of suffragettes.

[82] EP-T, *In the Land Of My Fathers,* p. 71.

[83] Quoted in Brian Heeney, *The Women's Movement in the Church of England 1850-1930,* The Clarendon Press, 1988, p. 129.

[84] EP-T, *Life is Good*, p. 132.

[85] *Ibid*, pp. 134-5.

[86] Burnett Hillman Streeter and Edith Picton-Turbervill, *Woman And The Church*, 2013 edition, Isha Books, p. 100. First published in book form in 1917 by Fisher Unwin, Edith's chapters were reprinted in 1953 by the Society for the Equal Ministry of Men and Women in the Church.

[87] *Ibid*, pp. 70-1.

[88] For these responses see 'Women in Church' Collection, 9/06 Microform, 6.1. Box 3. TWL, LSE.

[89] The book is reprinted in Crampton, *A Head Above Others*, pp. 107-251.

[90] *Ibid*, p. 131.

[91] EP-T, *Musings of a Laywoman on the Life of the Churches,* John Murray, 1919, p. 110.

[92] EP-T, *Christ and International Life*, George H. Doran, New York edition, 1921.

[93] Before becoming a wartime Minister he had been Vicar-General to the Archbishop of York.

[94] EP-T, *Life is Good*, p. 155. In 1929 she claimed that she had been in sympathy with Labour for a long time before joining the party. *Labour Woman,* 1 July 1929.

[95] 'Why I vote Labour', *Labour Press Service* in Rose Davies Papers, 3/DXIK 44, Glamorgan Archives, Cardiff.

[96] Mari Takayanagi, 'Parliament and Women c. 1900-1945', King's College London, PhD, 2012, p. 33.

[97] Quoted in Beaumont, 'Fighting for the "Privileges of Citizenship"', p. 469.

[98] 'The American Plan as seen by an Englishwoman', The American Social Hygiene Association, 1919, p. 11 in Josephine Butler pamphlets, TWL, LSE.

[99] See Elizabeth Robins' Diary for 20 December 1917 and 16 May 1918 in Robins Papers, The Fales Library, Elmer Holmes Bobst Library, New York University, Series 1A, Box 6. Margaret Dreier Robins was married to Elizabeth's brother, Raymond Robins.

[100] *The Times* 27 November 1925.

[101] *MG* 14 November 1922

[102] 'What PICTON-TURBERVILL Stands for!' 1922 Election Box, People's History Museum, Manchester.

[103] Saving on expenditure was one of the big concerns of the time. There was a political party called the Anti-Waste League.

[104] For Balfour see Joan B. Huff, *Lady Frances: Frances Balfour, Aristocrat Suffragist*, Troubador, 2017.

[105] *Our Own Gazette* 40/10, November 1922.

[106] Ibid 40/11, December 1922.

[107] Conservative: 13,520, Labour: 7,993, Liberal: 7,256.

[108] This forged letter, purporting to be from the President of the Third International, appeared in British newspapers four days before polling. It urged revolutionary activity. Since the

Labour government had recognized the Soviet Union, it gave the impression that it was in league with Communism.

[109] The Conservative easily won the seat from the Liberals but Edith came second, polling 7,418 votes.

[110] EP-T, *Life is Good*, pp. 159-60. MacDonald's secretary Michael Franklin joined Edith at an open-air meeting in her constituency during her 1929 electoral campaign. Her sister Violet spoke in Aberavon against MacDonald.

[111] The Wrekin is a hill: a prominent landmark in East Shropshire. Edith's constituency had a population of more than 70,000 and included Wenlock, Newport, Oakengates, Shifnal and Wellington. It had first returned a Labour MP in 1923. In 1997 much of the old constituency was included in the constituency of Telford though a revised constituency called The Wrekin still exists.

[112] *Great Thoughts,* October 1936.

[113] Helen Jones, *Women in British Public Life 1914-50: Gender, Power and Social Policy*, Pearson Educational, 2000, p. 83.

[114] *Time and Tide* 28 May 1926.

[115] *The Times* 19 August 1926. The letter provoked some disagreement

[116] EP-T, *Life is Good*, p.56 where she calls it the Parc Gwylt [sic] explosion and states incorrectly that it took place in July. Hansard, 19 December 1929, ccxxxiii, col.1728.

[117] *MG* 20 May 1929.

[118] Deirdre Beddoe, *Out of the Shadows:A History of Women in Twentieth-Century Wales*, University of Wales Press, 2000, p. 104.

[119] Martin Pugh, *Women and the Women's Movement in Britain,* Macmillan, 2nd edition, 2000, p. 170 argues that it was felt that 'this staunch middle-class churchwoman' could appeal to the middle class voter. Edith is unlikely to have described

herself thus but it appears to have been a shrewd selection strategy.

[120] For an analysis of the women MPs see Brian Harrison, 'Women in a Man's House. The Women MPs 1919-1945', *Historical Journal,* 29/3, 1986, pp. 623-54.

[121] Margaret Bondfield became Minister of Labour and Susan Lawrence Parliamentary Secretary to the Minister of Health (with Ellen Wilkinson as her Parliamentary Private Secretary.

[122] EP-T, *Life is Good*, p. 192.

[123] *Great Thoughts*, February 1937, part of a series of articles in which she explained the workings of Parliament to the public.

[124] Hansard, 28 November 1930, ccxlv, col. 1710.

[125] See Pedersen, *Eleanor Rathbone.*

[126] In a letter to *The Times* on 23 November 1935, Edith challenged this, arguing that Edward I had summoned four Abbesses to Parliament. Lady Astor replaced her husband in a by-election after his elevation to the Lords.

[127] *MG* 26 November 1924.

[128] According to the Tory Lieutenant-Colonel Moore. Hansard, 30 July 1931, cclv, col. 2612.

[129] *Ibid*, 8 May 1930, ccxxxviii, col. 1217.

[130] *Ibid*, 29 July 1930, ccxlii, col. 386.

[131] *Ibid*, 9 July 1931, ccliv, cols. 2281-2382. See too her comments on the status of women in India in a book review in *Labour Woman,* January 1931.

[132] There were four standing committees, with each session named A to D, plus a Scottish Standing Committee. Edith attended Committee A for 26 out of 42 meetings in 1929-30, and Committees C and D on 17 out of 23 occasions in the following session.

[133] Takayanagi, 'Parliament and Women' PhD chapter 5, and Idem, '"They have made their mark entirely out of proportion to their numbers." Women and Parliamentary Committees, c.1918-45' in Julie V. Gottlieb and Richard Toye, *The Aftermath of Suffrage: Women, Gender and Politics in Britain, 1918-1945*, Palgrave Macmillan, 2013, Chapter 10.

[134] Elizabeth Vallance, *Women in the House*, Athlone Press, 1979, Appendix 5, p. 186.

[135] Quoted in EP-T, *Life is Good*, Appendix.

[136] *Ibid*, pp. 206-7.

[137] For this section, see *The Times* 18 October 1976, which reproduces Edith's letter from MacDonald; EP-T, *Life is Good,* pp. 173-4 and Chapter XV and David Howell, *MacDonald's Party: Labour Identities and Crisis 1922-1931,* especially pp. 327-41.

[138] Edith voted against the government in the second (successful) reading of the National Economy Bill in September, giving it power to carry out the economy plans.

[139] *MG* 20 March 1930.

[140] EP-T, *Life is Good*, pp. 276-89; Pedersen, *Eleanor Rathbone*, pp. 245-6.

[141] For this section, see Hansard, 11 December 1929, ccxxx111, col. 442; 22 January 1930, ccxxxiv, col.203; 26 June 1930, ccxl, cols. 1478-1480, 1499, 11 May 1931, cclii, cols. 951-3; CO 825/22/9, CO825/25/5, CO825/27/7, National Archives, Kew; *Mui Tsai in Hong Kong and Malaya. Report of Commission*, HMSO, 1937; EP-T, *Life is Good*, Chapter xvii; *MG* 19 March, 31 August 1936, 16 August, 13 October, 4 November 1937; *Observer* 14 November 1937; *Daily Telegraph* 10 March 1939; *The Times* 1 March 1937; Norman Miners, *Hong Kong under Imperial Rule 1912-1941,* Oxford University Press, 1987; Susan Pedersen,

'The Maternalist Moment in British Colonial Policy: The Controversy over "Child Slavery" in Hong Kong 1917-1941', *Past & Present*, 171, May 2001, pp. 161-202; David M. Pomfret, 'Child Slavery in British and Far Eastern Colonies 1880-1945', *Past & Present*, 201, November 2008, pp. 175-213; Rachel Loew, 'Do you own non-Chinese Mui Tsai? Re-examining race and female servitude in Malaya and Hong Kong 1919-1939', *Modern Asian Studies*, 46/6, 2012, pp. 1736-1763; Hansard, 11 May 1931, cclii, cols. 951-3; A.C.W. Lee & K.T. So, 'Child Slavery in Hong Kong: Case Report and Historical Review', *Hong Kong Medical Journal* 12/6, December 2006, pp. 463-6.

[142] This was a refuge run by the Chinese Society for the Protection of Women and Girls.

[143] Pedersen, 'Child Slavery', p. 193.

[144] See Loew, 'Do you own non-Chinese Mui Tsai?', p. 54.

[145] *Manchester Guardian* 4 November 1937.

[146] Her eldest sister Violet died in Cheltenham in 1951, aged eighty-one.

[147] RCONT 1, EP-T Talks, Files 1 and 2, BBC Written Archives Centre, Caversham Park, Reading.

[148] She could be quite proprietorial about her conception of Wales. When the journalist Glyn Roberts sought in *Time and Tide* (14 July 1934) to puncture some of what he saw as exaggerated claims of Welsh eminence, she responded (21 July and 28 July).

[149] Britain's longest running political programme began in November 1929. Originally entitled 'The Week in Parliament', it was developed by the Talks director Hilda Matheson. See Kate Murphy, *Behind The Wireless: A History of Early Women at the BBC*, Palgrave Macmillan, 2016, Chapter 6; RCONT 1, EP-T Talks, File 1, BBC Caversham.

[150] Radio Talk Scripts, BBC Caversham. She was paid seven guineas for this.

[151] Letter of 27 August 1931 in RCONT 1, EP-T Talks, File 1, BBC Caversham.

[152] Memos of 11, 13 July 1934, 31 January 1935, 1 June 1942, 27 April, 27 September 1943 in Ibid.

[153] Temple, *The Story of Algar Temple*, p. 71.

[154] *The Times* 25 January 1954. This section draws upon the interview Brian Harrison conducted with Edith's nephew Wilfred Picton-Turbervill in 1977: 8 SUF/B/174, Box 1, Disc 35, TWL, LSE.

[155] *Who Was Who,* V, 1951-60, Adam & Charles Black, 1961, p. 875.

Frances Hoggan, European student.
With thanks to Roger Ford

Frances Hoggan, Welshwoman.
With thanks to Roger Ford

Margaret Wynne Nevinson (second from left) at a women's suffrage demonstration. *Author's collection, from the Late Myrna and Philip Goode*

Edith Picton-Turbervill by Flora Tomkins, oil on canvas, NMW A 5091, *by permission of Amgueddfa Cymru/National Museum Wales*

Myvanwy and Olwen Rhŷs, Llyfr Ffoto 6055/9,
by permission of Llyfrgell Genedlaethol Cymru/
National Library of Wales

Tutors at St Anne's, 1943. Olwen Rhŷs is the first on the left in the back row (sitting), *courtesy of St Anne's College, Oxford*

Margaret Haig Thomas, Viscountess Rhondda, oil on canvas by Alice Mary Burton, 1931

Menna Gallie, author's collection,
from the late Annest Wiliam

4

Family Footsteps

The Rhŷs Sisters[1]

Myvanwy and Olwen Rhŷs were part of a remarkable Welsh family living in Oxford from the latter part of the nineteenth century. This essay traces the lives of these two sisters who, as members of the intelligentsia, became involved in the protracted struggle for educational and political equality for women. Their parents provided considerable support and the parental legacy remained long after their deaths. So we start by considering how their lives and fame affected their daughters.

Lady Elspeth, their mother, died in April 1911, and their father, Sir John Rhŷs, four years later in December 1915. The first Professor of Celtic at Oxford University and the Principal of Jesus College, he is known as the founder of modern Celtic Studies and credited with establishing Welsh philology on a scientific basis. He was knighted in 1907 for public service that included being a member of the Welsh Land Commission, and elected to the Privy Council four years later.

When Sir John died, *The Times* described him as 'The Principal of the Principality',[2] acknowledging both his position in his Oxford College and his pre-eminence in Wales.[3] A telegram from the Prince of Wales conveyed sympathy to the family and College.[4] Myvanwy and Olwen commemorated their parents with a striking and unusual terracotta memorial at Holywell cemetery, that peaceful oasis in the centre of Oxford.

Both parents had experienced geographical and social mobility. John Rhŷs (known as JR) was the son of a small farmer-cum-lead miner in rural Cardiganshire (Aberceiro near Ponterwyd). In 1860, at the age of twenty, after five years as a pupil-teacher, he entered the Normal College, Bangor. Elspeth (née Hughes Davies), an accomplished linguist, had been born on a farm near Llanberis in 1841. Unusually for the time, she progressed from being a pupil-teacher in North Wales to the Borough Road Teacher Training College for Women in London.[5]

The couple met when they were both young teachers on Anglesey in the early 1860s. JR had a teaching post there at Rhosybol School where he was reputed to study Greek before breakfast, French at noon and Latin in the evening.[6] Elspeth was already headmistress of the British School for Girls at Amlwch. His first gift to her was a French-German dictionary. They studied French together. Later, when Elspeth was in Berlin and John in Leipzig, he taught her Latin by post and sent her literature 'more often than trinkets'.[7]

After leaving Anglesey, Elspeth briefly became head of Broughton British School near Chester. She then taught English in Boulogne. Over the next few years she was in Paris, Switzerland, Germany and Rome (where she studied drawing in the studio of the artist Signor Buzzi). Her impressions of Germany were published in an article in the weekly organ of the Welsh Calvinistic Methodists, *Y Goleuad*.

In 1865 JR won a scholarship to Jesus College. By 1869 he was a Fellow of Merton. He studied in France and Germany at some of their finest universities. When the couple finally married in 1872 after an engagement that had lasted five years, their honeymoon was in Paris.

Their daughters perpetuated their parents' approach to study, traditions and values, yet in their own distinctive ways. Many women who advocated the vote and other women's rights were reacting against the strictures of Victorian family life. Not so the Rhŷs daughters. Their parents had both been active suffragists and involved in a number of liberal and Liberal causes.

If these privileged daughters had a burden to bear, it was that expectations were constantly high. Unlike many of their contemporaries who needed to prove that women were capable of thinking and acting for themselves, for Myvanwy and Olwen it was more a case of having to measure up to their parents' achievements, reputation and popularity. JR was described in *Welsh Outlook* as 'One of the most learned, one of the most unassuming, one of the most kindly and one of the most lovable of men'.[8] *Cymru Fydd* declared that "for children who have such parents and such a happy home to turn out commonplace would be to reverse the order of nature by gathering thistledown from fig trees'.[9]

When Elspeth died a month before her seventieth birthday, the periodical *Y Gymraes* reproduced a picture of her on its front page and an extensive obituary by the Aberystwyth academic Professor J. Young Evans.[10] It ended by drawing attention to the scholarship of the two daughters. They were presented as part of a remarkable family unit, each member displaying prodigious intelligence. And they, like their parents, were claimed for Wales.

A love of languages helped to define this family. Each member spoke four or five. The daughters were portrayed as part of the Rhŷs phenomenon, proud products of an educated, Liberal and intellectual environment, worthy heirs in this success story. They sealed JR's transition from humble origins to international acclaim.

Myvanwy had been born on 1 August 1874 in Rhyl, North Wales, when their father was HMI for Flintshire and Denbighshire schools. She was not, however, the first child. Baby Gwladys, born in May 1873, had lived for just over a year. The anniversary of her death on 10 June 1874 was noted annually in JR's diary. Olwen's birthday was 4 March 1876, just nineteen months after Myvanwy's. The sisters' proximity in age, the fact that there were no other surviving siblings, and that neither woman married nor had children, helped to make them especially close, as did shared linguistic skills. Although their lives followed quite similar grooves that would, for some, have spelt rivalry, they remained remarkably close throughout their lives. Myvanwy's diary constantly referred to Olwen and they corresponded frequently when apart.

Their parents were native Welsh speakers. The family spent summer holidays with Elspeth's parents in Llanberis (Gwladys was buried nearby at Nant Peris). Elspeth shared JR's interest in Celtic epigraphy and accompanied him on field trips in search of Ogam inscriptions.[11]

Local tales suggest that the girls learned to read and spell simple Welsh words such as *Nain* and *Taid* (Grandma and Grandpa) by their father scratching words on stones they found as they walked in the countryside near Llanberis. This story[12] served to fuse neatly the scholar's interests with an appealing image of learning that was closer to Hedge schools than to formal education.

The family moved to north Oxford in 1877 when JR became the first Professor of Celtic at Oxford University. In that same year a Royal Commission ended the marriage bar for university dons. For JR it was a return to the city where he had first studied as a student. Tom Ellis, future Liberal MP and leader of *Cymru Fydd* (the Home Rule for Wales movement) was a student there at this time and wrote to his sister, recalling how he had heard Rhŷs conversing in Welsh in Oxford with his small daughters.[13]

The 1881 census shows two Welsh servants in the Rhŷs household. A decade later the servants were English-born but the housekeeper, the North Walian Elizabeth

Hughes, stayed with them. JR became principal of Jesus College in 1895. The family divided their time between the Lodgings at Jesus and a north Oxford villa they called Gwynfa (Paradise) at 35 Banbury Road. Each summer they returned to Wales for a month and usually attended the National Eisteddfod.

These parents were also fiercely ambitious for their daughters. This might well have turned at least one of them against the studying that was integral to their upbringing. The pressure on the girls was intensified by the fact that, unusually for the time, this was a small nuclear family more akin to the ideal family size of modern than Victorian society. There were no other children alive to fulfil hopes. Yet both daughters appreciated their parents throughout their lives: 'What it is to have a good father' was how Myvanwy opened her diary on 8 June 1899.[14]

When she was six, Myvanwy's mother proudly wrote that she 'works large addition and sums also subtraction and multiplication ... she is quite a little student now. She reads fairy tales by herself'.[15] In the early 1880s the Rhŷs household included a resident French tutor.

The young girls went to France with their mother in the spring of 1881. Myvanwy wrote to 'My dear Papa' from St Cloud explaining that she liked attending the convent school and that 'I understand nearly every thing they say to me in French'. She added, 'I hope I shall know much more before I come home'. They had visited the Louvre and found there 'the most beautiful pictures that I have ever seen'.[16] She might have signed her letter 'from your little girl Myfanwy'[17] but it hardly reads like the correspondence of a six year old.

The sisters went on to Oxford High School for Girls, established in 1875 by the Girls' Public Day School Trust.[18] They soon distinguished themselves in this academic environment. Both girls won form prizes for French. In 1891 alone they received certificates from the Associated Boards of the Royal Academy and Royal College of Music and in turn both won the Ada Max Müller scholarship for proficiency in German.[19]

That same year Myvanwy also secured the Gold Medal of the National Society of French Teachers in England. To qualify, entrants had to come top of French in their own school. The strongest candidates from 150 colleges and public schools sat a written exam in French literature and language. Five were shortlisted to face an oral test. Myvanwy was just sixteen but shared the medal with a native Frenchman who, like other candidates, was somewhat older than her.[20]

She won this medal twice then in 1893 it was her sister's turn. Olwen had recently received the best marks in the country for her Higher Certificate French.[21] The *Western Mail* remarked that 'Languages are acquired by the Rhŷs family almost as easily as bad habits are acquired by the weak'.[22]

An article in *The Queen* concluded that Myvanwy's career 'cannot fail to be a brilliant one'.[23] Somewhat sycophantic newspaper articles, from the *Aberystwyth Observer and Merionethshire News* to the *South Wales Daily News*, proudly noted the ceremony at London's Mansion House where the Lord Mayor presented the medals. This was seen as a sort of vicarious triumph for Wales despite the fact that Myvanwy had been educated in Oxford.[24]

Cymru Fydd published an article expressing a wish that Wales would be blessed with many girls like Myvanwy Rhŷs. It carefully chose to attribute her early success to her mother's home education when the children were small, rather than to Oxford High.[25] Letters to the family from figures such as the educationalist, lecturer and writer O.M. Edwards praised Myvanwy's great success.[26]

As the essay on Frances Hoggan shows, Myvanwy and Olwen's parents advocated publicly equal educational opportunities for girls. In 1882 Elspeth chaired the first public discussion in Wales on women's education. JR served on the seminal Aberdare Committee of 1880-1 as well as education commissions in Ireland and the United States, and played a key role in the developments that resulted in the Intermediate Education Act of 1889.

JR later sat on the Council of the University College of North Wales. And it was to Bangor that Myvanwy went as an Exhibitioner (awarded £25) in 1891. The proportion of female to male full-time students in university education in Wales was more than double that of England: by 1900, 38% of students were female compared to just 15% in England and 14% in Scotland.[27]

The College had opened in 1884, with women admitted from the outset. They were awarded external London University degrees. Numbers were modest: by 1890 there were 97 students in all, 42 of them female. Myvanwy lived in the University College Hall for Women (opened three years earlier), which was administered by a limited company. At first all seemed fine. She studied Latin and Greek. Elspeth described her daughter as being in 'a splendid condition' after her first term. She completed the year successfully.

But problems emerged during her second year. They were not of Myvanwy's making but stemmed from allegations made by Frances Emily Hughes, Lady Principal of Myvanwy's Hall, and sister of Elizabeth Price Hughes, first Principal of Cambridge Training College, later Hughes College.[28] They concerned the behaviour and morals of a twenty-six year-old student called Violet Osborn who had left the Hall and was lodging in town as an 'out-student'. Such students were only permitted to visit the residents if they were invited, and Miss Hughes sanctioned their visits. She, however, refused to allow Osborn to do so, believing her to be a bad influence on young students like Myvanwy and that she was 'out to catch a professor'. Osborn would later marry one of the Bangor academics, the Latin professor E.V. Arnold. He sat on the Hall's board of directors to which Hughes took her complaints – to no avail – and spoke in Osborn's favour.

Hughes told Elspeth (who was staying in Bangor) that Osborn was an unfit companion for Myvanwy. In turn, Elspeth passed on these claims to Oxford friends. This helped to spread unwelcome publicity. Osborn heard about the allegations and complained to the College. She even gained the support of prominent advocates of women's education such as Dr Sophie Bryant and Frances Buss (who had earlier been on the Hall's executive committee but resigned after a disagreement with Hughes).

The situation escalated into a scandal, partly fuelled by the press, who delighted in headlines such as 'Principal versus Lady Principal'. Attention and significance became attached to the situation, not least because it revealed a burgeoning power struggle between the College authorities and Women's Hall, with implications for the future of women's education.[29]

Hughes refused to attend a Senate enquiry (as an employee of a limited company rather than a College official, she was not obliged to do so). She would not withdraw her allegations when her charges were declared to be without foundation and Miss Osborn's conduct and character to be honourable. The College Council later endorsed the Senate's decision, though half a dozen members resigned in protest at the unfair treatment of Hughes.

The scandal reverberated way beyond Wales. It was raised in Parliament, and there were two libel cases. Elspeth had to give evidence at Chester Assizes in 1893 when Hughes sued the *Weekly Dispatch* for libel. Hughes was replaced.

This dispute revealed complicated political, religious and gender divisions. It also demonstrated some questionable behaviour that today would be described as 'politically incorrect', namely undue familiarity towards women students on the part of male professors, especially the professor of philosophy (who later resigned his post). Both the press and most historical interpretations have made light of this and failed to recognise the almost impossible position in which women like Hughes were placed. If they failed to protect their vulnerable female charges they were attacked. Yet if they exercised moral pressure they risked being ridiculed. One casualty of the sorry situation was Myvanwy: the attendant publicity and ill feeling surrounding the relationship between the College and Hall resulted in the family removing her from her course at Bangor.

Myvanwy kept a diary. Parts of the pre-1900 diaries were written in a code that involved transliterating English into the Greek alphabet (with some modifications).[30] It enabled this student of classical Greek to write more frankly than in the rest of her diary. Servants and many others who might come across it would not be able to decipher her words.

Myvanwy always enjoyed a sense of drama. Using her code enabled her to rehearse her feelings about the Bangor situation. Deciphering it reveals that, for her, the villain of the piece was Violet Osborn's supporter Professor Arnold. Myvanwy expressed her disdain for him and speculated as to his motives, timing, and moves. She was convinced that he had anticipated an attack on 'Vi' and that Hughes had confronted him about her at an early stage. Myvanwy was especially resentful of the way that he allowed her mother to 'bear all odium' when, in her opinion, he was the one fomenting the scandal.[31]

Myvanwy returned home but carried on studying. Her diary shows that on a typical day in 1893 she attended what she called 'a terrific Sophocles lecture' at Oxford, puzzled over algebra, had a music lesson and went to a dance. The diary of the housekeeper Mrs Hughes shows the sisters, like their hospitable parents, enjoying social life in Oxford and beyond.[32] Both young women rode bicycles – that symbol not only of Oxbridge students but also of the liberated woman of the 1890s – and attended the theatre. Olwen was active for years in the Oxford Home Students' Dramatic Society: in 1912 she was stage manager for a production of *The Trojan Women* (Hilda Matheson, later a senior figure in BBC radio, played Andromache).[33]

Despite the commitment to study, this was a household that entertained frequently: a friend told Myvanwy that the funniest stories in Oxford were heard at the family's dinner parties.[34] International academics, politicians, Welsh luminaries and popular figures such as the novelist Marie Corelli dined with them. There were college dinners too. Reporting on a dinner at Brasenose, Olwen jokingly told Myvanwy that 'It was very staid and sober. Father and I are both too young and frisky for such entertainments'.[35]

Undaunted by her earlier experiences, in 1895 Myvanwy won a Winkworth scholarship to read for the classical tripos at Newnham College, Cambridge. Not surprisingly, she felt pressure to succeed and worked extremely hard. Her parents had to ensure that she took a break after studying for finals. The Principal of Newnham, the mathematician Eleanor Sidgwick (sister of Arthur Balfour and wife of the philosopher Henry Sidgwick who in 1870 had helped to initiate the first lectures for Cambridge-based ladies), wrote to Elspeth. She explained that Myvanwy had 'worried herself silly over her work and made it her goal and much more of a strain than it could have been had she taken it more quietly'.[36] She hoped, though, that she would, in time, return to undertake further study at Newnham.

Myvanwy's undergraduate exertions paid dividends. Each class in the classical tripos was at this time divided into three and she attained a 1.3, that is, a Lower First.[37] She was one of the two most successful women in the classical tripos of 1898. The following year she was back at home learning Russian and Italian, taking dancing and music lessons and doing callisthenics. She also worked on a essay for a Cambridge prize. At first she was half-hearted – 'it hung heavily around my neck heavy as lead' – but she was from a family that understood the work ethic.

The preacher and theologian Dr Cynddylan Jones, who had been a pupil-teacher with the teenage JR, remembered him as highly intelligent but largely attributed his success to extremely hard work, literally burning the midnight oil.[38] The accounts that Elspeth told her daughter of teaching and studying in Paris in the 1860s suggest that she too had known little leisure time when young.

In the spring of 1899 Myvanwy attended a dancing class then wrote in her diary that she 'had the bliss of being introduced to the tall man called Heywood'.[39] Such comments were, however, unusual. The previous year when someone had suggested she write a novel, she had replied that she felt ill equipped to do so as she knew no men.[40] Romances with men or women do not seem – at least in the written record they chose to leave – to have featured much in the lives of these self-sufficient sisters.[41] A Frenchwoman[42] who met them in Dieppe remarked that it might not be easy for these intelligent and moral women to find worthy husbands.

That summer Myvanwy, like the rest of the family, was caught up in the revelations about the Dreyfus Case in France.[43] She noted that they were 'living, sleeping, eating, drinking' its twists and turns and denounced 9 September (when Captain Dreyfus was found guilty of treason with extenuating circumstances) as 'A day without its equal in the Annals of Shame'. She hoped people would boycott the French exhibition.[44]

JR was not, however, prepared to 'let me say goodbye' to the Cambridge essay and by December Myvanwy found that it had taken her over, forming 'the main thread of my existence'. It paid off. She won the Gibson Greek Testament Prize for her 148-page analysis of the sources and content of the Logos.[45]

She had not, however, been awarded her undergraduate degree. Although women had been admitted to university exams since 1881, they nevertheless remained graduates without degrees and excluded from formal membership of the university. Not until after the Second World War would Cambridge admit women on the same terms as men and adopt Girton and Newnham as colleges of the university. The first women's degrees would be awarded in 1948.

However, like Margaret Wynne Nevinson, who gained a degree through an enlightened scheme at St. Andrews University, and Frances Hoggan, who obtained her medical licence from Dublin, Myvanwy found a way for her work to be recognised. In 1905, the opening of degrees to women at Trinity College, Dublin provided a temporary loophole for those who were barred by their gender from receiving the degrees they had earned. For a limited period Trinity offered an 'Ad Eundem' degree to qualified women. Myvanwy travelled there with her father to receive her BA. By the time of the 1911 census she was described as a researcher in History. She was based at home again in Oxford but travelling widely.

Olwen too was well travelled and seized opportunities to improve her French. In 1897, for example, she went to Geneva with her mother, where she spent a few months attending university lectures. Twenty-five years later she was back there, following lectures in linguistics.[46] The time spent on the continent by these sisters shows them following in the footsteps of their Europhile parents. In 1907 Olwen accompanied her father to the United States for just over a month.

Olwen's prime educational commitment was to Oxford. In June 1878 a meeting at Jesus College resulted in the formation of the Association for the Higher Education of Women (AEW). The following year the Society of Oxford Home Students was started for those living locally, and it became an umbrella organisation for women undertaking academic study.[47] Both sisters became Life Members. Home Student members enrolled in the AEW, received tuition from its educational staff and were admitted to university lectures. The AEW organised the examinations for women but they were set and marked by university teachers. In 1901 Olwen was awarded first class honours in Modern Languages in the university's women's exams.

But such information hides as much as it reveals. The university did not accept this as a degree. Three years later Oxford instituted the Final Honours School of Modern Languages and this was open to women. Yet the university still refused to accept the special women's examinations. Only in 1920 were women formally admitted to university membership and privileges. And despite having already been a temporary resident tutor at Somerville College, and the Home Students' Association enjoying the privileges of a recognised society of women students of Oxford University since 1910, Olwen now had to suffer the indignity of taking a complete course of pass degree public examinations. She had been tutoring French students for the AEW for two decades.

When Myvanwy undertook research in west Wales in 1921, Olwen accompanied her but spent most of her time ensconced in Carmarthen's Ivy Bush Hotel and Aberystwyth's Bellevue Hotel, swotting for her June exams. On 14 May she wrote in her diary: 'I Euripideed all day practically till half-past nine after which I read a silly book. I then got up to line 600 of the *Alcestis*'.[48] She finally received her MA degree in 1924. In her book on women at Oxford, Vera Brittain singled out Olwen's unfair position. Gender certainly mattered. A brother would have been entitled to his degree long before this.[49]

The following year Olwen became the first Home Student to be appointed a university examiner (in French in Pass Moderations), demonstrating how ludicrous her position had been. She sat on the Home Students' governing body for some years and played an active role in the old students' association. Some of their meetings were held at her home. In 1929 she became a Home Society lecturer in Old French, a position she held until 1946 by which time the Home Society was known as the St Anne's Society. In 1952, shortly before Olwen died, St Anne's College became a full College of the University.

The disjunction between the Rhŷs sisters' evident ability and the failure of the Oxbridge education system to recognise this, would have been one factor in encouraging them to support women's suffrage. Their lives were already women-centred and in their support of suffrage they were also following in their parents' footsteps. The Pankhursts are the best-known example of a family dedicated to women's suffrage but as the historians Katherine Bradley and June Balshaw have noted,[50] suffrage support was frequently a family affair. All the Rhŷs family members were suffragists, and even Mrs Hughes the housekeeper attended meetings.

Elspeth had heard John Stuart Mill speak in the 1860s. When the family lived in Rhyl, JR and the early suffrage leader Lydia Becker of the Manchester National Society for Women's Suffrage twice shared the platform at suffrage meetings. He 'chuckled over her confounding of the local Solomons' and compared the status of Victorian women with those of the twelfth century.[51] A letter sent to Elspeth in 1888 from Lydia Becker refers to Elspeth's continued membership of the suffrage society and asks if she will join the General Committee.[52] Elspeth also worked behind the scenes to help the Cause. For example, in May 1905 the Anglesey MP Ellis Griffith wrote to assure her that 'In response to your command I went down to the House yesterday to vote for the Bill'. He was at pains to stress that he had always supported women's suffrage: 'I add this because I rather fear you think otherwise'.[53]

The first drawing-room meeting on women's suffrage in Oxford had been held in 1873[54] before Myvanwy and Olwen were born, but it was JR who chaired its first public meeting on women's suffrage, at the Corn Exchange in 1878, not long after the family moved to Oxford and before the foundation of Somerville, Lady Margaret Hall and the Society of Home Students.

The constitutionalist National Union of Women's Suffrage Societies (NUWSS) was established in Oxford in September 1904, five years before Mrs Pankhurst's

Women's Social and Political Union appeared there.[55] JR was made vice-president of the Oxford Women's Suffrage Society (OWSS) and was its president from 1909, a position he held until his death in 1915.[56] It boasted 200 members by 1908 and more than 500 by 1914, by which time Oxford women students had their own society and the OWSS branch had also become part of a wider NUWSS Federation comprised of Oxfordshire, Buckinghamshire and Berkshire.[57]

JR was active in a number of suffrage societies. The moderate Men's League for Women's Suffrage was especially popular with academics and had branches in universities such as Bangor and Manchester. He was a member of the Oxford University branch, established in 1912 with Gilbert Murray, Regius Professor of Greek its president. Both men were also active in the Men's Liberal Society for the Parliamentary Enfranchisement of Women.

In January 1906 JR stated at a suffrage meeting that he did not for a moment think that the Liberal MPs would refuse to do political justice to women. He added that if they failed women, it would be 'entirely their own fault if at the next election they were "jilted" by the women suffragists'.[58] It must have been galling for this staunchly Liberal family to see their leader Asquith oppose women's suffrage when he became prime minister.

The first honorary secretary of the OWSS was Myvanwy. On 13 June 1908 she and Alys Russell headed the Oxford contingent of 85 women and a few male sympathisers in the vast NUWSS demonstration (estimated to be between 10 and 15,000 strong) from London's Embankment to the Albert Hall.[59] It was the fortieth year of Mrs Fawcett's service to the Cause so at the Albert Hall an equal number of women each gave her a bouquet of flowers. Myvanwy presented a bunch of blue irises tied with a blue ribbon and a message reading 'Honour to a Pioneer from Oxford Women's Suffrage Society'.

Myvanwy attended the fortnightly committee meetings of the OWSS regularly (sometimes they were held at the Lodgings or Gwynfa). In 1909 alone the committee met 25 times and held more than 50 meetings of one sort or another. Myvanwy stood down as branch secretary in May 1909 due to demands outside Oxford but remained on the committee until November 1912, when Olwen replaced her. Over the next few years this youngest member of the family attended committee meetings whenever possible. In 1913-14, for example, she attended 19 out of 30 meetings.

In January 1913, Mrs Fawcett and other leaders of the NUWSS asked key supporters to write brief sympathetic messages that could appear in the press when the Franchise Bill, (which urgently needed to include a women's amendment), reached the Committee Stage in Parliament. Olwen was approached.[60] Her message stressed that 'the sense of injustice long felt by thoughtful women is steadily growing especially among the younger generation and its removal is essential to the best development of the nation'.[61] Ten days after requesting this support, the Speaker of the House of Commons ruled against the amendment.

That November was a time of increased militancy. JR attended a deputation of NUWSS men to Lloyd George.[62] No longer did JR express the confidence in the Liberals that had been evident in his 1906 speech. His appeal instead sought to touch a raw nerve. Referring to the Chancellor's work on national insurance and land reform, he presented votes for women as a third great measure of democratic reform.[63] Together, he said, they would form 'a triple monument to show ages to come the greatness of the humanitarian genius. Welshmen were fond of *triads*[64] and if the Chancellor of the Exchequer failed to see the logic of that *triad* he could hardly call him a true *Kymro'*.

The Rhŷs family had long supported Liberalism. It was Elspeth who had proposed the formation of an Oxford branch of the Women's Liberal Association back in 1888. She became a vice-president and, four years later, president of the Mid Oxfordshire branch. In 1905 Olwen became secretary of the Oxford branch. Jesus College awarded Lloyd George an honorary Fellowship.

The Lloyd Georges were personal friends. They stayed with the family on more than one occasion. In June 1912 Mrs Lloyd George and her two daughters were guests at a dinner party for fourteen.[65] Jesus College awarded Lloyd George an honorary Fellowship. But what many felt to be a Liberal betrayal of women's demands – evident since a government announcement late in 1911 had effectively scuppered the proposals of the promising all-party Conciliation Bill – must have been increasingly difficult for the Rhŷs family. Although they would have condemned the suffragette attack on Lloyd George's new (empty) house on Walton Heath, his equivocal actions in relation to the granting of women's suffrage put a strain on the family's support for him and the Liberal Party.

Elspeth, however, did not live to experience these disappointments over Liberal leadership, or the partial victory that women won in the Representation of the People Act of 1918. She died in April 1911. Although she had been in poor health for a few years, her death was unexpected, and JR was in Paris at the time.

During the latter part of the pre-war struggle for suffrage, the Rhŷs daughters and Olwen in particular fulfilled the social role formerly performed by their mother, helping with the entertaining required from a college Principal. Nevertheless, the remaining three members of the family still travelled frequently within and beyond Britain. In 1912 alone, Olwen visited Germany and Italy. Myvanwy spent time in Paris, and was abroad with her father in the spring.

Olwen continued to campaign for the vote into wartime. In 1916 she represented her locality at a national NUWSS council meeting in Chelsea – a reminder that women's suffrage did not fizzle out during the First World War even though the Suffragettes had suspended their activity.[66]

Olwen juggled with many demands during the war. Through the Oxford suffragists she helped Belgian soldiers and also organised entertainments for soldiers' wives via the Belgian Relief Committee. An old family friend thanked Myvanwy in November 1914 for the invitation to their hospitable home, adding that he was aware that they were expecting Belgians to be staying with them for an unknown length of time.[67] Olwen also helped with the Union Jack Club for non-commissioned servicemen.

JR's death on 17 December 1915 was a shock. Although Olwen was at home and the chief mourner at the funeral, Myvanwy was travelling in Switzerland and, despite departing for Oxford immediately, could not get home in time.

The sisters' lives had followed in the grooves laid down by their parents, but their subsequent experiences took them into new territory, prompted in large part by the exigencies of war. Olwen had the opportunity to become temporary bursar at Somerville early in 1916 but decided instead to volunteer with her Oxford friend (also a suffragist) Eden Lewis to join the Quakers in French War Victims Relief work. She wrote in her diary on 7 February 1916: 'I am offering myself to the Quakers in July'. The Rhŷs connections in high places were demonstrated when Olwen asked Lloyd George's secretary for a letter to help them obtain permits for Switzerland from the French consulate.[68]

In early August Olwen arrived at the Hotel Bellevue at Samoëns, a Quaker convalescence home for refugees in the Haute Savoie.[69] The obstetrician and suffragist Dr Hilda Clark (from the Quaker family of shoe manufacturers) was the key figure behind this. It had opened in April 1916. Although initially conceived as a sanatorium for convoys of *repatriés* from Germany, at first it was used for needy women and child refugees in Paris. Those in other overcrowded centres (especially if likely to contract tuberculosis) were also sent to the fresh mountain air of Samoëns.

In summertime Olwen worked in a sunny, sheltered valley but in the winter it was bitterly cold and snowy. Many extremely vulnerable patients came from the war zone. There were clothing and food shortages, burst pipes and low morale. They were under-staffed and Hilda Clark persuaded the somewhat reluctant Olwen to take on responsibility as *Directrice*. Olwen also had to travel to

Annemasse Hospital where those from concentration camps in Germany were sent before being moved on. Some were selected to recuperate at Samoëns.

It was a baptism of fire. Although patients tended to improve, the health of the staff suffered. Olwen contracted measles in April 1917. 'A shame in such a beautiful creature'[70] wrote Clark, who nursed her at Samoëns. Olwen recuperated in France and Switzerland before returning to her post in mid-May. Her diary for this period was written up later. Most entries simply show one word: Samoëns.

Exhausted, she left in mid-October. She accompanied Clark to her family home in Somerset where she spent the rest of the year recuperating from shingles, brought on by the pressure of her work. Olwen felt guilty about having abandoned Samoëns: 'Feel I ought to have stayed on. I am regretting all my shortcomings' she confided to her diary on Christmas Eve.

She moved to the Alexandra Hotel in Lyme Regis in the New Year. Hilda Clark initially accompanied her. It was confirmed in January that the Samoëns centre was to be closed and Clark wrote to Olwen accepting responsibility.[71] Clark added in her diary that the Relief Committee appeared to blame Olwen and 'do not realise what a success she was, and that the failure is entirely my fault'. Olwen had 'made mistakes too – but she never wanted to do it'. Clark saw it as her own fault that she had not anticipated that Olwen needed extra help there.

Olwen stayed on in Lyme until April. Both Clark and Myvanwy visited her when they could get away. The sisters happily conjugated verbs together on walks as they had done when younger. Myvanwy wanted to work in Italy so was brushing up on her Italian. Clark's diary for 1917 to 1919 is peppered with references to the sisters, especially Olwen. Clark met Myvanwy a number of times in Paris but was especially smitten by Olwen, who suffered from migraines and quite delicate health. Clark enjoyed taking care of Olwen but her diary suggests that she felt 'de trop' whenever Myvanwy was present.

When Myvanwy came to Lyme on 12 January 1918, Clark wrote that it was 'awfully nice to see her but I feel sad at the close of this time with Olwen'. Conscious of how close the sisters were, she was sure that Myvanwy would 'rather have O to herself'. That spring, having observed that they were both rather 'nervy' about the war news, Clark's diary noted that not only were they both 'much more highly strung' than their actions suggested but they also remained something of an enigma: 'I wish I knew whether they really like having me – but I shall never understand them'.[72] Meeting Olwen in London almost four years later, Clark found her as reserved and elusive as ever and remarked: 'One cannot make the full of friendship if people will not give out rather more'.[73]

Myvanwy spent much of the war abroad. Like the famous Welsh patrons of art and the arts, the Davies sisters, who worked in Red Cross canteens, she too volunteered for French canteens. By 1918 she was supervising two new canteens near Fontainebleau run by the OWSS.[74] Whenever possible, the sisters met up, whether in Europe or Britain.

One difficulty, however, was that they no longer had a

home of their own. Olwen spent part of the spring staying with the Lewis family in north Oxford. By the summer she was based in Portsmouth, employed by the War Pensions Committee. To her surprise, she enjoyed the work. It involved making reports on the domestic circumstances facing women whose menfolk had died or been badly wounded. In the evenings she helped Clark (who pre-war had been the county borough tuberculosis medical officer) at a TB dispensary in the town. They shared a flat in Portsmouth. Olwen was away on a course in Dorset in the autumn but by the following February she was helping again in the dispensary.

After the Armistice, Myvanwy was seconded to the Italian army in Belgium to organise a canteen. Despite her experience at Samoëns, the spring of 1919 saw Olwen learning Serbian at every conceivable moment, ready for work with the Serbian Relief Fund.[75] In July, having purchased pyjamas from Harrods and canteen overalls from Dunhill's, she and Eden Lewis travelled across Europe to Belgrade (Clark joined them in Trieste). By August, Olwen was in a beautiful, remote countryside sleeping in a tent in a field. She was taken on visits to camps to learn how provisions were distributed.

She then undertook a tough sixteen-hour journey to Niš, the only woman on a soldier's train. In this ancient Serbian city, where Constantine the Great had been born, Olwen worked in clothes distribution at Unit 6, providing peasants with clothing in return for produce. A thousand bales of clothing had been sent out to Niš.[76] She was not happy there. 'Poor little shrimp. Try and cheer up!' wrote Myvanwy, who was doing Friends War Victims Relief work at Pargny (in the Somme area) and then at Ypres. She added, 'I expect the experience is valuable as you say, though you must be terribly cut off'.[77] Before long Olwen was sent back to Belgrade to look after the Fund's flat there, though she felt that this was worse as she was underused. A report for the Fund by Olive Rhys (Olwen) and a co-worker shows them stationed at the outpost of Medvedje early in 1920.[78] A typhus outbreak had been stemmed but there were many cases of influenza.

Returning to Niš and Banja, Olwen helped in the distribution centre and the orphanage.[79] Eden Lewis was now with her. They also did stints in the dispensary. Olwen tried out her Serbian on the children and sorted piles of clothes. She wrote to tell Myvanwy how wolves roamed nearby in the mountains and that they were 'plunged in Serbian manners and customs'.[80] Myvanwy was pleased that Olwen was at last getting the kind of work she had hoped for but worried that her younger sister was too meek and lacked confidence in herself.

The sisters were now in their forties. They kept in touch by letter and fretted if they did not hear from each other for more than a few days. Olwen addressed her older sister as 'Darling Muffins' and she responded with 'Darling Olwen'. On 6 January 1920 Myvanwy wrote 'I live in hope of a letter from you. I have had nothing for eight days and am most anxious'.[81] At the end of the month Myvanwy wrote from Reims, 'my dear little sister, I do not at all like being so cut off from you'.[82]

She told Olwen that she hoped to go to Italy. By Easter she was in Rome recovering from 'The most melodramatic day I ever lived!'[83] She had gone to Sicily with a friend. Travelling in a Thomas Cook motor car to see an ancient site, a bandit had fired at them, demanding money. Myvanwy was taken to hospital but not seriously injured. Considering the places the sisters worked in and their exposure to danger and disease, they were, however, fortunate to have escaped so lightly for so long.

They continued to support war victims. At the end of the year Myvanwy was trying to arrange (via the Quakers) for money to be sent to an old German friend who was starving in Dresden.[84] But their days of risking their lives and health far from home were over.

Olwen assumed a different responsibility. Here she was also following in her father's footsteps: assessing the quality of teaching in Welsh schools. She became an assistant examiner in French for the Central Welsh Board of Education (CWB) created in 1896. It inspected and examined the pioneering Welsh Intermediate (Secondary) Schools that predated the state secondary system established in England in 1902.[85]

From 1917 the CWB was subject to the overriding authority of the new Secondary Schools Examination Council. Olwen has left an account of her examination of pupils in mid and North Wales in the summer of 1919.[86] Although she spent only a few weeks conducting her visits, it was demanding, intensive work, involving a lot of travelling to and within remote locations. There had been a large increase in the number of Welsh Intermediate (Secondary) Schools. Oral examinations had to be conducted as well as written work scrutinised.

Olwen travelled to Oswestry on 10th June, examined an excellent Intermediate School in Llanfyllin, then the boys' school at Welshpool the next day, followed by the girls' school. The next few days saw her examining in Newtown, Llanidloes, Aberystwyth and Tregaron. By the time she reached Machynlleth she was feeling sick and had a headache.

She was told there that her assessments were out of kilter and considerably lower than those of other examiners. The position of Modern Languages within secondary schools had been strengthened but there were still comparatively few graduate teachers of Modern Languages and in the districts that Olwen examined, French was not usually started until the second year of secondary schooling.[87]

In Towyn, where the headmaster had known her father, she was embarrassed when he asked her opinion of his French master. After examining boys at Dolgellau, the Board altered her itinerary. Her final examinations were in Barmouth and Bala then she returned to London on 25th June.

Myvanwy spent much of the 1920s in European cities and London (usually staying at clubs such as the Ladies Town and Country and the University Women's Club), as did Olwen out of term time. Oxford life had become very different from the old days: in 1922, for example, Olwen was lecturing, coaching students, giving elementary school teachers French classes, and living in an Oxford bedsit. But in 1929 the sisters acquired their own home in Oxford. They named the house in Barton Lane, Headington after the old family home Gwynfa.[88] Both women remained dedicated to scholarship. In the 1930s Olwen was secretary of the Oxford Branch of the Modern Language Association.

Myvanwy's later years were dominated by biographical research into her father's life. It had begun before his death. She had written to Olwen in 1913, asking her to visit the folklorist Henri Gaidoz on her forthcoming visit to Paris.[89] JR had stayed with Gaidoz's family back in 1868 and Myvanwy wondered how he had spent his time. Did he meet the great Breton scholar Ernest Renan?[90] She had eight questions that needed answering.

In March 1916 just a few months after JR died, Olwen and Myvanwy had unearthed his early letters and diaries in the attic and began sorting them as well as making preparations to leave the Lodgings.[91] Over the next few years the war had absorbed time and energy. But in 1918 Myvanwy contacted many people for their memories. Her godfather was A.H. Sayce, Professor of Assyriology at Oxford and a close friend of her father's for fifty years.[92] She drew on his and other colleagues' reminiscences.[93]

She appealed in the *Times Literary Supplement* and *Manchester Guardian*[94] for readers who had corresponded with JR to lend her their letters. A tiny notebook in her papers in the Bodleian lists things to do. They included securing a detailed map of the part of Ceredigion where her father had lived, checking whether people mentioned in family papers were still living there and enquiring about individuals connected to the family, from Aberceiro to New York.[95]

Myvanwy travelled extensively in pursuit of information. The first Welsh journey in her father's footsteps was in the spring of 1918 when, accompanied by Olwen, they visited Dr Henry Owen at Poyston Hall, Pembrokeshire (childhood home of Edith Picton-Turbervill's ancestor, Sir

Thomas Picton). A lawyer and noted antiquarian, Owen boasted a library that was magnificent in style and content. He and JR had shared an interest in inscriptions on stones. In 1905 JR had become chairman of the Honourable Society of Cymmrodorion. Owen was its vice chairman and treasurer.

There followed what Olwen called an extensive 'biographical hunt'. It encompassed a visit to the National Library in Aberystwyth, where the sisters saw 'what promises to be a fine building'. The marble bust of JR by Sir William Goscombe John, (originally presented to their father by Henry Owen) from the Cymmrodorion Society had been bequeathed to the library.[96] It looked good, Olwen thought, and she admired the flower arrangements in front of the library: pansies, snapdragons and poppies.

Moving further north, they visited their father's birthplace and locations where he had later lodged and studied. At Pant y Ffynnon they sat on hay in a barn where he once had lessons. In Capel Bangor they talked to a Mrs Owen, who had sold him farthing candles. They visited graves, and filled in details about JR's childhood. There was plenty of tea and talk, much of it in Welsh.

They also went to Llanberis to learn more about Elspeth's upbringing. Olwen admitted in her diary that she had been somewhat snobbish when young and now regretted not having known more about her mother's birthplace and family. People assured them that whenever their father had returned, he had seemed the same unspoiled person. Olwen was uncertain that they had gleaned much new information but found the visit humbling: 'to realise what you had to do for your education was worthwhile'.[97] Myvanwy then travelled on to Cardiff to meet more of her father's erstwhile colleagues. Three years later, the sisters returned to JR's home patch and saw the mine where their grandfather had laboured.

During the 1920s Myvanwy worked on medieval historical research, exploring pipe rolls in the Public Record Office, and reading volumes in the British Museum. She also pursued her father's history. She was based in digs in London but often worked at women's clubs, such as the University Women's Club and the Pioneer Club. The latter, which dated back to 1892, she found 'a dismal hole – so dark and full of gushing ladies who love one another'.[98]

She also made yearly trips to Wales, staying often at the Gwalia Hotel in Llandrindod Wells for leisure and doing research in the National Library at Aberystwyth, as well as making yearly visits to Europe. The Rhŷs daughters had been well provided for financially but unsurprisingly given the economic climate of the 1920s, there was periodic concern about their investments, the details of which Myvanwy left to Olwen.

Myvanwy's diary for the interwar years suggests at times a somewhat lonely existence for this independent scholar with no fixed abode. On Easter Monday 1926 she travelled from digs in Tollington Park in North London to work at the British Library.[99] After a morning in the Reading Room she had a snack at a nearby tearoom, returned to study and then, finding few restaurants open, ate a 'dubious' meal on her own at Lipton's.

Myvanwy lacked the regular employment and collegiality that Olwen could enjoy in Oxford. Although she had been an active suffragist, she does not appear to have been involved in feminist organisations in the interwar years. Olwen was her sole surviving close family member and the approved social space for women on their own in London was very different from that for men. However, as Katherine Holden's study of singleness reminds us, the way that spinsterhood has been perceived makes it easy to confuse being alone with loneliness.[100] In the main Myvanwy's detailed diary conjures up a picture of a very busy woman who enjoyed the *relative* freedom provided by her class and single status.

Myvanwy never achieved the status and success of the erstwhile Cambridge student Eileen Power,[101] who became a renowned medievalist and LSE professor. She did, however, publish a well-regarded article on folksong in the progressive weekly *The Nation* in 1907, and her painstaking research, involving deciphering and documenting medieval Latin, resulted in a hefty volume (close on 500 pages) entitled *Ministers' Accounts for West Wales 1277 to 1306* for the Cymmrodorion Record Series.[102] Published in 1936 and describing its author as 'Sometime Scholar of Newnham College', it provided the text and translation, and was intended as the first of two volumes. The eminent medievalist Professor Tout[103] was thanked for encouraging Myvanwy, as was Olwen, who checked the totals of the accounts. It was well reviewed and is still cited today.[104] The second volume never materialised. As for Myvanwy's biography of her father, that was never published.

An entry in Olwen's diary on 10 July 1920 shows that Myvanwy was not the only one interested in researching her father's life. Olwen records someone by the name of Ellis arriving in Oxford – possibly the Liberal politician

Sir Ellis Jones Ellis-Griffith.[105] Their visitor stated that he wanted to write a biography of Sir John and this cast Myvanwy 'into a perplexity as to whether she ought to have handed it over to him but in the main we were both agreed that it was not desirable'.[106]

Twenty years later Myvanwy was still working on her project. Her 1940 diary shows her making some headway. By May she had completed drafts of five chapters, spurred on, it would seem, by fear as the Germans advanced on Paris. She made arrangements with Eden Lewis (now in Devon) to take care of the manuscript if need be, fearful that many years of work might go up in flames.

The Sir John Rhŷs archive at the National Library of Wales holds draft versions of Myvanwy's manuscript. There are six chapters, all handwritten and in English, as well as preparatory notes based on her reading. There is background material about the state of nineteenth century Welsh rural life and details on the history of education in Wales at the time.

The opening chapter traces JR's family history, acknowledging that facts were 'woefully meagre'.[107] He had not been very communicative about his childhood, lacking, as Myvanwy put it, 'the Celtic passion for pedigrees'. His daughters never knew his parents or siblings, even though Myvanwy met some relatives in Wales and in America. Myvanwy stressed that her grandfather Hugh Rees might have had Sunday School as his only means of instruction and spent his life in a very remote location, but he valued knowledge. His ideal had been to send his son to theological college at Bala, and he instilled in him 'a proper appreciation of the language and traditions of his people'.

Myvanwy also portrayed this paternal grandfather as something of a dreamer and suggested that some of her father's mental alertness came from his mother who died prematurely of diphtheria. She stressed the 'burning love of knowledge' that shaped her father's life, but was also at pains to recognise 'his strong humanity' and work for others.

The biography was somewhat reverential despite the fact that Myvanwy was writing some time after the Lytton Strachey watershed that challenged the tone of nineteenth century respectful life stories through his 1918 publication *Eminent Victorians*.[108] But it is hardly surprising that this memoir of a beloved father is uncritical.

It does not flow easily, but we only possess Myvanwy's draft manuscript. There is no published version. Who would want to be judged on their rough drafts? A final version might well have been somewhat different and more polished. Unfortunately this was never produced. What we do have though, is informed and based on detailed research over time and an invaluable account that deserves further attention.

In the summer of 1945, aged sixty-seven, Myvanwy was knocked down by a car and spent some weeks in hospital. The sisters had left Gwynfa and were living in private hotels. At this point Olwen was at the Forest Lodge Hotel in Headington, Oxford and Myvanwy was at the Ivy House Hotel in Marlborough, Wiltshire.

Olwen's letters to her sister were concerned with wartime rationing and her fears, and make sad reading. She referred to everything seeming 'so unreal and nightmarish' and fretted about Myvanwy's health. On 28

November 1945, the day on which the Sir John Rhŷs lecture was given at the British Academy in London, Myvanwy died.

As *Thicker Than Water*, Leonore Davidoff's aptly titled study of siblings between 1780-1920 shows, they frequently provide life's longest relationship.[109] For Myvanwy and Olwen, the term 'sisterhood' seems to have had a double meaning. The death of her sister, after all they had shared, must have been devastating for Olwen, even though the society that had just returned to peace had become tragically inured to loss.

Olwen was now in her late sixties, teaching French three mornings a week, giving a little Italian tuition and studying in the Bodleian. She still corrected entrance papers and interviewed candidates for admission to St Anne's, and marked numerous student translations. At the same time her publisher Blackwell was pressing her for the manuscript of her book. An edited volume entitled *An Anglo-Norman Rhymed Apocalypse* it was produced in collaboration with Sir John Fox for the Anglo-Norman Text Society and published in 1946. In that year Olwen finally retired.

The published output from these two women amounts to rather less than might have been expected from lives that early on had promised so much and appeared so privileged. In 1904 the then president of the United States Theodore Roosevelt had told JR in a letter that he would like to meet Myvanwy when she visited Washington.[110] Richard Jones, Professor of Literature at Vanderbilt University, urged her to see the editor of the *Review of Reviews* who could make suggestions about her getting into print.

Jones wondered whether Myvanwy would consider a joint book with him on the *Idylls of the King* and its predecessors.[111] This was during the second of three trips she had made to the United States in three years as a young woman.

Had she perhaps peaked too soon? The daughters had, in a sense, been hot-housed in their youth. Perhaps the burden of expectancy for the Rhŷs offspring was too great for them to be able to fulfil their own, let alone others' aspirations.

Yet, in many ways they were unfortunate in being adults in the first half of the twentieth century. Not only did they live in a period when expectations for women remained limited but they also had to endure the demands and dislocation of two world wars. Much of their energy was expended far from the safety of scholarly research. When war broke out in September 1939, interspersed with the grim daily news and descriptions of Olwen putting up squares of black paper on the windows and attending meetings in the blackout, Myvanwy's diary recorded her continuing research into medieval Calendars of Inquisition Post Mortem,[112] and the likelihood that her research would not get published.

However, just as their father left a valuable legacy of public service and both parents had spent their early adult lives teaching, so their daughters deserve recognition for more than their publications. Olwen was a pioneer in higher education for women. Like JR, she was a philologist though stressed that 'Philology was never my sujet de prédilection'.[113]

She taught the linguistics of Old French but as her old friend, the eminent Modern Languages tutor at Somerville

Mildred Pope put it, she was also 'a lover of literature and of language as a means of expression of thought and feeling'.[114] Olwen appreciated the 'shades of meanings of words and constructions'.

It was several generations of students who really gained from Olwen's erudition. One of her wartime students, who became a head teacher at a girls' grammar school, remembers arriving at St Anne's as a 'shy country girl' who was made to feel comfortable in the challenging classes (on the development of the French language and old French texts) held by the learned, but never intimidating, Miss Rhŷs. If a student made a mistake, she simply uttered 'Oh, my poor friend'. She was gentle, encouraging and remained very elegant.[115]

Olwen died on 10 April 1953. One former student, M. F. Appleby of the Foreign Office, recalled in an obituary how her 'beauty and brilliance' had been a legend of her childhood and persisted to the end. 'To us', she wrote, 'she was the personification of Oxford'. This suggests just how much had been achieved by this woman who was, for so long, denied her degree.

This obituary was, however, also something of a caricature of the otherworldly academic woman, raising questions about the pitfalls of generalising from such sources. Olwen we are told, was 'out of touch with ordinary worries' and 'to make a bed or a cup of tea were tasks outside her experience'.

Yet this was not so. Olwen had immersed herself for long hours in war service in gruelling conditions, from tuberculosis dispensaries in Hampshire to a remote part of Serbia. In 1918 she had done a term's training (including exams) at White Lodge, a school of domestic science attached to Sherborne School for Girls. Here Olwen had learned to smock, to cook roast dinners, make blackberry and apple tarts, sago moulds, type, do double entry bookkeeping, laundry, first aid and polish stairs until her back ached.[116] Hilda Clark's diary shows that it was Olwen who made curtains and chair covers for the flat the women were sharing in Portsmouth in 1919.

Students would have seen only one side of their tutor, and Olwen was especially self-contained. Hilda Clark, who was used to clever, busy sisters and other strong-minded women, declared her to be 'the most difficult person to understand I ever lived with'.[117] She was more versatile than many suspected and certainly far from ignorant of domestic demands.

However, for a woman of her background and time, training for such work was perceived as a means to an end, for use in service for others rather than in taking care of herself. That, her upbringing had taught her, was not really *her* task even though for much of the Second World War Olwen (always more practical than Myvanwy) helped the housekeeper-cum-cook Dorothy in the Gwynfa household, where they had taken in a lodger.[118]

Olwen's will reflected her commitment to study and students. St Anne's was left £1,000 for research work in Medieval Romance Language and Literature or Medieval History.[119] The College established the Olwen Rhŷs Scholarship. It still exists today, covering the college fees of one graduate a year.

As a gesture in memory of Myvanwy, Olwen left an equal sum to Newnham College, Cambridge for research work in Medieval History. Following in the footsteps of her father, after other legacies were settled, the residue from the remaining £22,000 was left to Oxford University for the promotion of Celtic study and research as the Principal of Jesus College, the Jesus Professor of Celtic and the University's Vice-Chancellor saw fit.

As for Myvanwy's long-term but incomplete biographical project, Olwen had asked Sir Idris Foster (who held the Chair in Celtic Studies at Jesus College) if he would finish the biography. This never happened, though she gave him the voluminous Rhŷs archive. The papers were eventually deposited in the National Library of Wales in 1978, when Foster retired. Thanks to this archive, and to JR's book collection in Aberystwyth University, the life and achievements of Sir John Rhŷs have been recorded for posterity.[120] The papers at Aberystwyth include details of Myvanwy's many years of research into her father's life and the sisters' correspondence in English and Welsh, whilst the Bodleian Library holds invaluable Rhŷs material, including the sisters' sporadic diaries.[121]

Miss Myvanwy Rhŷs MA also enjoyed another distinction. In 1930 she was elected to the Council of the prestigious Honourable Society of Cymmrodorion.[122] She noted in her diary that she was the only lady present at the annual meeting in London.[123] Yet the society's report of this event says nothing about Myvanwy as a scholar of Welsh history in her own right. She is simply described as 'daughter of a former chairman of the council'.[124] She did, however, become a vice-president a few years later.

Myvanwy and Olwen followed in their eminent parents' footsteps in a number of ways. Together they suggest a remarkable, close and progressive family. Yet their life stories, encompassing the late nineteenth and half of the twentieth century, suggest that they also deserve recognition as two highly intelligent and plucky individuals in their own right. Their early scholarship was eulogised by the press but this camouflages the fact that, like other late Victorian women, they also had to overcome considerable hurdles in their determination to pursue academic success. Not until they were middle-aged did they even possess the right to put a cross on a voting form in a national election.

Notes

[1] This essay was developed from the Centennial Lecture I gave at 'From the Celtic Hinterland: Sir John Rhŷs Centennial Commemorations' at the National Library of Wales, December 2015, the second of two conferences exploring his life and work. JRP = Sir John Rhŷs Papers in the National Library of Wales, Aberystwyth. Myvanwy and Olwen's diaries and papers are in the Bodleian Libraries, University of Oxford. Unless otherwise indicated, manuscript references are from this source.

[2] *The Times* 10 December 1915.

[3] In his time this small college grew in size and reputation, becoming one of the more progressive Oxford colleges. See M.G. Brock and M.C. Curthoys (eds.), *The History of the University of Oxford: Volume viii. Nineteenth Century Oxford. Part 2*, Clarendon Press, 2000, p. 124.

[4] *The Times* 22 December 1915. See T.M Charles-Edwards, 'John Rhŷs. Celtic Studies and the Welsh Past' in Neil Evans and Huw Pryce (eds.) *Writing a Small Nation's Past. Wales in comparative perspective 1850-1950*, Ashgate, 2013, pp. 165-77.

[5] According to Myvanwy, JRP, B2/1/2, Box 103. This may well have been part of Borough Road Normal College.

[6] JRP, B2/1/1, Box 103.

[7] Ibid, Myvanwy's words.

[8] *Welsh Outlook*, 3/1, January 1916.

[9] *Cymru Fydd,* Series 4/2, February 1891.

[10] *Y Gymraes,* xv/179, August 1911 in JRP B2/2/1

[11] Ogam/Ogham is an alphabet that was used (especially in the 5c and 6c AD) for Irish and Old Welsh inscriptions on stone.

[12] *Aberystwyth Observer and Merionethshire News* 22 January 1891 in JRP B2/2/2.

[13] The letter was printed in *Baner ac Amserau Cymru* 11 March 1891.

[14] MS. Eng. Misc. e680, 8 June 1899.

[15] JRP, B1/1/1, Letter of 18 November 1880.

[16] JRP, B2/2/1, Letter of 19 May 1881.

[17] She occasionally spelt her name thus, using the modern Welsh spelling.

[18] Myvanwy's diary for 1893 shows that Elspeth held a High School Committee meeting in their drawing room at their Oxford home. The housekeeper Mrs. Hughes also mentions a High School Committee in her diary, JRP, B3/4, Diary, 8 January 1897, and various meetings of Liberal women.

[19] *Jackson's Oxford Journal* 24 May 1890, 30 May 1891 (Myvanwy won it two years running but on the second occasion it passed to another pupil). Ada Müller's mother Georgiana was the founder and president of Oxford's anti-suffragists. Her father, Sir Friedrich Max Müller, was a noted philologist and orientalist.

[20] JRP, B2/2/2.

[21] *Carnarvon and Denbigh Herald* 13 January 1893.

[22] *Western Mail* 21 December 1893.

[23] *The Queen* 24 January 1891.

[24] JRP, B2/2/2.

[25] *Cymru Fydd,* Series 4/2, February 1891.

[26] JRP, B1/1/2, Letter of 4 February 1891.

[27] Carol Dyhouse, 'The British Federation of University Women and the Status of Women in Universities 1907-1939' in *Women's History Review,* 4/4, 1995, p. 469.

[28] See Essay 1. For the scandal see W. Gareth Evans, 'A

Victorian Cause Célèbre', *Planet,* 102, December 1993-January 1994, pp. 80-86; David Roberts, *Bangor University 1884-2009*, University of Wales Press, 2009, pp. 108-111; J. Gwynn Williams, *University College of North Wales Foundations 1884-1927*, University of Wales Press, 1985, pp. 104-7; *Western Mail* 4 March, 28, 29, 31 July, 5 August 1893; *North Wales Chronicle* 24 December 1892, 4 March, 29 April, 2 September 1893. For a more sympathetic reading see Sara Delamont, 'Distant Dangers and Forgotten Standards: Pollution control strategies in the British Girls' School 1860-1920', *Women's History Review*, 2/2, 1993, pp. 246-7.

[29] The first two Principals of its Cardiff equivalent (Aberdare Hall) were not even paid a salary. Beth Jenkins, 'Women's Professional Employment in Wales.1880-1939', Cardiff, University, PhD 2016, p. 14.

[30] She did not attempt to render non-Greek sounds like 'w' and 'j' with Greek letters. Neither did she attempt phonetic equivalence elsewhere. So, having decided for example, that κ would represent the letter c however pronounced, quite often the result was alphabetical hybrids. Thus 'which' became 'whiκh'.

[31] MS. Eng. Misc. e676 from p. 47.

[32] JRP, B3/4

[33] St Anne's College Library Archives, G.6. *The Ship*, 1.

[34] MS. Eng. Misc. e676, 1893 nd.

[35] JRP, B2/2/1, Letter nd.

[36] JRP, B1/1/2, Letter of 23 July 1898.

[37] Newnham College Register, 1895 entrants, Newnham College Archives, Cambridge.

[38] Ibid, B2/2/1, Letter of 6 March 1916.

[39] MS. Eng. Misc. e679, p. 72.

[40] MS. Eng. Misc. e677, undated Notes.

[41] Admittedly, not all of Myvanwy's code has been deciphered. What has been sampled suggests that she reverted to code when writing about the foibles of others rather than recording her own actions or feelings.

[42] She was the sister-in-law of the eminent French philologist Paul Meyer. The sisters stayed at his home in 1901-2 whilst pursuing their studies in Paris. http://schuchardt.uni-graz.at/id/letter/817.

[43] This political scandal deeply divided French society from 1894. Dreyfusards saw the conviction of Captain Dreyfus for treason as an appalling example of anti-Semitic behaviour, a gross travesty of justice, and applauded Emile Zola's intervention. Not until 1906 was Dreyfus exonerated.

[44] MS. Eng. Misc. e681, 30 August, 9 September 1899.

[45] Logos comes from the Greek for 'word', 'discourse' or "reason'. Myvanwy's research was on the New Testament conception of the Logos. In the Gospel of John, Christ was 'the Word' made flesh.

[46] MS. Eng. Misc. e700, 9 May 1922. In 1921 she did a course in French phonetics at University College, London.

[47] See St Anne's College Annual Reports, 1911; Brock and Curthoys, *The History of the University of Oxford*, p.288.

[48] MS. Eng. Misc. e699.

[49] Vera Brittain, *The Women at Oxford: A Fragment of History*, Harrap, 1960, p.160.

[50] Katherine Bradley, '"Faith, Perseverance and Patience": the History of the Women's Suffrage Movement in Oxford, 1870-1918' in Katherine Bradley and Helen Sweet (eds.), *Women in the Professions, Politics and Philanthropy 1840*, Trafford Publishing, 2009, pp.189-225; June Balshaw, 'Sharing the Burden: The Pethick Lawrences and Women's Suffrage' in

Angela V. John and Claire Eustance (eds.), *The Men's Share? Masculinities, Male Support and Women's Suffrage in Britain, 1890-1920*, Routledge, 1997, pp. 135-157.

[51] JRP, B2/1/1, Box 103.

[52] JRP, B1/1/2, Letter of 9 March ny. (but 1888). Becker was the first secretary of the National Society for Women's Suffrage.

[53] Ibid, B1/1/2, Letter of 12 May 1905.

[54] *Women's Suffrage Journal* 1 July 1873. Becker spoke at the meeting held at Lincoln College.

[55] Oxford and district had its share of militant action from 1912.

[56] Chaired by Jessie Payne Margoliouth, daughter of the Dean of Canterbury and wife of the Revd. D.S. Margoliouth, a Fellow of New College and, like her father, an Arabic scholar. Bradley, '"Faith, Perseverance and Patience"', pp. 196-7.

[57] Myvanwy also sat on a sub-committee in 1907 to organise a campaign across the county.

[58] *Oxford Times* 11 January 1906.

[59] *Ibid* 29 June 1908; Uncatalogued Papers of Helena Deneke, Box 19. Minute Book 1904-15, Report for 1907-8, Bodleian Libraries, University of Oxford.

[60] JRP, B3/1. Letter of 13 January 1913.

[61] Ibid.

[62] This was one of several deputations to Lloyd George. The radical war correspondent Henry W. Nevinson (who had been an Oxford student and was Margaret Wynne Nevinson's husband) was a representative for the militant Men's Political Union. He was disappointed that Lloyd George did not rise to their challenges. The following year he published a 3d tract called 'The Claim on Oxford' for its Oxford University branch.

[63] *Oxford Journal* 26 November 1913; *The Times* 29 November 1913.

[64] The preservation of folklore and history in triple groupings.

[65] JRP, B3/4, 7 June 1912.

[66] MS.Eng. Misc. e698, 17 February 1916. Discussions included a debate on 'To what extent the suffragist is pinned to the skirts of Labour during the war'.

[67] MS. Eng. Lett. e.131. A. H. Sayce, Letter to Mifanwy [sic] Rhŷs, Bodleian Libraries, University of Oxford.

[68] MS. Eng. Misc. e698, 9 April 1916. The Rhŷs Papers include affectionate letters from Megan Lloyd George to Myvanwy, for example on 6 and 31 March 1916, JRP, B2/2/2, Folder 2.

[69] For this section see MS. Eng. Misc. e699 and the five-year diary of Hilda Clark, 1914-19, HC/6/21 in the Hilda Clark Papers, Alfred Gillett Trust (formerly the Clark Archive), Street, Somerset; FEWVRC/Missions/2/2/4/1, Reports on Samoëns, Friends' House Library, London and Sandra Stanley Holton, *Quaker Women: Personal Life, Memory and Radicalism in the Lives of Women Friends (1780-1930)*, Routledge, 2007.

[70] Hilda Clark Diary 15 April 1917.

[71] Ibid 8 February 1918. See too 21 January 1918.

[72] Ibid 31 March 1918.

[73] Ibid 16 December 1921.

[74] An urgent appeal in the summer of 1917 from the French authorities requested British women to manage rest-huts and canteens. One was established near Châlons and another near Reims. Workers were expected to stay for four months. Box 19, Deneke Papers.

[75] She continued to support the Fund after returning home. In 1920, for example, she subscribed £47 to this 'work of

mercy'. *The Times* 9 August 1920. The sisters supported Polish and Russian Relief work. Olwen also sent £20 towards the rebuilding of the University of Caen in Normandy. Founded by John of Lancaster in 1432, it had been completely destroyed by aerial bombing.

[76] FEWVRC/ Missions/9/5/4/3. Memorandum on the work of the Serbian Relief Fund, 30 March 1919, Friends' House Library, London.

[77] MS. Eng. Lett. d337, Letters from MR, 13 January 1920.

[78] FEWVRC/Missions/9/5/2/2, Friends' House Library.

[79] MS. Eng. Misc. 1920, MS. Eng. Misc. e699.

[80] MS. Eng. Misc. e683, 29 December 1919.

[81] MS. Eng. Lett. d337, Letters from MR, 6 January 1920.

[82] Ibid 31 January 1920.

[83] MS. Eng. Lett. d333, 23 March 1920, loose leaf diary, Bodleian.

[84] FEWVRC/Missions/12/3/18/1, card to Ernest Holliday, 12 December 1920, Friends' House Library.

[85] See W. Gareth Evans, Robert Smith and Gareth Elwyn Jones, *Examining the Secondary Schools of Wales 1896-2000*, University of Wales Press, 2008, pp. 6-12.

[86] MS. Eng. Misc. e.699, 10 June-24 June 1919. See too ED 35/34/7, National Archives Kew.

[87] See Evans, Smith and Elwyn Jones, *Examining the Secondary Schools*, pp.22-9.

[88] JRP, Appointments Diary, Box 88 A4/2.

[89] JRP, B3/1, Letter of 7 April 1913.

[90] Renan published an unprecedented comparative approach to Celtic literature: *Essai sur la Poésie des Races Celtiques* (1854). JR met him as part of the Cambrian Archaeological Association's visit to Brittany in 1889.

[91] MS. Eng. Misc. e698, from 7 March 1916 to the end of the month.

[92] For Myvanwy's correspondence with Sayce see MS. Eng. Lett. e131.

[93] In 1920, for example, she stayed with Sayce in Edinburgh, discussing his early impressions of his friend.

[94] On 1 August 1918.

[95] MS. Eng. Misc. 9 97/1-4.

[96] In 1929 Myvanwy gave the 1913 oil painting of her father by Christopher Williams to the National Museum of Wales.

[97] Ms. Eng. Misc. e698, June 1918.

[98] MS. Eng. Misc. e685, 21 August 1923. For details of these clubs see Peter Gordon and David Doughan, *Dictionary of British Women's Organisations 1825-1960*, Woburn Press, 2001.

[99] MS. Eng. Misc. e686.

[100] Katherine Holden, *The Shadow of Marriage: Singleness in England 1914-60*, Manchester University Press, 2010. In July 1919 Hilda Clark's diary refers to O having a 'trying time with man [sic] who wants to marry M'. 'M' may well have been Myvanwy (Olwen had dined with Hilda Clark that evening) but, if so, nothing more is known about him. Hilda Clark Diary, 4 July 1919.

[101] See Maxine Berg, *A Woman in History: Eileen Power 1889-1940*, Cambridge University Press, 1996 and Alice Clark, *The Working Life of Women in the Seventeenth Century*, George Routledge, 1919.

[102] The society had established its Record Series in 1892 to support the publication of archive material. This was volume xiii.

[103] He also taught and encouraged the future Labour politician, Ellen Wilkinson.

[104] See *Manchester Guardian* 8 December 1936 and a review in *History,* 23/89, June 1938, p. 84 that refers to the 'Almost super-meticulous care' given to the reproduction of the Latin texts. Margaret Sharp (ed.) *Counts of the Constables of Bristol Castle in the Thirteenth and Fourteenth Centuries,* XXXIV, Bristol Record Society, 1982.

[105] Another, less likely, candidate was R. Ellis Roberts who was briefly editor of the *New Statesman.*

[106] MS. Eng. Misc. e699.

[107] For the draft chapters see JRP, B2/1/1, Box 103.

[108] Hermione Lee has, however, warned against too stark a divide between Victorian biography and twentieth century 'new biography'. Hermione Lee, *Biography: A Very Short Introduction*, OUP, 2009, p. 73.

[109] Leonore Davidoff, *Thicker Than Water: Siblings and their Relations 1780-1820*, Oxford University Press, 2012.

[110] In JRP, A1/1/35, Letter 13 February 1904.

[111] JRP, B2/2/1, folder 2. Letter of 20 February 1904.

[112] In feudal society these were local enquiries carried out on behalf of the crown to ascertain what income and rights might be due after the deaths of tenants-in-chief.

[113] In *The Ship*, 43,1953, pp. 21-3.

[114] *Ibid*.

[115] Personal communication, January 2017.

[116] It began as a school of domestic science in 1912 for old girls and other students, providing training in all branches of house management. However, as early as 1903, Elizabeth Hughes, the family's housekeeper, recorded that Olwen had started going to cookery classes in Oxford. JRP, B3/4,24 September 1903.

[117] Hilda Clark Diary 18 February 1918.

[118] See Myvanwy's account of these years in her diaries for these years. For example, on 27 September 1942 Olwen gathered beans from the garden. 'Darling O spent the rest of the morning cutting them up. I tried but my knife would not cut and I whimpered and cried off'. MS. Eng. Misc. e695, 8 September 1942.

[119] *The Times* 28 August 1953.

[120] The collection (117 boxes) was uncatalogued for a further thirty-three years.

[121] In December 1920 Myvanwy explained in a letter that she had lost her diary. FEWVRC/ Missions/12/3/18/1, Friends' House Library.

[122] This venerable organisation, originally founded in the eighteenth century by London Welsh men, was influential in developing national institutions within Wales as well as Welsh literature and culture. For further information see www.cymmrodorion.org.

[123] MS. Eng. Misc. e686, 20 November 1930. Myvanwy was not the first woman to sit on the council but it was rare. Mrs W. Cadwaladr Davies did so in 1907-8. See too Essay 1.

[124] *Transactions of the Honourable Society of Cymmrodorion*, 1929-30. Report of the Council for the year ending 9 November 1930. Olwen was also a member of the society, as was Lady Rhondda. See too Essay 1 above, p. 84.

5

1922

A Year in the Remarkable Life of Lady Rhondda[1]

Life writing has long assumed ingenious forms. One recent and popular trend has been for the partial biography. This has even been reduced to covering merely a year in the life of an individual. It can be a valuable snapshot, a means of illuminating our understanding of both a person and a period. James Shapiro provides an inspiring example of this, both in his biography *1599: A Year in the Life of William Shakespeare*, (2005), and in his subsequent volume, *1606: William Shakespeare and the Year of Lear,* (2015) which matches playwriting to the historical moment.[2] Jonathan Schneer's *London 1900:The Imperial Metropolis*[3] is an evocative exploration of the city and its relationship with the British Empire, whilst Juliet Nicolson's *The Perfect Summer* makes 1911 the biographical focus of a time before the First World War appeared to change everything.[4]

I've taken a year in the life of Margaret Haig Thomas, Lady Rhondda. I've plumped for 1922 but could have opted for several other dates that loomed large in her personal and professional calendar. 1913 was one such year. Margaret was thirty then and living in Monmouthshire near Caerleon with her husband Humphrey Mackworth. This only daughter of the immensely wealthy industrialist and Liberal politician D.A. Thomas, and Sybil Haig Thomas of Llanwern, was the secretary of the Newport branch of the suffragette Women's Social and Political Union. She was arrested after setting a letterbox box alight in Newport. She had travelled to London for her incendiary materials (as with Edith Picton-Turbervill, the London train was significant in her literal and symbolic journey). She smuggled her ammunition in a flimsy covered basket as she travelled home – surely for the only time in her life – in a third-class railway carriage. Margaret narrowly avoided detection on this occasion but her arson attack was noticed and she was briefly imprisoned that summer. She responded by going on hunger strike while in Usk Gaol for her militant suffrage activity.

Alternatively, I might have selected 1926 a year indelibly linked in Welsh history with the General Strike and protracted miners' lockout as the essay on Menna Gallie demonstrates. As a director of a number of coal companies, 1926 inevitably had a big impact on Margaret but it was also the year in which she was elected as the first and, to date, sole female president of the Institute of Directors, a position she held for a decade. At this time she became a key figure in the revival of pressure for extending the vote to all British women, and she and Mrs Pankhurst (recently returned to London after running a tea shop in the south of France), spoke at what proved to be the last mass demonstration in London for equal rights. Margaret chaired the group organising it and helped to orchestrate the activities that culminated in the equal franchise legislation of 1928.

1926 also gave Margaret a new role as editor of *Time and Tide*, the weekly review she had founded in 1920 and funded for the rest of her life. One of the most innovative, imaginative and adaptable of papers, it reflected the views of the thinking woman and man, especially the newly enfranchised woman over thirty. Margaret would remain editor until her death in 1958.

Another possibility was 1933, so momentous for European history. Margaret's autobiography *This Was My World* was published that year, though she would live for a further quarter of a century. It provides a somewhat partial account in more ways than one. It is, nevertheless, a useful source for historians of Wales, with its focus on her early years. The lives of better-off young Welsh women have tended, at best, to be tagged on to modern historical accounts of Welsh society in the late nineteenth and early twentieth centuries, so her reflections are especially valuable since they provide a different kind of militancy from that usually associated with South Wales. 1933 marked a new stage in Margaret's personal life as she and her paper's literary editor Theodora Bosanquet, Henry James's former amanuensis, decided to set up home together.

I could have selected a date during Margaret's final decade. In 1950 she became the first woman president of a Welsh college: the University College of South Wales and Monmouthshire, the forerunner of Cardiff University. At the end of her five-year stint she received an honorary degree from the University of Wales. As she had dropped out of Oxford University after just two terms – something she had long since regretted – she especially welcomed this. For years she had advocated higher education as of paramount importance for young women.

Yet although claims can probably be made for any year to have witnessed changes with long-term implications, 1922 seems particularly well-qualified, prompting significant shifts on a national and international scale, as well as providing a valuable frozen snapshot of Margaret's development as a public figure.

That year the findings of Sir Eric Geddes' Committee on National Expenditure set in train what became known as the 'Geddes Axe', accelerating severe cutbacks in spending on education, housing and health as part of a policy of post-war retrenchment. The British Broadcasting Company (the BBC's initial name) was created in October, and a month later daily broadcasting began. The Carlton Club meeting of MPs soon led to the fall of the Lloyd George coalition (there followed in 1923 the famous committee of Conservative MPs, known as The 1922 Committee). The November general election saw Labour replace the Liberal Party as the main challengers to the

Conservatives, with Ramsay MacDonald, Labour's leader, in charge of the opposition. It also marked a political watershed for Wales: MacDonald's decisive electoral success at Aberavon reflected a decisive shift towards the hegemony of Labour in Wales. The Labour Party won half the seats there, sweeping the board in the mining valleys.

T.S. Eliot's *The Waste Land* was published in book form in December, the month that saw the first female solicitor in Britain. 1922 also witnessed Winifred Coombe Tennant of Cadoxton Lodge in the Neath Valley as the first female British delegate to the League of Nations, and London gained its first female mayor, Ada Salter, who also became the first woman Labour mayor in Britain.

Time and Tide picked up on any 'Firsts' for women. It also commented on and discussed – seriously and satirically – the key cultural and political events of the day, whether through editorials, news features or, from 1922, in the 'Weekly Crowd' poems of Eleanor Farjeon, who was also penning verses for the socialist press.[5] There were plenty of newsworthy events, some ominous, from further afield. The British Protectorate over Egypt was terminated in February and Egypt became independent. Civil war began in the Irish Free State that summer, whilst October saw the Fascist March on Rome. Mussolini became Prime Minister of Italy.

1922 was a seminal year for one of Margaret's most important public campaigns for equality: the long battle for women peers in their own right to take their seats in the House of Lords. It was to have major constitutional repercussions and was of immense significance in the long struggle for women's equal rights. The year also provides an excellent example of the variety of demands that Margaret juggled in what was her most productive decade. It marked too a watershed in her personal relations, and this had an impact on her links with Wales.

When Margaret's father D.A. Thomas died prematurely in 1918, he had recently been made Viscount Rhondda as a reward for his wartime work. A supporter of women's suffrage, he had taken the highly unusual step of obtaining special permission from the king for the right of his beloved (and only legitimate) child to inherit his title.

Keen to play her part in the new post-war world in which she had finally received the vote and witnessed the first few women MPs, Margaret stated her intention to petition the king to receive a Writ of summons to Parliament, as did other new Peers of the Realm. She was well aware that peeresses in their own right – currently two dozen of them – did not *sit* in the Lords but she believed that the new Sex Disqualification (Removal) Act of 1919 (which had enabled, for example, women jurors) boosted her claim. It stated that a person should not be disqualified on the grounds of sex from exercising a public function.

Margaret's petition was referred to the Committee for Privileges of the House of Lords. Her case was heard on 2 March 1922 and she was granted her Writ by a majority of seven to one. On that day Myvanwy Rhŷs noted in her diary: 'Women in House of Lords. Lady Rhondda's application allowed without opposition'.[6] The glad tidings were broadcast in the press from Argentina to Ceylon. The *Manchester Evening News* even wondered whether a Lady Archbishop or Lord Chancellor would follow.[7] No report from this committee had been resisted since 1869, and even then the motion had not been carried. Margaret seemed to be in an unassailable position and about to take her rightful seat. But the Lord Chancellor, Lord Birkenhead, saw matters differently.

Birkenhead was a powerful man. As Edith Picton-Turbervill explained (in a 1937 article about the workings of Parliament), he was one of three people – the others were the Prime Minister and the archbishop of Canterbury – in charge of the country when the monarch was abroad.[8] He was not only the head of the judiciary but also the presiding officer of the House of Lords. He argued in the Lords against the acceptance of the writ, effectively challenging the relevance of the 1919 legislation and stating that its purpose was to remove existing disabilities rather than confer new rights. He secured an enlarged committee to reconsider Margaret's case and 'packed' it by placing himself and other opponents of women's rights on it.

On 18 and 19 May Margaret, her mother and the former actress Elizabeth Robins nervously attended the hearing. Birkenhead indulged in detailed and arcane arguments of constitutional law and succeeded in swaying the committee. A clear majority now rejected Margaret's claim. Birkenhead produced a lengthy report. As F.E. Smith, he had led the Commons attack on the compromise proposal for women's suffrage known as the Conciliation Bill. Indeed, he challenged the automatic right of anybody, female or male, to a vote, and held that, at times of crisis, women's opinions might 'prove a source of instability and disaster to the State'.[9]

The whole issue of women in the Upper House touched a raw nerve for both Birkenhead and Margaret. It struck at the heart of this clubbable man's world, threatening the ultimate male sanctuary. He told Baroness Ravensdale that 'he would rather have us anywhere than the House of Lords'.[10] For Margaret too, much was at stake here. For her claim was not just for herself. She recognised that it signified a vital stage in the completion of parliamentary equality and as Cheryl Law has pointed out, 'a symbol of entry to the ultimate seat of traditional political power'.[11]

The press made the most of the situation in cartoons and articles. Margaret did not give up. But she had a long battle ahead, since there were plenty of other antediluvian peers as well as some enlightened and progressive ones. She became known as 'the Persistent Peeress',[12] and it was not until 1958 that the first women – life peers – were able to take their seats in the Lords. They did so just after Margaret's death. Not until 1963 did hereditary peeresses gain this right, and only then was Britain permitted to sign up to the United Nations Convention on the Political Rights of Women. Now Margaret's portrait hangs in the House of Lords.

1922 saw Margaret involved in equality issues on several fronts. She had founded the Women's Industrial Council that sought to help women's employment opportunities post-war, and she chaired (from 1920) the Consultative Council on General Health Questions set up under a new Health Act. The shortcomings of the Sex Disqualification (Removal) Act of 1919 had been partly responsible for Margaret starting the Six Point Group (SPG) two years later with its progressive six point Charter demanding effective legislation. The points tackled issues such as child assault, the age of consent, and equal guardianship rights for men and women. It even sought equal pay for teachers. Gender equality was paramount in this social betterment programme that received considerable publicity in *Time and Tide*.

In 1922 Margaret was busy as the SPG's chairman (she never liked the term chairwoman). Lloyd George's coalition government introduced its own Criminal Law Amendment Bill in February, and the SPG responded, pushing for eighteen as the age of consent. Margaret addressed a big meeting at London's Queen's Hall in March where she impressed the young Vera Brittain. In *Testament of Youth* she recalled Margaret's passionate speech, her flushed face and indignant blue eyes.[13]

So inspired were Brittain and her good friend Winifred Holtby that the young women now cut their political teeth addressing audiences at Hyde Park on behalf of the SPG. They would both play an important part in Margaret's life in years to come. The legislation was passed in the summer. Sixteen became the age of consent. This was a compromise, but better than the age of thirteen, and it showed the effectiveness of the SPG as a pressure group.

1922 was an election year. The SPG devised an imaginative tactic to name and shame those MPs whose record on women's rights was not good. Before the election it published in *Time and Tide* a Black List cutting across party allegiances: the paper was resolutely non-party at this time. It named opponents. A White List praised supporters. Since there were few women MPs, the latter list included not only the Tory Lady Astor and Liberal Mrs Wintringham, but also Captain Wedgwood Benn and Isaac Foot. The role models were treated to an annual luncheon at the Hyde Park Hotel. A Drab List exposed those who had not lived up to their promise.

Margaret, the daughter of a Liberal, had rejected party politics in the wake of Prime Minister Asquith's opposition to women's suffrage. Nevertheless, in November the journal *Welsh Outlook* suggested that she was the one Welsh woman who could be a real parliamentary leader. She was now president of the National Women Citizens' Association, formed in 1917, part of a burgeoning movement with branches throughout the country dedicated to promoting women as active citizens in post-war society.[14]

How the press at home and abroad treated Margaret is revealing. This can be seen in the way that American newspapers depicted her during a visit to the United States in August 1922. This trip was primarily a welcome holiday after the gruelling battles over the peerage and a busy time with her weekly newspaper, as well as involvement with campaigns for women's rights and business matters.

Margaret travelled with Elizabeth Pridden, an old school friend from St Leonards School in St Andrews, who was now a teacher at this prestigious Scottish school. The two women stayed in Connecticut at the gracious Stonington Manor. But Margaret could never resist publicity for her causes – she used to declare 'Publicity is Power' – and she was, after all, a journalist. So she gave various interviews.

The *New York Evening Mail* called her 'a handsome, well-built viscountess'.[15] Predictably, much attention was paid to her appearance. One paper commented that she was 'a vivacious young woman' with the rosy cheeks of a seventeen year old. She was almost forty. The *New York Tribune* noted that Margaret was the British Empire's leading businesswoman, yet possessed 'a quite old-fashioned femininity', and was 'refreshingly wholesome' in appearance.

Yet although some papers used her appearance as reassurance that the masculine worlds of business and politics had not adversely affected her femininity, others implied the antithesis. A Los Angeles newspaper described her as 'tall, athletic, with the stride of a comely man' in her sternly utilitarian, well-cut clothes, short skirts, low heels and no hat. The *Boston Sunday Post* noted that her face assumed 'almost masculine lines' when talking about suffrage. The 'taint' and fear of suffrage was always there just beneath the surface. Another paper remarked that Margaret's handclasp was 'quick and firm'.

At a time when issues of gender identity were increasingly addressed but often by indirect means, the British press portrayed *her* gestures knowingly. The *Daily Mail* was not alone in describing Margaret 'whistling at the top of her voice like a jolly errand boy' as she walked down to street level from her office in Victoria Street. Margaret was frequently the token woman in the insistently masculine boardrooms running heavy industry and only too used to being seen as different by those she worked with as well as by those who saw her from afar.

She now sat on the boards of more than thirty companies, embracing mining, shipping, railway and other interests, often sharing directorships with two Welsh men: her father's protégée Henry Seymour Berry and D.R.

Llewellyn. It was rare for women to be prominent in big business yet Margaret chaired eleven boards.

1922 was a tough year for the South Wales coal trade. At the Consolidated Cambrian's AGM in March, Margaret and the Board were told that for the first time there would be no dividend on ordinary shares. But if the economic situation was serious for employers after the 1921 strike, it was grim for those losing or seeking work. British male unemployment alone now exceeded two million. In contrast, Margaret's private accounts show that her total income amounted to £9,072 for just the first half of 1922.[16] In 1922-4, the average annual earnings for women across seven occupational classes were £103.

Margaret was also unusual in that her professional life encompassed both big business and Bloomsbury. In October 1922 a London paper noted: 'It is, I fancy, in Viscountess Rhondda's drawing-room that I have seen more women writers to the square inch than anywhere else'.[17] Readers of *Time and Tide* were treated to accounts of the monthly meeting of the Consultative Committee of Women's Organisations, as well as discussion of infant health and National Baby Week (Margaret was vice-chairman in 1922). But in amongst such news and features were also detailed reports, sometimes covering several pages, of items usually deemed of masculine interest: minutes of the AGMs of Welsh colliery companies on whose boards Margaret sat. Between mid-March and early April *Time and Tide* readers could learn more than they probably wanted to know about not just Consolidated Cambrian but also North's Navigation, D. Davis and Sons, and the Welsh Navigation Steam Coal Company.

Margaret was not yet *Time and Tide's* editor – that followed four years later – but it was, of course, indisputably her creation and, in a sense, her private fiefdom. Its pioneering all-female board was, after all, largely composed of friends. Indeed, although Margaret protested that *Time and Tide* and the SPG were not synonymous, it and other organisations benefitted enormously by having such an opportunity for publicity.

Margaret was clearly prepared to finance more than just her staff and the printing of the paper. Early in 1922, in the name of the paper, she took counsel's opinion on the legality of Glasgow's corporation recent dismissal of married women and received the go-ahead to protest against this in print. She also wrote regularly for the paper, providing signed, unsigned and pseudonymous articles. She contributed fortnightly reviews of plays for the paper under the pseudonym of Anne Doubleday.

The presence of regular features about Wales in a weekly paper that was produced in Fleet Street (and later from Bloomsbury) was, to say the least, unusual. As one correspondent would put it in 1949 when *Time and Tide* ran nine substantial articles on Wales, quite apart from coverage of many things Welsh: 'It is so seldom that one finds in the London Press any indication that more than one nation occupies the area of England and Wales'.[18] Welsh affairs had prominence in the paper from the start, whether reports of sheepdog trials in Aberystwyth or Eisteddfodau and, especially in later years, issues about the self-determination of small nations.

From the First World War onwards Margaret's centre of gravity had shifted from Wales to London. She had been born in Bayswater but spent her childhood and youth in Wales. Nevertheless the London ties had always been strong. Her parents had a flat in Ashley Gardens, Victoria and for three years Margaret attended Notting Hill High School. But she always identified herself as Welsh.

During Lloyd George's premiership she was part of the London Welsh elite (the *crachach*) who graced dinner tables, worked with Margaret Lloyd George in organising Welsh stalls at bazaars, and provided funding for Welsh causes. Lloyd George had stayed at Llanwern in 1909: a photograph of this visit includes Margaret sitting demurely in the front row, looking more like a schoolgirl (complete with shirt and tie) than a married woman in her mid-twenties and militant suffragette. Although Lloyd George and her father had most certainly had their differences, D.A. Thomas' premature death in 1918, hastened by overwork, enhanced his posthumous reputation (most notably as the man who had successfully introduced wartime food rationing to Britain). During the Coalition Margaret was especially well placed in London society.

But whether Margaret's commitment to Wales amounted to anything more than a somewhat romanticised and, at times, expedient notion of Welshness is debatable.

During the First World War she had carefully drawn on patriotism and a sense of national identity in order to persuade young Welsh women to volunteer for women's service in France. But such rhetoric was common then, and propaganda was part of her job.

Private papers show that she was generous to Gwent causes, such as the Royal Gwent Hospital, in the early 1920s. Yet Margaret's espousal of things Welsh was selective. For example, she had always been quite dismissive of her paternal grandmother Rachel Thomas, suggesting that she was a not very interesting or intellectual woman. Yet Rachel Thomas had been highly regarded in Welsh speaking literary circles. A member of the Gorsedd, active in the Cymmrodorion Society and very knowledgeable about genealogy, the Welsh press had compared her to Lady Llanover, the renowned patron and promoter of Welsh cultural life. When Rachel Thomas died in 1896, three special trains conveyed mourners to the public funeral in Aberdare.

Admittedly Margaret had only been twelve when she lost her grandmother, but in later years, despite being an avowed feminist, she played down the significance of a relative whom she might have drawn upon as an early role model. She paid far more attention to her mother's relatives than to her more *arriviste* Thomas connections. Her choices suggest her sense of status, allied to a lack of interest in indigenous Welsh-language culture. She did not speak Welsh, and had grown up in the anglicised south of Monmouthshire, a county that was itself tagged on to Wales in a somewhat complicated relationship. Margaret's relationship to Wales also reflected the liminality of that borderland position, and as a woman whose life straddled Wales and England she, like many of her compatriots, was in danger of falling into the interstices, being perceived as Welsh in England and English in Wales. Her names Thomas and Rhondda were Welsh, but beyond providing her wealth and her title, the latter hardly represented her 'world'.

In 1922 Margaret was known as Lady Rhondda, but

she was also shaking off her other name, that of Mackworth. This was an important factor in shifting her attention away from Wales even though she would continue to visit her mother Sybil in Llanwern every few months for several decades and would, in her last years, rediscover the joys of her mother's Radnorshire home Pen Ithon, where she had spent her holidays as a child.

The First World War had been for Margaret, as for many other women, liberating as well as a time of loss. It had given her public responsibility in terms of highly responsible jobs, and it provided the personal space that she needed. Her marriage in 1908 to Humphrey Mackworth, whose chief interest in life seemed to be hunting, had not been a total disaster but the couple were not compatible. As Margaret put it:

> Humphrey held that no one else should ever read in a room where anyone else wanted to talk. I, brought up in a home in which a father's study was sacred, held, on the contrary, that no one should ever talk in a room where anyone else wanted to read.[19]

Although more tolerant of his wife's suffrage activism than were many husbands, suffrage had absorbed much of Margaret's time and energy pre-war so probably kept the marriage going in these years. The couple had no children. Humphrey was based in Bristol with the army during the war. With Margaret living in London by 1918, they drifted apart.

By early 1922 Margaret had taken out a lease on her London flat Chelsea Court on the Embankment. Helen

Archdale, a committed feminist and former suffragette who edited *Time and Tide,* moved into the flat below. Widowed and with three children, she became Margaret's partner and also her personal secretary. Margaret paid for her children's education. The two women also shared a cottage in Kent and later a large fifteenth century house, not far from Sevenoaks. The rest of Margaret's life would remain woman-centred and primarily focused on south-east England.

By the early twenties there were nearly four-and-a-half times more divorces than there had been pre-war, despite the fact that it remained very costly and shaming. In 1922 Margaret confronted the breakdown of her marriage. Humphrey had already issued her with an ultimatum: unless she lived ten months of the year in Monmouthshire, they should divorce. He was, though, not hoping for a divorce. She felt differently, and was easily the wealthier of the two. They decided that she would sue for divorce on the grounds of his desertion *and* adultery and that he would not contest this. Neither of these claims was strictly true but, at this point, whereas a wife's unfaithfulness alone was considered sufficient grounds for a man to gain a divorce, for a woman wishing to end her marriage, it was necessary to prove more than her husband's infidelity alone. Ironically, had they waited a year, the Matrimonial Causes Act of 1923 would have slightly simplified their case, since adultery by either partner was now accepted as sufficient to grant a divorce.

In 1921, therefore, Margaret and Humphrey set the scene for his desertion by unofficially colluding in the pretence that he had deserted her. In letters designed to be read in court they had to show that Humphrey had sought to separate and Margaret to resist this. On 1 May 1922 Margaret, accompanied by her mother, appeared at London's Law Courts. Margaret was a public figure and paid the price. Newspaper placards proclaimed 'Lady Rhondda's Wrecked Happiness'.

It was a particularly bad time to have to appear in court. Divorce cases were seen by the Sunday and popular press as wonderful opportunities for entertaining and often scurrilous reportage. At the same time it was an opportunity to suggest moral laxity and to re-impose notions of what constituted acceptable femininity in the face of feminism and the suspect freedom that women seemed to be enjoying post-war. In July 1922 the divorce trial in a sensational Society case, Russell versus Russell, involved so much sexual scandal and suggestive reporting that George V complained to the Lord Chancellor (John Russell's mother was Lady Ampthill, Lady of the Bedchamber).[20]

The situation would soon change. The Criminal Justice Act of 1925 forbade photographs to be taken in court, and the Judicial Proceedings Act of the following year prohibited the publication of detailed press reporting of divorce cases.[21] But in 1922 reporters and photographers were free to 'go to town' on scandals. They helped to sell papers at a time when there was a serious circulation war and newspapers still held sway. The *Daily Mail* alone sold more than 1.75 million copies a day.

Even the broadsheets reported how the Visitors' Book of the Midland Hotel St Pancras was produced in court and Lady Rhondda asked whether she recognised any signatures for the night of 5 July.[22] She identified her husband's handwriting. Beneath it was the name Margaret. When asked if she had stayed in the hotel that night, she denied it. Hotel employees were called to attest that they had seen Sir Humphrey Mackworth there, accompanied by a lady (in effect a professional co-respondent hired for the night). The court heard that they had stayed one night. The chambermaid confirmed that she saw them in bed together in the morning. No defence was made. Humphrey's adultery was confirmed.

On 21 December Margaret was granted a decree nisi. The sordid farce had been played out in court and in the press and at a cost that was not just financial. It was now Christmas time. Margaret departed, with her mother, on a cruise for what were literally calmer waters, so ending 1922. It had been a tumultuous year in her public and personal affairs, yet one that signalled the many obstacles that this ambitious and determined woman could expect to face as well as the challenges that she chose to embrace.

Notes

[1] This essay is expanded from a talk I gave to the Honourable Society of Cymmrodorion in London on 18 November 2014. It also draws upon Angela V. John, *Turning the Tide: The Life of Lady Rhondda*, Parthian, 2013.

[2] Published by Faber.

[3] Published by Yale Nota Bene in 2001.

[4] Published by John Murray in 2006.

[5] For a discussion of the variety of views expressed in the paper and the specific contribution of Farjeon see Catherine Clay, *Feminism, Journalism and Literary Culture: Time and Tide 1920-1939*, Edinburgh University Press, forthcoming, Chapter 2.

[6] MS. Eng. Misc. e685, 2 March 1922, Bodleian Libraries, University of Oxford.

[7] For this and other press responses to Margaret's claim see Scrapbook C8 in the D.A. Thomas Papers, National Library of Wales, Aberystwyth.

[8] Edith Picton-Turbervill, 'Glimpses of Parliament', *Great Thoughts,* January 1937.

[9] Quoted in John Campbell, *F.E. Smith, First Earl of Birkenhead*, Jonathan Cape, 1983, p. 280.

[10] Baroness Ravensdale, *In Many Rhythms*, Weidenfeld & Nicolson, 1953, p. 95.

[11] Cheryl Law, *Suffrage and Power: The Women's Movement, 1918-28*, I.B. Tauris, 2000 edition, p. 112.

[12] Alice Fraser, '"The Persistent Peeress"', *Independent Woman*, December 1948.

[13] Vera Brittain, *Testament of Youth*, Virago Press edition, 1978, p. 584.

[14] For an account of their work in one locality see Joanne Smith, 'From Suffrage to Citizenship: The Cardiff and District Women Citizens' Association in Comparative Perspective 1921-1939' in *Llafur*, 11/4, 2015, pp. 26-41.

[15] The comments published in the American and British newspapers cited here can be found in C8, D.A. Thomas Papers.

[16] In private family papers.

[17] In C8, D.A. Thomas Papers.

[18] J. Wynne Lewis in *Time and Tide* 21 May 1949.

[19] Viscountess Rhondda, *This Was My World,* Macmillan, 1933, p. 110.

[20] See Lucy Bland, *Modern Women on Trial: Sexual Transgression in the Age of the Flapper*, Manchester University Press, 2013, Chapter 5.

[21] See *Ibid*, Chapter 3 and Lynda Nead, 'Visual Cultures of the Courtroom: Reflections of History, Law and the Image', *Visual Culture in Britain*, 3/2, 2002.

[22] See, for example, *The Times* 1 May, 22 December 1922.

6

Place, Politics and History
The Life and Novels of Menna Gallie

This Essay is dedicated to the Memory of Annest Wiliam, Menna Gallie's cousin.

When Menna Gallie died in the summer of 1990 at her home in Newport, Pembrokeshire, she was only seventy-one. White-haired and suffering from arthritis, she looked older. To the last, she maintained her wit, capacity to strike out at injustice and gift for storytelling. A superb raconteur, she held court for all who cared to listen, delighting in this ancient tradition and adept at turning even mundane daily events into glorious pieces of drama.

Yet, curiously, when I first met her in the 1970s, she uttered not a syllable for an hour. For my arrival at her home had coincided with an episode of *Pride and Prejudice* on television. Menna much admired Jane Austen's writing and that first meeting ended with a long discussion of English literature. Since Professor Bryce Gallie, Menna's Scottish husband, had retired from his position as Professor of Political Science at the University of Cambridge, the Gallies had made their Pembrokeshire bolt hole their permanent home. My mother was their neighbour, living five doors away, and I was to spend a lot of time with them in the house they called Cilhendre. It was named after the village in her novels.

Menna had studied English alongside some History and Economics at University College, Swansea. She later taught English at various schools (even doing a little tutoring for Raymond Williams at Cambridge University). But her first language was Welsh. She never spoke anything but Welsh to her mother though wrote letters to her in English. She translated Caradog Prichard's novel *Un Nos Ola Leuad* into English under the title *Full Moon* and began translating his *Afal Drwg Adda* (as Adam's Bitter Apple).[1] For her own novels, English was her medium. Yet, as Menna put it so well, 'I was a Welsh speaker who without fail, spoke and wrote with a Welsh accent'.[2]

Menna Humphreys had been born in 1919[3] in Ystradgynlais in Breconshire. Her mother Elizabeth Humphreys (née Williams) was from west Wales, but her father William Thomas Humphreys was a North Walian. He was a colliery engine fitter when Menna was a baby though spent most of his working life as a woodcarver and builder. But inevitably in these colliery communities, the General Strike and Lockout of 1926 dominated the childhood of Menna and her two older sisters.

The family moved to Creunant in the Dulais Valley when Menna was eleven. She was a clever child, and won a place at Neath Grammar School. Going to university marked an important break. War began when she was still a student in Swansea. She did her last Finals exam the day that Paris fell and married the philosophy lecturer Bryce Gallie a month later, just a few days before he left for the army. Menna's war work was for the Inland Revenue in Llandudno and London, though her two children were born back in Ystradgynlais. After the birth of her son Charles in 1944, Menna modelled with her baby for the Polish artist Josef Herman who had recently arrived in Ystradgynlais. 'Attachment', a pastel of Menna with her second child Edyth, is in the National Museum in Cardiff. Herman also did scores of sketches of her since, as Menna put it, he could 'always sell a quick nude'.[4]

Herman famously arrived in the community for a fortnight and stayed for eleven years. Menna valued their friendship and was greatly influenced by this immensely talented artist who introduced her to a wider world of European literature and Jewish culture. It is worth comparing the artist's description of Ystradgynlais with Menna's vision of Cilhendre in her first novel. Herman wrote vividly about the 'Violet roofs at the foot of green hills', the 'Pyramids of black tips surrounded by cloudlike trees the colour of a dark bottle' and how the sun transformed the grey streets to copper brown. On a sunlit evening the village was 'glazed', and the River Tawe, 'which has always two colours more than the sky', showed both red and 'the blackness of coal and yellow of clay'. The hills would be bright blue.[5] Menna too painted her village in colours. The sun polished the walls of houses built of river stones 'lavender grey, cloud grey, sea grey, pink and purple'. The side of the valley that faced the sun was golden and pink. The other side revealed hills 'in deep shadow, deeply blue'.[6]

Most of Menna's married life would be spent, however, not in the Welsh valleys but in another kind of close – even closed – community which she observed carefully: academia. From these experiences came her writing.

When asked, in 1959, the year in which her first novel was published, why she began to write, Menna provided several explanations. The story was set in Wales yet it was the experience of living in Northern Ireland that had prompted it. From 1954 to 1967 Bryce Gallie held the chair in Logic and Metaphysics at Queen's University, Belfast. The rich use of the English language and its symbolism in these surroundings influenced Menna. Living in County Down on the Castle Ward estate at Strangford Lough gave her a useful distance from Wales and a vantage point from which to reflect back. She was also approaching forty. As she put it, she was aware that until then she had been wife, mother and secretary (she typed her husband's lecture notes). But there had not been 'much time to be me, not much time to remember or think about the idea that's long since slipped tidily down the sink with the dishwater, or been wrung out hard with the nappies'.[7]

Now she had some space. She had a rich store of family stories to draw upon, a vivid imagination and had long been a consummate letter writer (her papers include letters to her husband in the army). She missed things Welsh though was aware that writing as an exile, what she called 'this remembering with love', was as dangerous as 'the jungle or Coney Beach, Porthcawl'.[8]

Over time Menna became increasingly wary of the temptation to romanticise during what she called 'the long *hiraethus* years' of living outside Wales.[9] 'How', she asked, in one of her most reflective and self-critical unpublished pieces (called 'The Two Valleys')'is one in love with the valleys to pull out the shrinking weeds of sentimentality?'[10] She identified the 'blandishment of distorted memory' as a further problem, quite apart from reconciling the gap between the remembered past and the disappointing 'reality' of a cherished community in the present. She also recognised the irony of her situation: 'What I owe to Ulster is of course the peace I've found in this so-called violent country'.[11]

Menna also provided an explanation for the subject matter of her first novel, *Strike for a Kingdom*. It was, she said, an obvious choice, being set in the Welsh valleys she knew so well and missed. But it was more than that. She stressed that it was crafted out of a sense of guilt. Menna's family had been in the minority in Ystradgynlais in 1926. Her maternal grandfather had gone underground aged ten but because her own father was not a collier, Menna and her sisters could not go to the soup kitchen, although their mother helped there. So, she explained, 'I think that when I wrote my novel I was trying to take part in that strike, that fight; here was the contribution that, to my shame, I felt my father had never made. Here was I at last taking soup with the other children'.[12]

Once established as a novelist, Menna provided a suitably poignant story to illustrate what provoked that book. Thus she told the tale of her father ritualistically dividing a bar of chocolate with his carpenter's ruler for his three daughters. Menna stood outside the front door, smoothing the empty wrapper after enjoying her chocolate. She noticed a little girl, daughter of a striking collier, watching her intently from a distance. She came up and whispered, 'Can I have the smell of the paper?' This, Menna later claimed, prompted her to compose her novel.[13]

Menna tended to write retrospectively about each of the societies she experienced. From the vantage point of a new location she reflected on the last. Location really matters in her novels and it is significant that the one place she lived in but did not put under the microscope was Cambridge. From the late 1960s, Bryce was a Fellow of Peterhouse, hardly the most appropriate of the Cambridge colleges for Menna who was an outspoken and committed socialist. She felt more foreign there, than in any of her other places of residence, including New York.[14] Despite being, by her own admission, essentially a shy person, she felt obliged to disparage pretension. In her novels she constantly dents pomposity. And although she disliked being labelled a feminist, she bristled against the way the wives of academics were perceived. In one novel written during these years, she described how these women tended to look a decade older than their husbands did. Under the strain of being 'the little handmaiden, slave' they 'get to look like caricatures of denial'.[15] With her customary subversion of literary titles she called an article for the *Cambridge Review*, 'Quietly following the Don'.[16]

The other places in which Menna lived became central to her novels.[17] Her first and third books are both located in the valleys of her youth. *Strike for a Kingdom* was essentially rooted in Menna's own experience. We first see Cilhendre through the eyes of a small girl. And this awkward little girl Nan with buckteeth, dressed as a fairy for the village carnival in that tough, hot summer of 1926, is a thinly disguised Menna.[18] Her account of this carnival is one of her finest pieces of writing: witty, poignant and freighted with significance.

Menna's other mining novel *The Small Mine* was also written in Northern Ireland. So too was her second book *Man's Desiring* which appeared in 1960. In the latter, place and identity are explored in a different way from the Cilhendre novels. Its theme is similar to that of the earlier and better-known *Lucky Jim* (1954) by Kingsley Amis who was a university lecturer in Swansea at the time. Victor Gollancz published both novels. Menna's story examines the journey of Griff Rowlands, collier's son from Creunant, to an assistant lectureship at a university in the Midlands, armed with cake from his Mam wrapped in the newspaper *Llais Llafur*.[19] One reviewer described this book as 'a sort of border ballad about the frontier between England and Wales'.[20] Here Menna indulged in a number of stereotypes despite her wariness of sentimentality. There were also comments on the class system and on the deceptions and petty snobberies of academics. The deracinated author confronted some of the awkwardness of social mobility, the difficulties of coming from one kind of community and the cost of shifting to another.

Man's Desiring is loosely set in the world the Gallies had just encountered at Keele. It was then a brand new university, the vision of A.D. Lindsay. Lindsay had been Master of Balliol College, Oxford when Bryce was a student there in the 1930s. Lindsay's protégé had joined him in this experiment at what was initially called the University College of North Staffordshire. Bryce, who later wrote a book about Lindsay and this new university, was its founding professor of Philosophy.[21] According to one of its early graduates, the true identity of the characters in Menna's novel was well known at the time.

Although *Man's Desiring* has not dated well, the comment of its character Lydia Kilmartin, an English lecturer, that she must keep her pride 'in this place of men, this academic man's world' suggests (as always with Menna's novels) that we need to look behind the bravado.[22] It gently reminds us just how tough it must still have been in the mid-twentieth century for the tiny percentage of women academics, determined to be taken seriously but lacking suitable role models.

The years in Northern Ireland had their turn in fiction when the Gallies lived in Cambridge. In 1970 *You're Welcome to Ulster* was published. Yet although it is set in Northern Ireland, the heroine is a Welsh middle-aged widow living in Cambridge. Wales and Welshness are always there in Menna's novels, tucked behind social and geographical mobility but ready to emerge at key moments.

In this instance the heroine is middle class. Upwardly mobile, Sarah's family had come from Cilhendre before moving to Cardiff. Fearing that she is fatally ill, she returns for a week's holiday to Northern Ireland where she had once lived and loved. This enables Menna to plunge the reader into contemporary politics.

The book reproduces excerpts from the 1922 Special Powers Act. It is Menna's most serious novel, examining a range of different arguments and positions, whether through IRA activity, shooting by the 'B' specials of the Ulster Constabulary or polemical dinner party discussions surrounding Civil Rights, Republicanism, class and religion.[23] Sarah, staying with Catholic friends, takes up again with her old lover, an outspoken journalist called James McNeil (the spelling of his name is not the same as that of the governor general of the Irish Free State).

During her time in Ulster, Menna was active in the co-religionist Northern Ireland Labour Party and outspoken about infant mortality rates and unemployment.[24] Loyalists stoned her at an open-air election meeting. She described herself as an ally of the 'ill-used Catholic minority' but did not condone the IRA or the use of any militant tactics.[25] Her ideal was an Ireland committed to constitutional socialism. The novel gives a vivid picture of the heightened tension in Northern Ireland as it lurched towards political crisis. Written at a time when the symbolically charged Investiture of the Prince of Wales was provoking some paramilitary activity within Wales, it also provided a warning against extreme manifestations of Welsh nationalist politics.[26]

The American edition of *You're Welcome to Ulster*, published by Harper & Row, includes what is called 'A Prelude'. It is set in a Welsh pub and sketches a furtive conversation between young militant Welsh men awaiting an arms cache from the Irish. Here we encounter Emlyn, who had been imprisoned for trying to blow up a reservoir, Griff the cultured organiser who believes that paving stones, petrol bombs and gelignite are 'the vocabulary of our time', Dafydd with his bourgeois Carmarthenshire background, and Efan, the scholarly ideologue.

This Prelude had not been included in the first UK edition.[27] It seems to have been written especially for the American market. A draft version in the Howard Gottlieb archive at Boston University calls it 'New 1st Chapter for US version'.[28] It was probably added to the US edition to establish a link between Welsh and Irish extremists, since a young Welsh nationalist on the run in Northern Ireland forms part of the novel's plot. The reader's report for Harper & Row had suggested that the religious and political controversy and events and their relationship to the Welsh runaway and the heroine were 'a little murky' and not 'adequately explained'.[29]

In one draft version of the opening scene, the central character Sarah walks into the pub but is ignored by the young militants.[30] As in the well-known episode in George Borrow's *Wild Wales*, the stranger is wrongly presumed not to understand Welsh. The published version removes Sarah from the scene and concentrates on the men's political discussion. This masculine setting for the Prelude contrasts with the focus in Chapter One on Sarah's fear that she has breast cancer. It is this that prompts her decision to revisit Ulster for a holiday.

The Prelude seems to have been Menna's attempt to make the narrative and context for the main plot more intelligible for US readers. A desire to explain to the wider world what was going on lay behind this book. Its publication inadvertently revealed some fundamental misunderstandings and how badly illumination was needed. It was carefully set on the eve of the Twelfth, highlighting how the past dictated the present. Yet one reviewer in California presumed that it was about Twelfth Night.[31]

During her years in Northern Ireland, Menna did numerous radio talks for the BBC, invariably drawing on her own life and experiences. They were always vetted. The Northern Ireland Home Service was well aware that they had an entertaining speaker – the listeners' appreciation index rated her well above the average[32] – but she was critical of what she saw as a conspiracy of silence surrounding religion and politics in the Irish society she inhabited. In a broadcast for the Welsh Home Service she admitted that she felt as though she were living in a colony where the watchword was not 'change' but 'keep'.[33]

Two years before *You're Welcome to Ulster*, she had published *Travels with a Duchess*. This account of two women behaving badly on one of the increasingly popular package holidays abroad was not as light-hearted a tale as it might at first appear. Unlike more modern stories of 'ladettes' or holiday romances, this novel was set in Dubrovnik, concerned middle-aged, middle class women and celebrated their friendship as well as, very candidly for its time, suggesting their need to affirm their (hetero)sexuality.

Menna had already visited Yugoslavia twice: once as Northern Ireland's delegate for PEN (the organisation of poets, essayists and novelists) and the second time on a fortnight's holiday with her Irish friend Peg. Here, as in other novels, Menna anticipated some of the issues that would exercise feminists a few years later. She provided a valuable corrective to the standard images of the swinging sixties. She demonstrated, for example, the indignity of being told that a wife cannot travel alone on a joint passport. Menna and Peg had experienced this personally at London airport as they set off on their holiday. Her first jottings on this subject were scribbled during their flight to Dubrovnik. Grabbing the nearest paper, she wrote on a BEA sick bag. Furious at their treatment and dreaming up retribution, she wrote:

> Here we sit hoping that we may be allowed to enter Jugoslavia [sic] because we are travelling not as two free, white Christian married & respectable women, but as two suspects, fleeing from our husbands without permission.
>
> Our passports are invalid & we are going behind the Iron Curtain – Goodbye England, Goodbye Wales,? [sic] next instalment follows in Dubrovnik???[34]

Only Menna's final novel *In These Promiscuous Parts* (1986) was set where she was currently living. It is about the small town of Trenewydd, a thinly disguised Newport, Pembrokeshire or Trefdraeth in Welsh (known colloquially as Ty'drath), where she spent her last years. Her booklet on the customs of north Pembrokeshire entitled 'Little England's Other Half' (1974) called this area 'the very heart of the Welshery'.[35]

Unlike Menna's other novels, which she had written at speed – and this stream of consciousness approach encourages the reader initially to devour them rapidly – *In These Promiscuous Parts* took a long time to craft. Not helped by arthritis, she also now lacked her customary physical distance from the society she was portraying. She appears to have been attempting to recapture something of the tone that informed her mining fiction.

Like these novels, it examines the workings of a small community. It posits officialdom versus local support, policing versus community sanctions, and locals versus incomers. The success of Menna's mining novels can be attributed to their combination of a tender portrayal of a community intimately understood from within, along with a keen sense of class and political awareness amongst its protagonists at a time of genuine crisis. Although Menna knew local people well – characters in the book as well as locations are still recognisable today – the sense of a crisis is, however, lacking in this final novel with its typically provocative title (a quote from Rudyard Kipling's *Just So Stories* of 1902). Menna admitted in a letter to me that, although her novel began moderately well, it 'goes off dreadfully'. She suggested that perhaps it was best to give it 'a tidy burial and forget it ever happened'.

This book was not published in the UK. The Menna Gallie Archive includes a letter from her agent suggesting that it was not quite in tune with current bestsellers. It was, however, published in the US by St. Martin's Press and well reviewed in the *New Yorker* and *New York Times*. It was in America that Menna was best known as a novelist. Harper & Row had published her first five books and *Time Magazine* reviewed her work. Praising her 'beautifully written' *Strike for a Kingdom*, it suggested that it was the sort of book that bestselling authors 'should be required to copy two or three times in longhand'.[36] Perhaps this was due in part to Menna's first two novels being compared, in a clutch of reviews, to the work of Dylan Thomas. Possibly the Welsh stereotypes and naming of characters such as Dai Dialectic and Jim Kremlin in *The Small Mine* seemed less hackneyed and outdated in America than here, though Jim Kremlin, for example, was the nickname for a real person from Menna's youth.

Menna's most successful novels were not only written retrospectively, they were also historical. *Strike for a Kingdom*, originally called 'Say the Pink Bells' is about 1926. *The Small Mine*, published in 1962, looks back to life in Cilhendre after the nationalisation of the mining industry. It was written after she spent two shifts down Cynheidre Colliery on a visit home. And Menna's descriptions of work – most notably the end of a shift – are especially powerful, inviting comparison with Josef Herman's paintings. Reviewers praised the compassion evinced in *The Small Mine* though some remarked that the plot was tenuous. Interestingly, one American critic was struck by Menna's representation of what he called 'communist zealots' since these men were 'evidently accepted by the other locals as men of probity and deep thought'.[37]

These mining novels revolve around a society that the author had observed first hand and represent a woman's perspectives, so they are especially valuable for the historian today. But when *Strike for a Kingdom* first appeared in 1959, it was essentially portrayed in Britain as an unusual detective story. Indeed, it was a joint runner-up (to an Eric Ambler novel) for the Crime Writers' Association of Great Britain's prestigious gold dagger award. A review by the crime writer Julian Symons referred to 'scene after brilliant scene'.[38]

The book was extensively reviewed and even translated into Japanese. Eleanor Roosevelt praised its 'feeling and depth of understanding'.[39] Described by the *Manchester Guardian* as a poet's novel, the *Herald Tribune* saw Menna as 'A born writer, indeed almost a poet' who 'seems to breathe her story, rather than manipulate it'.[40] An enthusiastic *Los Angeles Mirror* called it 'by far the best of the highly-regarded new transatlantic novels that have come from a crop of new writers...one of those small gems which come along only too infrequently. Beg, borrow or buy it'.

Reviewers also portrayed Menna's fiction, sometimes rather patronisingly, as extremely funny. The *Sunday Times* saw in it the 'rich comic rhetoric of a novel by Gwyn – or a story by Dylan – Thomas', both of whom she knew. And she does seem to have been influenced by the latter's lyrical freedom. A short story about her time in New York opens with her account of the leaving of Wales. It refers to 'the fat, black-silked aunties and the sat upon little uncles and the cousins with moustaches and jobs and sometimes even umbrellas. We were going to America in the morning' (this last sentence nodding to Jack Jones's *Off to Philadelphia in the Morning*).[41] In *The Small Mine* Joe Jenkins walks down Railway Street through the 'fine, diligent, determined rain'.[42] The *News Chronicle*, with its own excess of adjectives, stressed how rare it was to find a 'genuine British woman humorous novelist', and praised the book's 'wonderfully heightened prose'.[43]

Alexander Cordell, another left-wing novelist of industrial South Wales, whose own fiction can be quite usefully compared with Menna's, wrote 'Make no mistake, this Menna Gallie can write'. He added, in an unfortunate attempt to be funny, 'Such is her pace that you need a skid-lid to handle her on the flat, never mind her hairpins'.[44] Unlike most novels about Welsh coalfield society, Menna's fiction was deliberately laced with humour. It was, though, often bittersweet, and these reviewers did not highlight the fact that Menna's work was also politicised writing. Interspersed with her wicked wit are damning indictments of social conditions. Listen to the description of the striking collier Tommy Davies: 'a nice quiet chap. He was used to sitting; he'd been on the Compensation for months before the Strike. Christ, he could cough'.[45]

Menna Gallie was a skilful storyteller and *Strike for a Kingdom* is in part a 'whodunnit' with all the classic features of that genre. It enabled her to tell a murder mystery in an unusual and dramatic setting, as would Reginald Hill in his Dalziel and Pascoe novel *Underworld* (1988) about Yorkshire miners. But this device is only the shell, albeit an important and carefully chosen one for Menna and, like an earlier mining novel with a murder, the great classic *Germinal* by Emile Zola, at its centre there are questions of class and loyalty.

Strike for a Kingdom is a subversive novel. Whereas most murder mysteries of the time remained conservative in their location (still frequently the country house), and characters (the working class literally serving the privileged members of the community around which the plot unfolded), Menna deployed the genre in a different way. At her novel's heart there is a protracted strike, a situation that marks South Wales out from England in terms of what actually happened historically, but one that is also a well-established feature in fiction from Wales. As John Jenkins has put it, 'here is a clever political novel masquerading as a harmless whodunnit'.[46]

To understand Menna Gallie's novels (and the five published in the UK came from the left-wing press of Victor Gollancz) we need to appreciate how she valued her Welsh socialist inheritance. Griff in *Man's Desiring* declares: 'Your politics are in your blood, like, it's not what you think, it's how your blood boils'.[47]

Menna's grandfather had helped found the Labour Representation Committee in South Wales. Keir Hardie had stayed at her grandparents' house and Menna used to delight in telling people that her monoglot *mamgu* (grandmother) had but two sentences of English. One was 'I like ice cream' (Ystradgynlais's Temperance Café run by a man from Patagonia produced a mean ice cream). The other sentence was 'Keir Hardie called me comrade'.

Menna's mother's roots lay in the Independent Labour Party (ILP). Influenced by the Spanish Civil War, Menna even joined the Communist Party briefly in the late 1930s but then spent the rest of her life as a Labour Party activist, wherever she was living. Her socialism helped to define her. As she explained in an interview: 'There was no question of one's politics. No other way of thinking –

you were a socialist'.[48] This was not the militant socialism of the male Marxist writers of the coalfield, but nonetheless it was part of a vibrant socialist tradition. As with the slightly earlier novelist Lily Tobias, a Welsh-born Jewish woman and Zionist who grew up in the mining community of Ystalyfera, just a few miles from Menna's home, but who spent much of her life in what became the State of Israel, socialism helped to shape her and provided some continuities as both women grappled with their own issues of identity.[49]

Central to *Strike for a Kingdom* is D.J. Williams, a striking poet-collier who is also a magistrate. He is a dignified man, this Justice of the Peace who is forced to query his very title. The first thing we hear about this class-conscious collier whose loyalties are being sorely tested, is that he is picking coal. D.J. values peaceful persuasion yet gets locked up for the night in the police cells. He is the kernel of this book and the Inspector, the other key figure in maintaining peace, is as foolish as D.J. is wise.

In his study of a century of Welsh writing in English as post-colonial fiction, Stephen Knight shrewdly notes that Menna was 'often more subtle than she chose to seem'. He sees the figure of D.J. as standing for David John Williams, the Carmarthenshire-born countryside writer and Rhondda collier who became a mature student at Aberystwyth and Oxford and later taught at Fishguard School. Most significant for Knight, was the fact that D.J was 'one of the three who made the major Nationalist statement by setting fire to the Penyberth bombing school in 1936'.[50]

But it is highly unlikely that Menna would have invoked

as her model the man who left the Labour Party to help found Plaid Cymru, given her antipathy to violence and wariness about Welsh nationalism. In *You're Welcome to Ulster*, the Welsh Nationalist Mabon Powell is a naive sixth former who bungles his mission and is way out of his depth when confronted with direct action in Northern Ireland. He is shown to have betrayed his labour origins and his very name. 'I'm not much of an -ist' declared Menna, 'except that I'm a socialist'.[51]

D.J. Williams was in fact based on Menna's uncle, W.R. Williams, a collier from the age of thirteen, a lodge and ILP chairman who, like D.J, had been to Ruskin College.[52] Known as W.R., he too was a poet as well as a collier who went on strike and got arrested. A magistrate, he also became the Labour County Councillor for Brecon and Radnor and chaired the education committee. D.J. deserves more attention as a literary figure, and not just because he is more subtly drawn than are some of Menna's characters nor because this tender portrait of the true dispenser of justice is based on a real person. D.J is significant historically because he is emblematic of a particular type of Welsh collier.

D.J stands for other learned Welsh colliers. He can be usefully compared to a figure like Ezra Jones, the miners' leader in *Cwmardy* and *We Live*, based on Lewis Jones's own mentor Noah Rees who also had a Ruskin background. But, unlike Lewis Jones, Menna was not writing as a Communist. She was at pains to stress that:

> ...they were not Marxists out to destroy Capitalism; they did not think of themselves as 'one of the Factors of Production', but they felt they were poor devils having a

> raw deal and they had had enough...This was a strike of Oliver Twists and the Owners had much in common with the Beadle.[53]

Menna Gallie was, in Knight's interpretation, consciously turning away from 'the genre of valleys political realism'.[54] Yet it can be argued that she was telling an alternative, equally valid, story that could also be encompassed within a definition of political realism. It reacted against interwar writing about Welsh coalfield society that, in her view, presented an overly bleak picture of a deprived people as the only really authentic Wales. Believing that the history of the Left was bedevilled by such stereotypes,[55] she sought to inject her stories with non-revolutionary elements of society: crime, the pettiness of village life, the hollowness of many marriages and the silliness of social climbing. All this is reclaimed as part of the fabric of a political and social realism.

Menna sought, not entirely successfully, to challenge the stock image of mining communities in her fiction. She stressed that, in contrast to the Rhondda and mining villages further east, the Swansea and Dulais valleys had 'no rows of wretched terraced houses thrown up by the wicked coal owner'.[56] Like her grandfather, men combined mining with farming on a small scale. The Cilhendre of the 1920s is described thus: 'a little huddle of pigeon-coloured houses following the curves of the River Tawe, which plaited its way among them'.[57] By the early sixties the deep pits in the valley had closed. Only private drift mines, too small to be part of the National Coal Board, remained. By the end of the decade, she was portraying Cilhendre as a place of 'desolation and demolition and a few dirty sheep', somewhere to leave rather than stay.[58] Menna's fiction traces the fate of her local community over time.

Menna also differs from the male coalfield novelists in her focus on and representation of its inhabitants. Her story is not set in the workplace but remains located within the colliery community. She includes the perspectives of children, and in *The Small Mine* they are the ones who have worked out who committed the dastardly deed.[59] And although writers such as Gwyn Jones in *Times Like These* wrote about mining families, the women in Menna's novels are often very isolated figures. The second chapter of *The Small Mine* opens with the simple sentence: 'Sall Evans was a lonely woman'.[60] Men and women appear to inhabit different worlds yet, as Jane Aaron has shown, 'there is nothing joyous about Sall's promiscuity'. Menna makes it evident how dependent the women of the community are on the men, whatever their position in life.[61]

At the same time her fiction is remarkable for its open discussion of women's sexuality. Reviewers could not resist calling her books racy or bawdy. It annoyed Menna that they tolerated men saying what they wanted but seemed outraged when women wrote about sex. In 1980, she remarked: 'There's a Victorian residual carry-over in literary response which would like to insist that women writers must be womanly'.[62] Raymond Stephens, writing in the *Anglo-Welsh Review* in the early 1960s, made the sort of comment that, I suspect, would not have been directed towards a male writer, when he suggested that 'What is perhaps needed is a greater application and consistency in controlling her emotions'.[63]

You're Welcome to Ulster provoked especially moralistic responses. In typically mixed mode it combined very serious political discussions with a renewed affair between the heroine and a married man. It anticipated the bringing together of the personal and the political which became so marked in 1970s feminism. It was disturbing for those expecting a story about the modern Troubles (and Menna was one of the very first novelists to confront this subject) to find it intertwined with a tale of sexual liberation, and vice versa.

Just after the book was published, Menna wrote a frank and heartfelt response to Germaine Greer's *The Female Eunuch*. This appeared in the *Cambridge Review* in November 1970. It seems to encapsulate her ambivalence about some aspects of the modern women's movement. Menna detected two, somewhat contradictory, voices at work in Greer's book: 'the intelligent feminist' and 'the sexually insecure exhibitionist'. In what seems to have been her most explicit written endorsement of feminism, she praised what she called Greer's 'good voice'. It provided:

> a good, feminist tract, persuasive and moving in its account of urban marriage and female misery. Her sympathy with unhappy women is genuine and infectious, and she is completely convincing in her descriptions of the frustrations and sorrows of the underprivileged, ill-educated, bored, disappointed wives and with the mothers of 'nuclear families'. One could not fail to be with her all the way. It's good to get this feminist ammunition and to have it so passionately expressed. [64]

Yet she was equally dismissive of Greer's 'other mouth'. Menna ridiculed her representation of men, the family and marriage as 'the enemy', accused her of generalising from personal experience and suggested that she was 'irritating, ignorant, prejudiced and insincere'. Menna was never one to mince her words and the sexually explicit language she deployed was far from the usual fare of this journal of 'University Life and Thought'. Menna may have disliked Greer's exhibitionism but in this review the fifty-year-old wife of a Cambridge Don could not resist trying to shock. Attacking Greer's critique of marriage, she not only defended the institution but also suggested that the trouble with marriage was the concept of adultery and an insistence on monogamy.

Menna Gallie's novels represent a distinct and distinctive perspective, shaped by (and reacting against as well as admiring) her particular Welsh upbringing and location, alongside a commitment to the labour movement and a female eye-view. Raymond Stephens noted that she was 'haunted by the desire for the good community'.[65] He saw this as part of her social rather than political values. Another way of understanding this concern is to conceive it instead as an integral part of a broader meaning of political, a meaning which had a particular resonance for women who came from within these communities. Whereas Stephens criticises the way that Joe is killed part way through *The Small Mine* and feels that the reader is left high and dry, Katie Gramich in contrast recognises that this is highly appropriate. Here, she argues, is a novel that is centred on the community rather than singling out heroes or heroines.[66]

Current research by John Jenkins into the representation of masculinity in Welsh mining novels confirms how Menna's perspective differs from that of the male writers of the coalfield.[67] The colliers she writes about refuse to subscribe to the notion of the heroic miner. The strike enables her to show us these men beyond the pit and within the community. And although 1926 is known as 'The Angry Summer', (a reference to Idris Davies's fifty-stanza poem), Menna's colliers are far from the classic Angry Man of fiction prompted by John Osborne's 1956 play *Look Back in Anger* and fashioned by English contemporaries.[68]

At the same time, we need to resist taking Menna's representation of her remembered past too literally. For example, she writes in *Strike for a Kingdom* about 'The almost incredible summer weather continued as though God was for once on the side of the colliers'.[69] It *was* a good summer but the historian Steven Thompson has shown that the weather was not exceptional in 1926.[70] Yet for colliers who normally worked in darkness, those months provided a singular experience, enabling them to notice and savour the sunshine. Menna, just a child at the time, would have been incorporating the received wisdom and perceptions of her elders. The media, politics and experience of returning to live in wartime Ystradgynlais as a wife and young mother after the deep mines had closed, would also have affected how she saw that community and eventually interpreted it from mid-twentieth century Northern Ireland.

In the early 1960s Menna suggested that much writing about Welsh working class society was parochial.[71]

Exposed to the politics of Northern Ireland, she also spent a year in the United States in 1963-4 where she was deeply shocked by what she saw and heard on a brief visit to North Carolina. She began to argue that race-relations were all-important and should be addressed 'from Crynant to Kenya'.[72]

The comparative neglect of Menna's writing within Wales can be partly attributed to her exile status. The androcentric approach of much literary and historical writing on Wales until comparatively recently has reinforced this. For example, Raymond Williams' lecture in 1978 on the Welsh industrial novel did not include Menna's work, even though it fulfilled his criteria.[73] To some extent Menna colluded in this. She saw her writing as an adjunct to being the wife of an eminent Oxbridge professor and writer of philosophical studies. Philosophy is well known as one of the most cerebral, esoteric and masculine of subjects. Against this background, Menna suggested that novel writing was the easiest and laziest form of writing.[74] It is, however, worth pointing out that after writing her first novel in three months then keeping the typescript hidden in a drawer for a year, it was Bryce Gallie who, after reading it, insisted that it be sent to a major publisher. Victor Gollancz accepted it.

In the early 1990s there were just a few lone voices calling for greater recognition of Menna's work. Angela Fish wrote an article in the *New Welsh Review*, and the historian and politician Hywel Francis, who comes from the Dulais Valley, drew attention to Menna's mining novels and how her writing reveals both local pride and wider horizons.[75]

The early twenty-first century has seen Menna Gallie's work re-evaluated, praised once more and appreciated in her own country as well as the United States. Honno Press has done much to make her voice heard by reprinting four of her novels in paperback in their Classics series and Menna's work appears in their anthology *Struggle or Starve*.[76] Just before he died in 2004, the novelist Alun Richards wrote in *Planet* about 'the deadly historical perception' evident in *Strike for a Kingdom*. Dai Smith included it in his Top Ten Welsh alternatives to the work of Dylan Thomas.[77] Jane Aaron and Stephen Knight emphasise her contribution to Welsh writing in English.[78] Menna's novels now feature on reading lists for students studying Welsh History and Literature. *You're Welcome to Ulster* appears on booklists about The Troubles. *Travels with a Duchess* has acquired its own historical significance with its accounts of a proud, unhappy Bosnian man and its description of Mostar.

The playwright Diana Griffiths turned both of Menna's mining novels into powerful Radio 4 dramas and 2015 saw a production of Griffiths's adaptation of *Strike for a Kingdom* by Swansea's Fluellen Theatre Company in association with the Josef Herman Art Foundation. Menna is now commemorated in a plaque erected on the wall of Cilhendre, her Pembrokeshire home.[79] Yale and Boston Universities include collections of Menna Gallie material and an extensive Menna Gallie Archive can be consulted at the National Library of Wales. It includes plays, short stories, talks and broadcasts as well as personal material and drafts of her novels. The Digital Library Atlas of Wales and its Borderlands includes Menna Gallie, focusing on *Strike for a Kingdom* and Ystradgynlais as part of an online interactive cartography that explores a small number of novels with Welsh locations.[80]

The work of a novelist much younger than Menna can be seen as a modern heir to *Strike for a Kingdom*. In 2014, Kit Habianic published *Until Our Blood Is Dry*. [81] Her title drew on a line in Idris Davies' 'Gwalia Deserta', in which those for whom a dream had become disaster, declare 'And we shall remember 1926 until our blood is dry'. This was the first novel by a woman about the impact of a strike on a Welsh mining community since Menna's ground breaking novel fifty-five years earlier.

As in Menna's case, this too was its author's first novel and she also came from a mining district (Caerphilly). The 2014 novel focuses on the miners' strike of 1984-5, and how it fundamentally affected the lives of women and men and notions of loyalty, love and community. It also had a long gestation period and, like Menna's novel appeared three decades after the seminal event. And although *Until Our Blood Is Dry* was written at a time when issues of gender equality were much more in evidence than they had been when Menna wrote her mining fiction, Habianic's sensitive handling of the way that her heroine became politicised, her accounts of the union and delineation of a range of masculinities, demonstrate continuities as well as discontinuities in mining communities. This novel was also written from a distance – in this case from London – but as with Menna's fiction, it benefits from having that distance allied to an old familiarity.

It may be that Menna Gallie's novels are best appreciated as *historical* cameos, in the sense that they give us a glimpse of how she chose to articulate and make sense of the locations in which she had lived. With the societies she depicted being transformed in recent years, so her writing has become more valuable, hence her belated recognition. This has been strengthened by a modern interest in women's history and gender, helping to propel this writer into the public eye in a way that differs from earlier attention. Setting Menna's perspectives alongside recent research – such as Sue Bruley's analysis[82] of the lives of women, men and children in 1926 using oral history – can illuminate both our understanding of gender and of communities that are becoming transformed beyond recognition.

Perhaps, though, Menna's writing most clearly reveals how an educated woman interpreted her past and present in the light of the time when she was writing, that is, from the late 1950s to the mid-1980s. *Travels with a Duchess*, *Man's Desiring* and the mining novels all suggest, for example, a dislike of sociology, an increasingly popular subject in the academic world when she was writing. It might even be said that Menna needed to become an historical figure herself for us to appreciate her significance. Yet the values that Menna Gallie cherished, most notably her brand of democratic socialism – summed up by the words 'as usual with D.J, wisdom prevailed'[83] – became muted at the very moment that this feisty woman's writing started to come into its own.

Notes

[1] Menna Gallie, *Full Moon*, Hodder & Stoughton, 1973.

[2] Menna Gallie Archive, National Library of Wales, Aberystwyth (MGA), ML1/16.

[3] Menna Gallie celebrated 17 March 1920 as her birthday: spending many years in County Down she enjoyed the association with St. Patrick and her second name was Patricia. Yet when researching her life for an entry in the *ODNB*, I discovered that her birth certificate told a different story, showing that Menna Patricia Elizabeth Humphreys was born at Dolycoed, Station Road, Ystradgynlais on 18 March 1919. See Angela V. John, 'Gallie, Menna Patricia (1919-1990) http://www.oxforddnb.com/view/article/98305

[4] Interview with Menna Gallie by Ursula Masson, 1984, SWCC AUD/544, South Wales Miners' Library, Swansea University.

[5] Reprinted in Nini Herman, *Josef Herman: A Working Life*, Quartet, 1996, Appendix 2, pp. 225-6 from *The Welsh Review*, 1946. The links between the writer and artist are explored in Angela V. John, 'Irrepressible: The Life and Fiction of Menna Gallie'. Josef Herman Annual Foundation Lecture, April 2013. Another version of this paper was given to the Eglwyswrw Heritage Society in April 2016.

[6] Menna Gallie, *Strike for a Kingdom*, Honno Press, 2011 edition, p.5.

[7] MGA, ML6/1.

[8] Coney Beach is the funfair in Porthcawl named after New York's Coney Island.

[9] MGA, ML1/16.

[10] Ibid.

[11] Ibid L1/9.

[12] Ibid ML1/16.

[13] Video of talk given by Menna Gallie at Onllwyn Miners' Welfare Hall for the 'Welsh Women Make History' day-school, *Llafur*, May 1985 (author's copy).

[14] MGA, L1/16.

[15] Menna Gallie, *Travels with a Duchess*, Honno Press, 1996 edition, p. 55.

[16] This plays on the title of Mikhail Sholokhov's classic Russian novel, *And Quiet Flows the Don*, serialised from 1928.

[17] She also wrote a draft novel entitled 'The Making of an Heiress' which was never published. It was set in the rural Carmarthenshire of her mother's family.

[18] MGA, ML6/1.

[19] A weekly paper meaning Labour Voice, printed in the Swansea Valley from 1898.

[20] *Time Magazine* 24 February 1961.

[21] W. B. Gallie, *A New University: A. D. Lindsay and the Keele Experiment*, Chatto & Windus, 1960.

[22] Menna Gallie, *Man's Desiring*, Victor Gollancz, 1960, p. 190.

[23] Idem, *You're Welcome to Ulster*, Honno reprint, 2010. See the Introduction by Claire Connolly and Angela V. John, pp. vii-xxii.

[24] See, for example, MGA, ML8/1.

[25] MGA, ML1/16.

[26] See Connolly and John, *You're Welcome to Ulster, Introduction*, also John Ellis, *Investiture, Royal Ceremony and National Identity in Wales, 1911-1969*, University of Wales Press, 2008, pp. 213-14.

[27] This was published by Victor Gollancz in 1970 and

included an exclamation mark at the end of the title that was missing in the subsequent Harper & Row US edition. The Prelude was, however, printed in the 2010 Honno edition.

[28] Menna Gallie Papers, Box 4, Notebook 1A5q, Howard Gottlieb Archival Research Center at Boston University.

[29] Reader's Report, Harper & Row correspondence, Box 101, Butler Library, Columbia University, New York.

[30] Menna Gallie Papers, Box 4, Notebook 1A5q, Howard Gottlieb Archival Center.

[31] MGA, L4/1.

[32] Menna Gallie file N118/90/1, BBC Written Archives, Caversham Park, Reading. She also did some broadcasts for the Welsh Home Service in English and Welsh, working with her actress cousin Annest Wiliam on several occasions.

[33] MGA, ML6/1.

[34] Ibid, LM 2/7. See too how it is told in the novel, Gallie, *Travels*, p.17.

[35] Menna Gallie, *Little England's Other Half*, Pembrokeshire Handbooks, 1974, p. 3.

[36] In Box 101, Harper & Row correspondence.

[37] MGA, L4/1.

[38] *The Times* 15 February 1959.

[39] Letter to Harper & Row 26 October 1959, Box 101, Harper & Row Correspondence.

[40] MGA, L4/1.

[41] Ibid, ML1/6.

[42] Menna Gallie, *The Small Mine*, Honno Press, 2000 edition, p. 41.

[43] In an advertisement for *Man's Desiring* included in 1962 edition of *The Small Mine.*

[44] Ibid.

[45] Menna Gallie, *Strike for a Kingdom*, 2003 edition, p. 8.

[46] Communication with John Jenkins.

[47] Gallie, *Man's Desiring,* p. 53.

[48] Interview with Menna Gallie by Ursula Masson. See too Aled Rhys Wiliam, 'Nofelydd y Cymoedd Glo', *Barn*, December 1996.

[49] See Jasmine Donahaye, *The Greatest Need: The Creative Life and Troubled Times of Lily Tobias. A Welsh Jew in Palestine*, Honno Press, 2015.

[50] Stephen Knight, *A Hundred Years of Fiction. Writing Wales in English*, University of Wales Press, 2004, pp. 129-30.

[51] Welsh Women Make History Video.

[52] Confirmed by Menna Gallie in the Interview by Ursula Masson.

[53] Gallie, *Strike for a Kingdom*, 2011 edition, p. 13.

[54] Knight, *A Hundred Years*, p. 129.

[55] See MGA, L1/2.

[56] Welsh Women Make History Video.

[57] Gallie, *Strike for a Kingdom*, 2011 edition, p. 5.

[58] Idem, *You're Welcome to Ulster*, 2010 edition, p. 225 which revisits Cilhendre.

[59] Knight, *A Hundred Years*, p. 130.

[60] Gallie, *The Small Mine*, 2000 edition, p. 17.

[61] *Ibid*, Foreword, p. ix.

[62] MGA, L1/16.

[63] Raymond Stephens, 'The Novelist and Community: Menna Gallie', *Anglo-Welsh Review*, 14/34, Winter, 1964-5, p. 61.

[64] Menna Gallie, 'For God's sake, hold your tongue, and let me love', *Cambridge Review*, 2199, 13 November 1970, p. 50.

[65] Stephens, 'The Novelist and Community', p. 53.

[66] Katie Gramich, 'Both In And Out Of The Game: Welsh Writers And The British Dimension' in M. Wynn Thomas (ed.) *Welsh Writing in English*, University of Wales Press, 2003, p. 262.

[67] See John Jenkins' forthcoming Cardiff University PhD provisionally entitled 'Masculinity, Genre and Social Context in Six Novels of the Welsh Mining Valleys'.

[68] See Peter Whitebrook, *John Osborne: 'Anger is not* about ... , Oberon, 2015 for a discussion of the Angry phenomenon. *Strike for a Kingdom* was published in the same year as Shelagh Delaney's bold, controversial play *A Taste of Honey* (first performed in 1958).

[69] Gallie, *Strike for a Kingdom*, 2011 edition, p. 125.

[70] Steven Thompson, '"That beautiful summer of severe austerity": Health, Diet and the Working-Class Domestic Economy in South Wales in 1926', *Welsh History Review,* 21/3, 2003, p. 558.

[71] 'The dominant problem of the sixties is surely that of race', she argued in June 1961. MLA, ML1/16.

[72] Ibid.

[73] Raymond Williams, 'The Welsh Industrial Novel', Inaugural Gwyn Jones Lecture 21 April 1978, Cardiff, 1979.

[74] Interview with Menna Gallie by Ursula Masson.

[75] Angela Fish, 'Flight-deck of experience', *New Welsh Review,* 2/18, Autumn 1992, pp. 60-4; Hywel Francis, 'Mwth, Wus and the O.Ds: learning from our Two Cultures', *Books in Wales*, Welsh Books Council, June 1994.

[76] Three of the four have been reprinted in several different editions over the past decade. Carol White and Sian Rhiannon Williams (eds.), *Struggle or Starve: Women's Lives in the South Wales Valleys between the two World Wars*, Honno Press, 1998, pp. 53-5, 90-3.

[77] Alun Richards, 'A Village Stiff with Colliers', *Planet*, 165, June/July 2004. Dai Smith's list is of English-language Welsh writers.
https://www.theguardian.com/books/top10s/top10/0,,1714699,00.html . See too Angela V. John, 'A female Dylan Thomas?' *HerStoria 8*, Spring 2011, pp. 15-17.

[78] Stephen Knight, '"A New Enormous Music": Industrial Fiction in Wales' in Wynn Thomas, *Welsh Writing in English*, pp.75-7, 84.

[79] Angela V. John, 'Memorialising Menna Gallie', *Cambria*,13/1, 2011-12, pp. 45-6.

[80] www.literaryatlas.wales

[81] Kit Habianic, *Until Our Blood Is Dry*, Parthian, 2014.

[82] Sue Bruley, *The Women and Men of 1926*, University of Wales Press, 2010.

[83] Gallie, *Strike for a Kingdom*, 2011 edition, p. 21.

Index

Initials indicate main subjects, as follows. EP-T: Edith Picton-Turbervill; FH: Frances Hoggan; MG: Menna Gallie; MRH: Myvanwy Rhŷs; MWN: Margaret Wynne Nevinson; ORH: Olwen Rhŷs; RH: Lady Rhondda. Page numbers in **bold** following the main heading for each biographical subject indicate the page range of the relevant essay, including the endnotes; the endnotes have not been indexed.